The Structure
of Verse

The Structure of Verse

MODERN ESSAYS ON PROSODY

Edited with an Introduction
and Commentary by

HARVEY GROSS

Revised Edition

NEW YORK   THE ECCO PRESS

Copyright © 1966 by Fawcett Publications, Inc.
Copyright © 1979 by Harvey Gross

All rights reserved

Revised edition published in 1979 by The Ecco Press
1 West 30th Street, New York, N.Y. 10001
Distributed in Canada by Penguin Books Canada Limited

The Ecco Press logo by Ahmed Yacoubi
Designed by Earl Tidwell

Printed in the United States of America

Library of Congress Cataloging in Publication Data

Gross, Harvey Seymour, 1922- ed.
    The structure of verse.

    Bibliography: p.
    SUMMARY: Essays by Eliot, Pound, Roethke, Graves,
Fussell, and others on prosody, meter,
rhythm—the art of making verses.
        1. Versification—Addresses, essays, lectures.
[1.   Versification   2. Poetics   I. Title.
PN 1042.G7   1978   808.1   78-6781
ISBN 0-912-94658-x

FOR HERBERT AND MILDRED WEISINGER

. . . con amore

Contents

PART THREE

POETS ON PROSODY

APPENDIXES

Preface to the Revised Edition

The Structure of Verse was originally published by Fawcett in May 1966. It was a successful title in their Literature and Ideas Series: from the time of publication to the end of 1970, when it went out of print, *The Structure of Verse* sold thirty thousand copies. A new edition now seems appropriate. I would surmise that many copies of the first edition are no longer in readable condition; a paperback book produced to sell for 95 cents was not intended to withstand the ravages of time and use. And, I am pleased to say, it has been widely used by students first studying the mysteries of prosody, and by critics and theorists engaging the complex problems of metrical form, the notation of scansion, and the import of rhythmic effect. I am also pleased to say that during the years *The Structure of Verse* has been out of print, I have received many requests, from scholars and poets, to reissue it.

What follows, however, is not a reissue of the first edition but a completely rethought and reworked collection that gives some account of recent developments in prosodic thinking—developments that include the impact of generative linguistics on metrical theory, the new refinements displayed by the musical scanners or 'timers,' and the wisdom and tact evidenced by critics like Paul Fussell and John Hollander who combine theoretical savvy with a sure historical grasp. Seven selections have been added to this revised edition, six have been deleted. The new selections are by Paul Fussell, John Hollander, Morris Halle and Samuel J. Keyser, Charles L. Stevenson, T. S. Eliot, Stanley Kunitz, and Donald Justice. In general, I have deleted selections from books that are widely known and

1

available and no longer need exposure here. But this was not a rigid policy: I have retained I. A. Richards' "Rhythm and Metre," which is reprinted from the classic *Principles of Literary Criticism*. It is in itself a crucial statement; it also gives theoretical grounding to, and thus complements, John Hollander's "The Metrical Frame."

Both the rubric and substance of Part Three have been changed. I had intended to reprint T. S. Eliot's "Reflections on *Vers Libre*" in the first edition, but at the time copyright restrictions prevented its use. Its present availability suggested a new and attractive grouping, Poets on Prosody. Accordingly, Ezra Pound was shifted from Part One to join Theodore Roethke, Stanley Kunitz, Donald Justice, and the friend who acknowledged him *il miglior fabbro*. It is, however, misleading to imply that only in Part Three do we listen to the poets talking shop. Robert Bridges, Robert Graves, Yvor Winters, John Hollander—all persuasive critics—are also poets whose work shows "the precise and loving care of the motion of meaning in language."* And it is notable that I. A. Richards, perhaps our century's most influential literary theorist, has been in the last two decades a prolific writer and publisher of poems.† The double urge to practice and preach is very strong.

I have written a new introduction that touches briefly on the relations between prosody and poetic practice, and the substance of the new essays. These represent current and differing modes of reading the structure of verse. At one extreme, we have the elegant synchrony of Halle and Keyser and the close, logically rigorous exposition of Charles Stevenson. At the other, we have the conversation with Stanley Kunitz: the subtly discursive and richly informed observations of a poet who has written superbly both in "the meters" and out of them. In my introduction I offer some polemical observations on the current concerns of literary theory; I also succumb to temptation and make suggestions on what might be some proper directions for prosodic study to take. (I believe it was Herbert Muller who said the real title of every book was *How to Be More Like Me*.) I should also note that while no anthology of essays by different authors can ever constitute that imagined 'real book' so indefatigably urged upon anthologists by publishers, I am confident in the reality of this collection: in both its variety and coherence.

It was Irving Howe who, as General Editor of the Literature and Ideas Series, suggested that I put together a collection of essays on prosody, and

---

*See R. P. Blackmur's "Lord Tennyson's Scissors" in *Form and Value in Modern Poetry* (Garden City, N.Y., 1957), p. 374.

†See his collection, *Internal Colloquies* (New York, 1971).

that *The Structure of Verse* might be an appropriate *parergon* to my *Sound and Form in Modern Poetry*. It was Daniel Halpern of The Ecco Press who asked me to do this revised edition. My thanks to both of them. I would also like to thank Stanley Kunitz for graciously agreeing to converse with me—in New York City on a hot day in July—and Charles Stevenson and Donald Justice for revising their essays specifically for this collection. Portions of my introduction originally appeared in a review published in *Comparative Literature*; I would like to thank its editor, Thomas Hart, for permission to rework my material here. I compiled the bibliography during the summer of 1977 when I held a fellowship at The Huntington Library. The resources of that superb collection were enormously helpful; I would like to thank Mr. James Thorpe, Director, and Mrs. Virginia J. Renner, Reader Services Librarian, for their cordial assistance.

Others have helped in ways neither metrical nor prosodical but have steadied the rhythms of my life. For aid and encouragement I would like to thank Donald and Joan Fry, and my dear friend and collaborator, Myron Simon. My secretary, Vincenza Scaduto, has helped with typing and copying. Finally, I owe special debts to my uncle and aunt, Sidney and Molly Gross, and to David L. Jonas: *sine eorum adjumento hic liber non scriptus sit.*

I have not regularized the differences between British and American spellings. Thus Graves, Richards, and Bridges write of *metre,* while Wimsatt and Beardsley and Halle and Keyser write of *meter.* I trust that this difference in the alphabetic representation of a key word will not unduly trouble readers.

H. G.

Stony Brook, New York
January 1978

Introduction
Toward a Phenomenology of Rhythm

Everything that we believe, we believe either through sight or through hearing. Sight is often deceived, hearing serves as guaranty.

—St. Ambrose

I

T. S. Eliot noted "the obvious fact that art never improves, but that the material of art is never quite the same." I would add that our ways of understanding and judging works of art do not necessarily improve—the methodologies of structuralism, despite their subtlety and refinement, have not supplanted Aristotle's *Poetics*. However, as the materials of art change and consequently artists seek out new techniques to transform experience and feeling into those symbolic forms which are works of art, criticism must shift its emphases and sometimes the objects of its inquiry. More than two decades ago (in 1956) John Crowe Ransom felt it was "a public scandal" that his colleagues among the New Critics, so renowned for their sensitivity and ingenuity, were singularly deaf "to hearing the music of poetry, or at least, to avoid misunderstanding, to hearing its meters." He assumed that the "authority of the meters is passing, or is past, because we have become jaded by the meters. . . ."[1]

Ransom's pessimism was certainly justified by the prevailing lack of theoretical concern with questions of prosody. Yet at the very moment of his complaint Ransom seemed unaware of the metrical direction taken by the

5

poetry of the fifties—a direction strongly influenced by the work of his student Robert Lowell. There was a significant change in the materials of art, and literary theory and criticism began to take a renewed interest in the larger matters of rhythm and the more "technical aspirations" (W. K. Wimsatt's phrase) of meter. It was in 1959 that Professors Wimsatt and Beardsley published their important "The Concept of Meter: An Exercise in Abstraction." In the following year appeared *Style in Language,* edited by Thomas A. Sebeok; Part Five of this important collection is devoted to synchronic and diachronic discussions of metrics and rhythmic effects.

My study, *Sound and Form in Modern Poetry,* was published toward the end of 1964, the first edition of *The Structure of Verse* in May 1966. Professors Halle and Keyser published their first essay in generative metrics, "Chaucer and the Study of Prosody," in December 1966. This essay, and their subsequent modifications of the theory it proposed, initiated an attempt to establish a grammar of English 'metricality.' Subsequent work through the end of the sixties and the early seventies tended to be along linguistic, grammatical lines. The late Professor Wimsatt's anthology, *Versification: Major Language Types* (1972), is peopled by authors who "show themselves, one and all, writers of a grammatical bent." Bringing this brief history up to date, I should mention John Hollander's learned and beautifully written *Vision and Resonance* (1975). Professor Hollander is as much concerned with the music of poetry as he is with the grammar of meter: I shall speak later of this important distinction.

During this period of intense interest in prosodic study, poets turned away from metered verse. Beginning with Lowell's *Life Studies* (1959), a freer prosodic style has prevailed; at the moment of writing, as Stanley Kunitz observes (q.v.), "All possibilities are open, even, I think, metrical verse." What we have witnessed is the normal cultural lag between criticism and creation; Ransom's lament for the passing of the meters was voiced in belated response to high Modernist style and the putative prosodic freedoms of Pound and Eliot. (Ransom seems to have forgotten that Yeats always wrote metered verse and that the freedoms of Eliot's prosody are under the most artful constraints.)

I do not doubt that this revised version of *The Structure of Verse* imperfectly reflects current prosodic practice; however, Part Three gives an account of how three generations of modern poets regarded the changing materials of their craft. Their theories concerning meter and rhythm of course issue out of their own poetic practices. Eliot's prosody moves toward and away from metrical bedrock; Pound's, more influenced by the aesthetics of the nineties than most of his critics will acknowledge, *aspires toward the condition of music;* Roethke's catches its rhythms from folk tunes, Mother Goose, and other sources of what, quoting Auden, he names as "memorable speech."

Poets get the lion's share of space in this anthology. Long ago Dryden observed, "Poets themselves are the most proper, though I conclude not the only critics. . . . I . . . think it reasonable that the judgment of an artificer in his own art should be preferable to the opinion of another man; at least where he is not bribed by interest or prejudiced by malice." It would be disingenuous of me to suggest that no malicious chords are struck in this collection; Pound, Graves, and Winters—to name three contentious prosodists of contending points of view—are hardly disinterested defenders of their particular theoretical positions. Their substance, and perhaps more important, their tone give some credence to J. A. Symonds' wry comment that prosody is "a region where each observer is apt to tax his fellow-workers with a want of intelligence."[2] It is hardly a secret that prosody has attracted cranks and faddists, that they resemble, in their feuding and polemics, those humorless scholars who devote their seemingly endless energies to the disestablishment of Shakespeare as the author of his own plays.

As a matter of policy, I have rejected for this collection essays animated by crank notions. These are usually impassioned expositions of a theoretical monism: that English verse, if we only listen carefully enough, is really quantitative in its basic structure; that English verse corresponds exactly to musical bar lengths in duple or triple time; that English verse is *entirely* a matter of this or a matter of that. English verse has been composed in many modes, some metrical and some non-metrical. Metrical verse appears in two basic forms: the strong-stress (or Old English meter) and the syllable-stress (or accentual-syllabic) form; these distinctions are carefully made by Bridges, Winters, and Wimsatt and Beardsley. No one 'law' explains all English verse; no single principle of stressing, isochronism, syllabic length or number animates the variety of forms in English verse. Halle and Keyser construct an impressive theory that accounts for the phenomenon of iambic metricality—for verse written in the syllable-stress tradition. But their "patterns" and "correspondence rules" hardly account for the pure syllabism of Marianne Moore, the "absolute rhythm" of Ezra Pound, or the visual prosody of E. E. Cummings. However, despite formidable obstacles and the hard facts of history, several generations of visionary scholars have sought a prosodic general field theory which, when finally formulated and applied, would give us ears to hear all the rich and strange music of English verse.

II

The late W. K. Wimsatt, for whom clarifying distinctions were always acts of faith, asked in some puzzlement what we should name the study that examines the phenomenon of meter, but also concerns itself with rhyme, stanza, sound effects systematically and unsystematically employed, and even with the way a poem appears to the eye. Professor Wimsatt felt "The classical term *prosody* once had great prestige and convenience for verse study. But it has been pre-empted by modern linguistics and . . . is used today to refer to phonetic features—chiefly stress, tone, quantity, juncture. . . ."[3] While I agree that phoneticians have their specialized uses for the term, *prosody* has hardly become their exclusive property. If their use of the term has caused it to lose prestige, it is a loss I have not felt. Quite to the contrary: *prosody* still carries overtones of musical delight and classical elegance. The Greek *prosoidia* had two meanings: "a song sung to or accompanied by music; the tone or accent of a syllable." My use of the term, then, comprehends what, in the broadest sense, we understand as the music of poetry; and, in a narrower sense, as the specific organization of the syllables, that is, the meter. Or as Stanley Kunitz (q.v.), who agrees that *prosody* is indispensable to poetics, puts it: prosody refers to "the inflection of the voice, the sound of the poem, the way it breathes . . . and the systematic reduction of it."

Prosody's double involvement with music and meter, and with the uncertain areas that lie between, has doubtless been responsible for its attracting theorists of opposite tendencies. The poem's meter (to cite Professor Wimsatt again) "offers itself as perhaps the clearest and most firmly definable objective correlative of our responses. . . . It has the most technical aspirations."[4] Consequently, investigators with scientific inclinations have tried, by means of the latest acoustical instruments or the most up-to-date linguistic theory, to establish once and for all the nature of that 'objective' but elusive phenomenon of metricality. Some of these investigators, notably Professors Halle and Keyser (q.v.), have cleared the landscape of much theoretical rubble and clarified many problems. It is their work that marks the last decade as a period of progress in metrical study.

Other investigators, especially those committed to 'performative' or temporalist scansions, move away from a concern with the grammatical nature of meter toward an understanding of the poem's larger music, toward its rhythm. Thus Charles Stevenson's essay, though included in Part Two, describes an English prosody which assumes that the ontological status of the poem's text is like a musical score. The prosodist then 'plays' his performance of the text.

> The account of a performance will include the following points: (1) There
> is a continuing play of feelings on the part of the subvocal performer
> (reader) or of the audience of a vocal performer: for example, his expecta-

tions that certain patterns will continue. These belong to the phenomenally subjective aspect of the experience; but they are a response to (2) the
phenomenally objective aspect of the experience.[5]

Professor Stevenson acknowledges the presence of a grammatically definable
meter, and that both the observance and departures from the metrical paradigm serve to release those surges of feeling which constitute the expressive
stratum of the poem. However, he is moving toward a 'phenomenology of
rhythm' (of which I speak more below); in describing "the phenomenally
subjective aspect of [his] experience," he is no longer advancing a restricted
(and restrictive) theory of English metricality but trying to deal with all of
the poem's recurrent patterns of feeling, with "its movement broadly conceived."[6] For Professor Stevenson the task of the theorist is to describe this
broadly conceived movement. Inevitably, in dealing with the total matter of
rhythm, the investigator must rely on the acuity of his own perceptions;
Professor Stevenson remarks, in his musical 'setting' of some lines by Edna
St. Vincent Millay, that "Much depends, let me repeat, on the style in
which the example is read."

Although the distinction between meter (the quality, quantity, number
of the syllables) and rhythm (the total music) is substantially recognized by
most theorists, and although there is much discussion devoted to the structural features of rhythmic forms, there has developed no comprehensive
theory on the genesis, nature, or function of rhythm. We have, to put it in
philosophical terms, neither an ontology nor an epistemology of rhythm.
Many poets have made valuable intuitive suggestions. T. S. Eliot and Stanley Kunitz have reported that a poem can first present itself to consciousness
as a wordless surge of rhythmic energy. The gift of the Muse is not conceptual, an ordering of ideas or lexical signs, but musical. But despite the rich
productivity of literary theorists during the last decade, no adequate theory
of rhythm has emerged. The generative metrists, drawing on the original
work of Halle and Keyser, continue to make their contributions toward
refining the concept of metricality; however, nothing in their approach has
been able to demonstrate that the metricality or non-metricality of a line of
verse has much to do with either its aesthetic effect or its aesthetic value. The
format of their work seems calculated to repel literary sensibility: a page in
Poetics, their leading journal, is apt to look like a demonstration in symbolic
logic or a computer printout.

The recent hermeneutic and semiotic movements, especially the fashionable French factions, have shown an extreme intellectualistic fastidiousness in dealing with the concrete realities of poetic structures. Like the now

old New Critics they have locked their interests into the meaning rather than
the texture of the literary work. However, they have gone much further than
the New Critics. They have been intent on transforming literary interpretation into a species of metaphysical discourse; as a result, much of their work
remains, at least for me, pinnacled in the intense inane of Pure Theory.
Those American critics coming under their influence have been less reluctant
to deal with the smudgy details of actual poetry; however, they have not
shown much interest in the problems of rhythm and meter. Occasionally a
revealing gesture is made. Geoffrey Hartman, one of our most sensitive
interpreters of poetic texts, in urging a theory of the literary vocation,
remarks:

> Since we are looking for a theory of *literary* as well as *functional* form,
> the essential ingredient is whatever makes the theory specifically relevant
> to literature. Otherwise we might quote Housman's "For Malt does more
> than Milton can/ To justify the ways of God to Man," and leave it at that.[7]

Professor Hartman has done what we all have done: quoted from memory and forgotten to check the text. Housman's lines ("Terence, this is stupid
stuff") read, in a fuller context:

> Say, for what were hop-yards meant,
> Or why was Burton built on Trent?
> Oh many a peer of England brews
> Livelier liquor than the Muse,
> And malt does more than Milton can
> To justify God's ways to man.

Professor Hartman links together Housman's jaunty tetrameter with Milton's more subtly modulated pentameter announcement that *Paradise Lost* is,
at least in intent, a theodicy. (Of course, Housman's recasting of Milton in a
less dignified meter achieves an ironic and flippant effect—a deliberate *misreading* that offers a world of comment on Victorian high seriousness.) Professor Hartman's linkage of the two meters misreads both Housman and Milton; it also indicates that Professor Hartman, intent only on the propositional
sense, did not hear the jarring rhythmic effect of *his* misreading.

My point may be only a quibble, and I certainly do not wish to impugn
the sensitivity of Professor Hartman's ear.[8] His misreading may have issued
from anxieties involving a too early exposure to *A Shropshire Lad,* an Oedipal
relationship with Milton, and memories of evenings down at Mory's. However, since we all seek a theory of literature whose "essential ingredient is
whatever makes the theory specifically relevant to literature," it may be of

some importance that our hermeneutics specifically include recognition of the poem's prosody. It is perhaps not quite a public scandal that recent literary theory—apart from the metrical investigations of the linguists—has shown such little concern for the aesthetic import of prosody. But when we consider the constricted nature of current theoretical interests we can understand this lack of concern. The interpretation of meaning is construed as a process of decoding or *deconstructing*; what is so treated (or mistreated) is a text whose status is not movement in a world of sound and whose contours are not "shapes in time," but an inscribed lexical sign fixed motionless on the page. Consequently there is no realization that meters and rhythms are also cognitive elements given to the reader's perception and available for interpretation. The "real" text is the written text; significantly one of the newest theoretical journals is called *Glyph*.

III

It is said that the world is divided between 'ear' men and 'eye' men. The semioticians and post-structuralist theorists are nearly all 'eye' men, as are the new grammarians of meter, the generative linguists. The linguists have, through increasingly subtle and ingenious techniques of scansion, reduced the poem to a "knowable object." They have codified the ways in which meter operates; their scansions have attempted to show that metricality operates within the confines of certain demonstrable 'laws.' They have charted the poem's physical features in diagrams, graphs, and "symbol strings"; this grammatical approach to prosodic study spatializes rhythmic structures and gives them visual status. However, the spatializing notations of scansion set up a process of reification: they 'see' things that cannot be heard, or are heard so faintly as to be aesthetically negligible. Nor have the two leading techniques of scanning (graphic and generative) proved fully adequate to the larger tasks of literary criticism. Scansion provides insight into the poem conceived as object: we can say of the following line, using the terminology of traditional graphic scansion, that the third foot is reversed; or using the terminology of Halle and Keyser, that an S occurs in the normally W fifth position and that stress maxima occur in the second and eighth positions:

> His silver skin laced with his golden blood.
> *Macbeth*, II, iii, 118

The versification, so described, is a clear and definable "objective correlative of our responses." Most (but not all) competent readers will scan it in the ways that I have. The metrical configuration of this line is an undeniable element of its total status as an aesthetic object—as undeniable as its striking iconography of violated royalty and of the horrible offense against God.

But the rhythm of the line (its broader movement, its 'music') inheres not only in its objectively describable meter; it is offered to the reader's consciousness charged with 'significance.' I am aware that this 'significance' is partly determined by the meaning and that, as Dr. Johnson warned, we can be tempted to "ascribe to the numbers the effects of the sense." I do not, however, wish to hedge my argument with too many qualifications. Meter provides the firmest structural base for the line, but the rhythm—which includes the violation of the meter, the repeated 's' and 'l' sounds, the modulation of the vowels—touches directly the sensitive membrane of the "auditory imagination" (to borrow a term from Eliot somewhat less exploited than the notorious "objective correlative").

Before I venture tentative suggestions about the significance of rhythmic forms, I should clarify some notions about what I call 'rhythmic presence' and the complex functioning of the auditory imagination. Obviously (as the poets have themselves testified) the rhythmic impulse originates with the poet, "far below the conscious levels of thought and feeling . . . sinking to the most primitive and forgotten, returning to the origin and bringing something back, seeking the beginning and the end."[9] In the process of creation, the poet objectifies this impulse through the formal structures of meter, patterns of sound, rhyme, syntax, and so on. The original impulse, at first without shape or articulation, gains body, becomes part of the "phonetic stratum" of the poem. Rhythm thus incarnated helps to establish the poem's "sensuous presence, which allows [us] to apprehend it as an aesthetic object."[10] Finally, the rhythm is offered to the reader's perception; at this point it becomes his experience and an activity of his consciousness.

Rhythm is a three-fold presence that can be located in the poet, in the poem, and in the reader's experience. The Compleat Prosodist, ideally equipped, should deal with the psychology of the creative process, the structure of the poem, and the reader's experience. In this collection we have divided the labor. Robert Graves gives a fancifully mythical account of the origins of the English meters. The linguists and graphic scanners give us the 'objective data' on metrical structure. Professor Stevenson and the poets are highly competent witnesses to their own experiences as readers and writers of verse.

Rhythms are offered to the reader's consciousness "charged with significance." Their significance comprehends both the ways they function and their putative import. From function to import we move along an axiological continuum. The metrical structure of Wordsworth's low-energy blank verse does little more than hold the lines together; their rhythmic import is signaled mainly by that familiar (and in Wordsworth's case, unassertive) phonetic patterning that distinguishes verse from prose. Rhythm functions neither mimetically nor expressively in lines like these:

> And all the neighbours, as he passed their doors,
> Came forth with wishes and with farewell prayers,
> That followed him till he was out of sight.
>
> *Michael,* 428-430

Wordsworth's narrative movement requires no particular rhythmic emphasis. But when we turn to lines like these, we grasp that rhythm functions in a more powerful way—with greater aesthetic effect:

> The Rainbow comes and goes,
> And lovely is the Rose,
> The Moon doth with delight
> Look round her when the heavens are bare,
> Waters on a starry night
> Are beautiful and fair . . .

Despite the Romantic program of particularity, Wordsworth's observations of nature are assimilated in his contemplation of them and deprived of sensuous immediacy: *Rainbow, Rose,* and *Moon* are near abstractions without visual vividness. The salient effect of these lines reaches us through the ear. The changing meter, the modulating 'o' sounds, the strongly stressed first syllable of *Waters* provide a more direct approach to the feeling in these lines than either Wordsworth's images or conventionalized pathetic fallacy.

The theory implicit in the above remarks is that rhythms allow access to 'felt experience.' "They make a direct appeal to and impression on the kinesthetic sense, which is an avenue through which we apprehend some vital aspects of reality."[11] What remains problematic are the *ways* rhythms make this appeal, and the precise nature of the reality so apprehended. 'Felt experience': but what is it being felt? Certainly the poet gives us through meter and rhythm the shape of inner psychologic processes: the feelings attached to tension, expectation, desire, fulfillment. The poet may also be using his rhythms in an attempt at direct representation; Keats's celebrated line,

> The hare limp'd trembling through the frozen grass

is often cited as an instance of metrical onomatopoeia, and in the words of
John Hollander, an instance of "'mimetic' effectiveness." It is a splendid
example of the communication of 'felt experience'; the crowding together of
the three strong stresses and the dissonant consonant cluster 'mp' not only
present the reader with an aural image of the movement of the freezing
animal but also trace with extraordinary vividness the activity of Keats's
consciousness—in this case an intense empathic response.

These abbreviated theories of rhythmic significance adumbrate a larger
referentialist theory of both poetic form and art in general. My sympathies
are generally on the side of referentialism: if rhythms are mimetic, they must
imitate aspects of human thought and action outside the poetic structure; if
expressive, they must serve as phonetic signs for human feeling and emotion.
Yvor Winters (q.v.), one of our most austerely formalist theorists, tells us
"rhythm is in a measure expressive of emotion . . . [it] permeates the entire
poem as blood permeates the human body: remove it and you have a corpse."
However, Winters makes only a local and limited analogy between rhythm
and organic process. Our other formalist theorists, Wimsatt and Beardsley
and Donald Justice, in their exclusive concern with meter, are more reticent
to deal with 'rhythmic significance.' For them meters are architectonic and
contextual, forming self-referring patterns of sound and meaning. Professor
Wimsatt, on occasion, does speak of the "local tension" generated by departures from the abstract metrical paradigm. The two reversed feet in this line
of Chaucer,

Wondring upon this word; quaking for drede . . .

"can be emphatic, vibratory, expressive." Such tension, offered to consciousness, serves as a sign of feeling and the function of rhythmic forms is
mimetic-expressive.

We are working, from the notion of rhythm as 'felt experience,' to a
corollary epistemology of rhythm. I can, in this introduction, only outline
the problems and possibilities of an elaborate theoretical task. Is the experience of rhythm given directly to our physical being without the mediation of
some (as yet undetermined) symbolic transaction? In lines like these, which
approach nonsense, this seems the case:

These were days when my heart was volcanic,
      As the scoriac rivers that roll—
      As the lavas that restlessly roll
Their sulphurous currents down Yaanek
      In the ultimate climes of the Pole—

> That groan as they roll down Mount Yaanek
> In the realms of the Boreal Pole.
>
> Poe, "Ulalume"

Poe's anapests are inappropriate to his dialogue of self and soul because their noisy marching drowns out any possibility of delicate modulation of feeling. We apprehend the rhythm through the crudity of a 'felt experience' that overrides the meaning; it is a species of low-level incantation which effects a dubious magic. I would venture that here the rhythm is a 'real' experience almost (but not quite) divorced from the poem's conceptual features.

In *Sound and Form in Modern Poetry* I proposed, with perhaps more assurance than tact, that rhythmic forms were, in the terminology of Susanne Langer, presentational symbols. Such symbols possess no specific sign function but are analogues to feeling. The phonetic patternings of meter and rhythm become articulate forms of feeling. However, I am now less confident that rhythm is, in Mrs. Langer's sense, "a real semantic" capable of any precise understanding.[12] Two problems stand as deterrents. If rhythms are truly analogues to feeling, then a particular rhythmic form must be isomorphic with the feeling it designates. That is, each element of the rhythmic form must correspond to the feeling in the way that the lines and points on a map correspond to the region mapped. If this were the case, we could write a grammar of rhythm as the linguists and graphic scanners have written grammars of meter. But no one reads a poem as he reads a map. Rhythms may *resemble* feelings in that the falling motion of some lines of verse,

> Winding across wide water, without sound.
> The day is like wide water, without sound . . .

may suggest to some readers a decrescendo of emotional dynamics.

A second problem is that we cannot isolate rhythmic form from meaning. Even in poems with the most insistent pulsing meters, what we ascribe to rhythm is often "the effects of the sense." This is especially true in lines where words occur that both describe and, through onomatopoeia, orchestrate the action:

> To a chirr of gongs
> And a chitter of cries
> And the heavy thrum
> Of the endless tread
> That they tread. . . .

The rhythmic significance of this ceremonial music is inseparable from the heavy denotational emphasis of its vocabulary. There is no technique of interpretation that can separate out the rhythm of this ironic *marcia funebre* from the resonance of words like *chirr* and *chitter, thrum* and *tread.*

I am at present skeptical that rhythmic significance will yield its secrets to the methodologies of any existing theory of signs. The prevailing structuralist preoccupation with *writing* reaffirms the New Critical emphasis on the poem's spatiality and its status as urn, Chinese jar, or "verbal icon." If, however, we also think of the poem unfolding as "a shape in time," then its temporal unfolding assumes in the consciousness of the reader ontological preeminence.[13] Rhythm, phenomenologically speaking, becomes a revelation of Being-in-Time; what we hear in rhythm are the qualities of our temporal experience, the noise that times makes. The poet may 'keep time' with an unbroken flow of slack and stressed syllables:

> And time that gave doth now his gift confound. . . .

Or he may 'break time' with a violent displacement of accent:

> Let me not to the marriage of true minds. . . .

We should stress, as do the musical prosodists, that the keeping and breaking are matters not only of articulated sounds but also of felt silences.

Rhythm also brings us into proximity to what Walter Ong calls "the ineluctable interiority" of all linguistic utterance:

> Language retains this interiority because it . . . remains always the medium wherein persons discover and renew their discovery that they are persons. . . . The pitch of utterance which bears toward the interior of the speaker—and by the same token toward the interior of the hearer, who repeats in his own interior the words of the speaker and thereby understands them—can never be done away with. . . .[14]

A phenomenology of rhythm might regard both the narrow and broad movements of poetry as a dialectic of that objective data supplied by the grammarians and of that which "can never be done away with": the mysterious but compelling fact that rhythm allows us direct cognition of that "interiority" retained by language. Such a phenomenological account would dissolve the artificial separation of subject and object: the regarding of a poem exclusively as "a mental transaction" unfolding in time, or exclusively as a palpable object frozen in space. What I hope is that prosodic study will proceed from the grammar of meter to the phenomenology of rhythm: from knowledge of the objective correlative to understanding of the auditory imagination.

NOTES

[1] "The Strange Music of English Verse," *Kenyon Review*, XVIII, 3 (Summer 1956), pp. 460–77.

[2] *Blank Verse* (London, 1895), p. 15.

[3] *Versification* (New York, 1972), p. xix.

[4] *Ibid.*, p. viii.

[5] Monroe C. Beardsley, "Verse and Music," in *Versification*, p. 241.

[6] Wimsatt, *Versification*, p. xv.

[7] "Toward Literary History," *Daedalus*, Spring 1970, p. 364. The passage is reprinted without correction in *Beyond Formalism* (New Haven, 1970), p. 367.

[8] The bad temper that has characterized much prosodic study is rooted in an easily deduced psychological fact: no scholar wants the sensitivity of *his* ear impugned.

[9] T. S. Eliot, *The Use of Poetry and the Use of Criticism* (London, 1933), pp. 118–19.

[10] Mikel Dufrenne, *The Phenomenology of Aesthetic Experience* (Evanston, 1973), p. 44.

[11] From a letter written to me by the late Richard P. Adams. Shortly before his death we exchanged views on the theory of rhythm. His suggestions have been extremely useful in clarifying my own ideas.

[12] For this critique of Mrs. Langer, I am indebted to Charles L. Stevenson. See *Language, Thought, and Culture*, ed. Paul Henle (Ann Arbor, 1958): especially pp. 202–10.

[13] Whether we conceive the poem as object-in-space or manifold-in-time, we are indicating a preference in analogy. All theory moves toward analogy; our preferences are often a matter of temperament.

[14] See "A Dialectic of Aural and Objective Correlatives," in *The Barbarian Within* (New York, 1962), pp. 29–30.

PART ONE

Prosody

History and Function

ROBERT GRAVES

Harp, Anvil, Oar

It is hard to resist the energy and enthusiasm of Robert Graves. He commands a vast if idiosyncratic scholarship; he brings a poet's imagination to both history and aesthetics. The anthropology Graves invokes to trace the origins of meter need not be regarded as science; however, Graves' recognition of the strong-stress and syllable-stress systems is of great value.

Perhaps more useful than Graves' mythology of literary history is his wisdom as a craftsman. He has closely observed English metrical practice; his comments on Donne, Shakespeare, and T. S. Eliot deserve attention if not necessarily assent. His insistence on purity of genre is an echo from the Augustan Age: prose is prose and verse is verse and let us not dilute good wine with water. The principle of metrical decorum has not been better stated or more vigorously advocated.

Last week I spoke about Marvan, the seventh-century poet of Connaught who revealed to the professors of the Great Bardic Academy how the poet's harp originated: namely when the wind played on the dried tendons of a stranded whale's skeleton in the time of Macuel son of Miduel. And how metre originated: namely in the alternate beat of two hammers on the anvil, while Lamiach was still alive. The three hundred professors could not follow Marvan here, having long ceased to think poetically. As historic or scientific statements his revelations are, of course, challengeable: not a grain of evidence can be cited for the existence of the whale, or even for that of Macuel son of Miduel. Nevertheless, as poetic statements they are exact. What is the whale? An emblem of the White Love-goddess Rahab, Ruler of the Sea, who used yearly to destroy her sacred kings in numerous cities from Connaught to the Persian Gulf; until at last the god Enlil, or Marduk (or Jehovah, according to the prophet Isaiah) killed her with the new-fangled weapon called a sword—the Babylonians claimed in a hymn that he sliced her like a flatfish. But the King of Babylon still had to do ritual battle with her every year, be swallowed, and spewed up again on the third day, as Jonah was. And though Jehovah's prophets chanted: 'O ye whales, bless ye Adonai, praise Him and magnify Him for ever!' they knew that Leviathan was unregenerate, uncontrollable and not to be fished up with any hook let down. Hence the author of the Apocalypse prophesied that one day 'there shall be no more sea'; by this he meant 'no more Rahab, and no more whales'.

The emblems of the Muse Trinity are a white dove in the sky, a white hind in the forest, a whale taking his pastime in the depth of the sea. Where, then, could one find a better figure of death than the white skeleton of a stranded whale? And wind, North Wind, the wind that (proverbially) pigs alone can see, the wind that, as I told you, Marvan carried in his mantle, the wind that fertilized the windswift sacred mares of Trojan Erichthonius and the prophetic vultures of Roman augury—wind (*spiritus, pneuma*) is the emblem of inspiration. The bones of Rahab the Whale may lie stranded on the shore; but, for a poet, there is more truth in her dead sinews than in Marduk's living mouth. When Macuel son of Miduel heard the wind howling tunefully in the Aeolian harp of the whale's skeleton, he bethought himself and built a smaller, more manageable one from the same materials. And when he struck his harp and cried: 'Sing to me, Muse!' this was no formal invitation—Rahab herself sang at his plea.

A close parallel, by the bye, may be found in English popular poetry. The ballad of the *Twa Sisters of Binnorie* tells of a drowned woman whose hair was used for harp-strings:

> And by there came a harper fine
> *Edinbro', Edinbro'*
> Such as harp to nobles when they dine.
> *Stirling for aye*
> He's ta'en twa strands of her yellow hair
> And with it strung a harp sae rare
> *Bonnie St Johnstone stands on Tay.*

He's done him into her father's hall,
    Edinbro', Edinbro'
And played the harp before them all,
    Stirling for aye
And syne the harp spake loud and clear
'Farewell my father and mither dear.'
    Bonnie St Johnstone stands on Tay.

And syne the harp began to sing
    Edinbro', Edinbro'
And it's 'Farewell, sweetheart,' sang the string
    Stirling for aye
And then, as plain as plain could be,
'There sits my sister who drownéd me.'
    Bonnie St Johnstone stands on Tay.

The harp is the prophetic voice of the yellow-haired goddess—the Muse-goddess was always yellow-haired—and she sings of love, and grief, and doom. Marvan, moreover, was careful to distinguish the fitful inspirational music of the Aeolian harp from the purposeful rhythmic clatter of the smith's anvil.

I am aware that I should here be discussing the English, not the Irish, literary scene. But Irish poetry is to English poetry, as—may I say?—the Pharisaic synagogue is to the Christian Church: an antecedent which historians are tempted to forget or belittle. The English have long despised the Irish; and though generously ready to acknowledge their debt to Anglo-Saxon, French, Italian, Latin and Greek literatures, are loth to admit that the strongest element in English poetic technique (though certainly acquired at second or third hand) is the Irish tradition of craftsmanship.

When two hammers answer each other five times on the anvil—*ti-tum, ti-tum, ti-tum, ti-tum, ti-tum*—five in honour of the five stations of the Celtic year, there you have Chaucer's familiar decasyllabic line:

> A knight ther was, and that a worthy man
> That fro the tymë that he first began
> To ryden out, he lovéd chivalrye. . . .

But Anglo-Saxon poetry had been based on the slow pull and push of the oar:

> Then I of myself / will máke this known
> That awhíle I was held / the Héodenings' scop,
> To my duke most dear / and Déor was my name.

The function of the Nordic *scop* seems to have been twofold. Not only was he originally a 'shaper' of charms, to protect the person of the king and so maintain prosperity in the realm; but he had a subsidiary task, of persuading a ship's crew to pull rhythmically and uncomplainingly on their oars against the rough waves of the North Sea, by singing them ballads in time to the beat. When they returned from a successful foray, and dumped their spoil of gold collars, shields, casques, and monastic chalices on the rush-strewn floor of the beer-hall, then the *scop* resumed his song. The drunken earls and churls straddled the benches, and rocked to the tune: 'Over the whale's way, fared we unfearful. . . .

Anglo-Saxon poetry is unrhymed, because the noise of rowlocks does not suggest rhyme. Rhyme reached England from France. It had been brought there by Irish missionaries who recivilized Western Europe after the Frankish invasions. These missionaries wrote and talked Latin, and *The Rhythm of St Bernard of Cluny*, the first rhymed poem of high literary pretensions written by an Englishman (during the reign of Henry I or II), follows the pure Irish tradition. Its complicated series of internal and end-rhymes, and its faultless finish, leave no doubt about this. Here are four of the three thousand rhymed lines:

Urbs Syon aurea, Patria lactea, cive decora,
Omne cor obruis, omnibus obstruis et cor et ora.
Nescio, nescio, quae jubilatio, lux tibi qualis,
Quam socialia gaudia, gloria quam specialis.

Prosodists have a Latin name for the metre: *Leonini cristati trilices dactylici*. St Bernard's *Rhythm* has been translated into English, pretty well (though with a loss of all the rhyme pairs except the end ones, which have become monosyllables), by the Victorian hymn-writer, J. M. Neale:

Jerusalem the Golden
    With Milk and Honey Blest,
Beneath Thy Contemplation
    Sink heart and voice oppressed:
I know not, O I know not,
    What social joys are there;
What radiancy of Glory,
    What Light beyond Compare!

Nordic verse-craft, as I was saying, is linked to the pull of the oar. Greek verse-craft is linked to the ecstatic beat of feet around a rough stone altar, sacred to Dionysus (or Hermes, or Eros, or Zeus Cronides), probably to the sound of the dactylic drum played by a priestess or a priest:

$$- \cup \cup / - \cup \cup / - / / \cup \cup / - \cup \cup / - \cup \cup / - -$$

The Greeks also admitted the iambic, traditionally named in honour of lasciviously hobbling Iambe, who (you may remember) tried to coax a smile from the bereaved Demeter at Eleusis. Iambic metre may have begun with Helladic totem dances which imitated the hobbling of partridge or quail:

$$\cup - / \cup - / \cup / / - / \cup - / \cup - / \cup -$$

There was also the spondaic measure derived from the gloomy double-stamp of buskined mourners, arousing some dead hero to drink the libations (*spondae*) that they poured for him:

$$- - / - - / - / / - / - - / - - / - -$$

A metrical line in Greek poetry represents the turn taken by a dancer around an altar or tomb, with a caesura marking the halfway point: the metre never varies until the dancers have dropped with fatigue. Similarly in *Beowulf* and other Anglo-Saxon poems, the oars' pull and push continues mercilessly until harbour is reached, or until the drunken diners fall off their bench to the floor, unable to rise again.

The Irish concept of metre is wholly different. All poets owed allegiance to the Muse-goddess Brigid—who may be decently equated with the Helladic Moon-goddess Brizo of Delos. Brigid had three aspects: the Brigid of Poets, the Brigid of Smiths, and the Brigid of Physicians. A Brigid of Smiths may seem anomalous, because English smiths have long ranked lower in the social scale than poets and physicians. In England smithcraft ceased, with the triumph of Christianity, to be an inspired profession; it was wrested by monks from the hands of the lame Smith Wayland (who served the Goddess Freya) and registered merely as a useful trade. Even as a trade, it is dying now: wedding ring, or scythe, or steel helmet is supplied by factories where not even a superstitious vestige of the Wayland cult has gone into the making. But the pagan smith, whether goldsmith, whitesmith, or blacksmith, approached his work with enormous care and magical precaution.

The religious connexion between poetry, smithcraft, and medicine is a close one. Medicine presupposes a knowledge of times, seasons, and the sovereign properties of plants, trees, beasts, birds, fish, earths, minerals. Poetry presupposes an inspired knowledge of man's sensuous and spiritual nature. Smithcraft—for the smith was also carpenter, mason, shipwright and toolmaker—presupposes an inspired knowledge of how to transform lifeless material into active forms. No ancient smith would have dared to proceed without the aids of medicine and poetry. The charcoal used on his forge had been made, with spells, at a certain time of the year from timber of certain sacred trees; and the leather of the forge bellows, from the skin of a sacred animal ritually sacrificed. Before starting a task, he and his assistant were obliged to purify themselves with medicines and lustrations, and to placate the Spites which habitually crowd around forge and anvil. If he happened to be forging a sword, the water in which it was to be tempered must have magical properties—May dew, or spring water in which a virgin princess had washed her hair. The whole work was done to the accompaniment of poetic spells.

Such spells matched the rhythm of the smith's hammers; and these were of unequal weight. A sledge hammer was swung by the assistant; the smith himself managed the lighter hammer. To beat out hot metal successfully, one must work fast and follow a prearranged scheme. The smith with his tongs lays the glowing lump of iron on the anvil, then touches with his hammer the place where the sledge blow is to fall; next he raps on the anvil the number of blows required. Down comes the sledge; the smith raps again for another blow, or series of blows. Experience teaches him how many can be got in while the iron is still hot. So each stage of every process had its peculiar metre, to which descriptive words became attached; and presently the words found their own tunes. This process explains Marvan's mysterious reference to Lamiach, who appears in the English translations of *Genesis* as 'Lamech'. Lamech was the father of Tubal the first smith, and Jubal the first musician. Nor did the smith (as many archaeologists assume) let caprice rule the number and shape of ornaments that he introduced into his work. Whether he was forging a weapon, or a piece of armour, or a tool, or a cauldron, or a jewelled collar, every element in the design had a magical significance.

An Irish poet versified to the ring of hammers; and the fact that rhyme and regular metre had become characteristic of English poetry by Chaucer's time implies that the smithy tradition of careful thought and accurate workmanship, which these call for, had also been to some extent adopted. The metaphor of beating out one's verse on the anvil is now, indeed, a poetical commonplace. But let me put it this way: though every English poet is a smith for the greater part of the year, he takes to the sea during the brief sailing season. Chaucer may seem to be a hammer-and-anvil poet when he writes:

> A knight ther was, and that a worthy man
> That fro the tymë that he first began
> To ryden out, he lovéd chivalrye. . . .

Ti-um, ti-um, ti-um, ti-um. Then he lays down the hammer and reaches for the oar. Instead of:

> Honoùr and freédom, trùth and coúrtesy,

he writes:

> Trùth and honoùr / freédom and coúrtesy . . .

and this has been the English verse-tradition ever since.

Skelton also reconciled the anvil with the oar in a metre which he used in his early *Lament for Edward IV,* and again at the close of his life in *Speke Parrot.* Note the Anglo-Saxon alliteration:

> *Miseremini mei* / ye that be my frendis!
> This world hath forméd me / downë to fall.
> How may I endure / when that everi thing endis?
> What creäture is bornë / to be eternáll?

and:

> The myrrour that I tote in / *quasi diaphanum,*
> *Vel quasi speculum* / *in aenigmate,*
> *Elencticum,* or ells / *enthymematicum,*
> For logicians to loke on / somewhat *sophistice:*
> Retoricyons and oratours / in freshe humanyte,
> Support Parrot, I pray you / with your suffrage ornate,
> Of *confuse tantum* / auoydynge the chekmate.

The history of Shakespeare's blank verse is a progression from the careful anvil work of, say, *The Comedy of Errors,* to *The Tempest,* where the oar is pulling in a very rough sea. *The Comedy of Errors* begins:

EGEON: Proceed, Solinus, to procure my fall,
And by the doom of death end woes and all.

DUKE OF Merchant of Syracusa, plead no more.
EPHESUS: I am not partial to infringe our laws;
The enmity and discord which of late
Sprung from the rancorous outrage of your Duke
To merchants, our well-dealing countrymen,
Who wanting guilders to redeem their lives,
Have sealed his rigorous statutes with their bloods,
Excludes all pity from our threatening looks. . . .

But in *The Tempest* the opening exchanges between shipmaster and boatswain are recognized as blank verse only because every now and then a regular line occurs to reassert the norm. (Heming and Condell in their edition of the *First Folio* print them as prose, and all cautious editors follow suit.)

(The BOATSWAIN appears when the MASTER summons him)

THE MASTER:	Good. Speak to the mariners; fall to't yarely.
	Or we run ourselves aground. Bestir, bestir!
BOATSWAIN:	Heigh my hearts, cheerily, cheerily my hearts,
	yare, yare!
	Take in the topsail! Tend to the master's whistle!
(to the MASTER)	Blow till thou burst thy wind, if room enough!

The rules of prosody apply only to anvil verse, or to sacred-dance verse, in which every syllable is evaluated and counted. Pope, for instance, says that he lisped in numbers for the numbers came; 'numbers' translates the Latin *numeri,* which imply a careful count of syllables. Pope never escaped from the 'numbers' theory: which posits an orderly sequence of metrical feet each with the same determined time value, every long syllable being given the value of the crotchet, and every short syllable the value of a quaver; though the Elizabethan critics, headed by George Puttenham, had emphatically rejected this theory. The only fundamental difference between Pope's notion of verse and Virgil's, or Horace's, was that the Latin convention of what made a syllable long or short had lapsed. Now, in Bernard of Cluny's *Rhythm,* for instance, the Latin rules of quantity are maintained: every syllable is regarded as long or short by nature, though a short syllable may become long by position; and a terminal vowel, or vowel plus *m,* will be elided and disappear. This, it must be realized, was a highly artificial convention: ordinary Latin speech, as heard in the home and Forum, seems from the scraps of camp songs penned by Suetonius to have been accentual, and the accent did not necessarily fall on the long vowel.

It amused educated English poets—such as Chaucer, Skelton, Ben Jonson, Milton, Marvell, Dr Johnson, and Coleridge—to compose Latin verses in Classical style; but the freedom to observe natural speech stresses (as opposed to the laws of quantity) not only in vernacular verse but in Latin too, if they pleased, had already been won for them by the hymnologists and carol-makers and Goliardic song-writers of the Middle Ages. The first two lines of the famous medieval students' drinking song:

> Mihi est propositum in taberna mori;
> Vinum sit appositum potatoris ori . . .

contain thirteen false quantities, and the first two lines of the equally famous hymn:

> Dies irae, dies illa
> Solvens saecla in favilla . . .

contain eight. (Don't bother to count them.) This is not due to ignorance. Who would dare accuse St Thomas Aquinas of ignorance because he rhymes *natus* with *datus?* Aquinas knew well enough that rhyme was a barbarism in Classical Latin poetry—and that Cicero had made a fool of himself with the internal rhyme of:

> O fortunatam natam, me Consule, Romam!

But he also knew that these quantities had been justified by Irish metrical example; the Irish did not acknowledge quantity, they relied on accent.

Skelton, in his *Devout Trentale for Old John Clerk, Sometime the Holy Patriarche of Diss,* actually alternated correct hexameters with Goliardic verse:

> Sequitur trigintale,
> Tale quale rationale,
> Licet parum curiale,
> Tamen satis est formale,
> Joannis Clerc, hominis
> Cujusdam multinominis,
> Joannes Jayberd qui vocatur,
> Clerc cleribus nuncupatur.
> Obiit sanctus iste pater
> Anno Domini MD, sexto.
> In parochia de Dis.
> Non erat sibi similis;
> In malitia vir insignis,
> Duplex corde et bilinguis;
> Senio confectus,
> Omnibus suspectus,
> Nemini dilectus,
> Sepultus est *amonge the wedes:*
> *God forgeue hym his mysdedes!*
>
> Dulce melos[1]
> Penetrans coelos.

> Carmina cum cannis cantemus festa Joannis:
> Clerk obiit vere, Jayberd nomenque dedere;
> Dis populo natus, Clerk cleribusque vocatus.

The Elizabethan critics, humanists to a man, were a little uneasy about this divergence from Classical metric theory, but there was clearly no help for it. Samuel Daniel, in his *Defence of Rhyme* (1603), found it necessary to lay down: 'As Greeke and Latine verse consists of the number and quantity of sillables, so doth the English verse of measure and accent.' They admitted, in fact, that the natural accent of current English speech decides whether a syllable should be long or short—even though the same word may change its value in the same line. Thus, for instance, the pentameter:

$$\bar{o}ff\breve{e}r\ h\breve{e}r\ /\ \bar{i}c\breve{e}s,\ \breve{o}r\ /\ \bar{a}\ /\ /\ l\bar{o}vel\breve{y}\ c\breve{o}m/f\bar{o}rt\breve{a}bl\breve{e}\ /\ ch\bar{a}ir$$

is quantitatively correct according to Ovidian rule, but does not scan. Moreover, the Virgilian hexameter, as Thomas Nashe forcefully explained in his answer to Gabriel Harvey's recommendation of it, is not natural to English:

> The Hexamiter verse I graunt to be a Gentleman of an auncient house (so is many an english beggar); yet this Clyme of ours hee cannot thriue in. Our speech is too craggy for him to set his plough in; hee goes twitching and hopping in our language like a man running vpon quagmiers, vp the hill in one Syllable, and downe the dale in another, retaining no part of that stately smooth gate which he vaunts himselfe with amongst the Greeks and Latins.

And so a strong sense has grown up among practical English poets that the natural rhythm of speech decides where accents fall; and that, therefore, the less artificial the words, the truer the poem.

Tell a schoolchild that Keats's *Faery Song* is an iambic poem with three four-foot lines followed by one of five feet, another of four feet, one of two feet, and finally a five-footer, rhyming AB, AB, C, C, D—and he will read it like this:

> Ah woe / is me / poor silv/er wing
> That I / must chant / thy lad/y's dirge
> And death / to this / fair haunt / of spring
> And mel/ody / and streams / of flower/y verge.
> Poor Silv / erwing / ah woe / is me
> That I / must see
> These Bloss/oms snow / upon / thy lad/y's pall.

But if the words are spoken in the manner most natural to their sense and feeling, this is how Keats will have meant it to be said; and you realize that the laws of prosody are, to verse, very much as copperplate models are to handwriting. Keats had a poet's ear for verse; and Shakespeare had; as Donne had; as Coleridge had; as Skelton had. But Keats was easily seduced. When he put on his singing robes and played at being a Classical poet, he became gorbliminess incarnate. In his *Ode to Apollo,* for example:

> Then, through thy Temple wide, melodious swells
>> The sweet majestic tone of Maro's lyre:
> The soul delighted on each accent dwells,—
>> Enraptur'd dwells,—not daring to respire,
> The while he tells of grief around a funeral pyre.

> 'Tis awful silence then again;
>> Expectant stand the spheres;
>> Breathless the laurell'd peers,
>> Nor move, till ends the lofty strain,
>> Nor move till Milton's tuneful thunders cease
> And leave once more the ravish'd heaven in peace.

> Thou biddest Shakespeare wave his hand,
>> And quickly forward spring
> The Passions—a terrific band—
>> And each vibrates the string
> That with its tyrant temper best accords,
> While from their Master's lips pour forth the inspiring words.

Keats should have known that to impose an artificial word-order, or an artificial vocabulary, on poems is a lapse in poetic dignity.

There is so much to say about professional standards in verse-technique, that I shall confine myself to generalities. For instance, that though the muscular *str* and *scr* words: *strain, strength, string, strangle, stretch, struggle, strident, extravagant, screw, scrape, scrawny,* and such easy skipping words as *melody, merrily, prettily, harmony, fantasy* match sense with sound, other words are not so onomatopoeic. A *strangely striped strip of satin* is far too emphatic in sound for the sense, and *a terribly powerful Florida hurricane* is not nearly emphatic enough. Yet to alter the spirit of an original poetic thought for the sake of metre or euphony is unprofessional conduct. So the art of accommodating sense to sound without impairing the original thought has to be learned by example and experiment. Under-emphasis or over-emphasis in a

word can be controlled by playing other words off against it, and carefully
choosing its position in a line, and making the necessary adjustments to
neighbouring lines until the ear at last feels satisfied. It is an axiom among
poets that if one trusts whole-heartedly to poetic magic, one will be sure to
solve any merely verbal problem or else discover that the verbal problem is
hiding an imprecision in poetic thought.

I say magic, since the act of composition occurs in a sort of trance,
distinguishable from dream only because the critical faculties are not dor-
mant, but on the contrary, more acute than normally. Often a rugger player
is congratulated on having played the smartest game of his life, but regrets
that he cannot remember a single incident after the first five minutes, when
he got kicked on the head. It is much the same with a poet when he
completes a true poem. But often he wakes from the trance too soon and is
tempted to solve the remaining problems intellectually. Few self-styled poets
have experienced the trance; but all who have, know that to work out a line
by an exercise of reason, rather than by a deep-seated belief in miracle, is highly
unprofessional conduct. If a trance has been interrupted, it is just too bad.
The poem should be left unfinished, in the hope that suddenly, out of the
blue, days or months later, it may start stirring again at the back of the
mind, when the remaining problems will solve themselves without difficulty.

Donne's chief failing as a love-poet was his readiness to continue the
inspired beginning with a witty development. For instance:

> Goe, and catche a falling starre,
> Get with child a mandrake roote. . . .

Here Donne paused, apparently remembered Villon's *neiges d'antan,* and went
on:

> Tell me, where all past yeares are. . . .

And then consciously searched for a rhyme to *roote.* But he had not the least
idea where the poem was taking him, except into a discussion of impossibility. So he continued in quite a different key:

> Or who cleft the Divels foot,
> Teach me to heare Mermaides singing,
> Or to keep off envies stinging. . . .

He paused again and apparently remembered Shakespeare's:

> Blow, blow thou winter wind,

> Thou art not so unkind
> As man's ingratitude . . .

and Dante's remarks about the bitterness of having to seek advancement from haughty patrons. So he ended the verse with the quite irrelevant:

> And finde
> What winde
> Serves to advance an honest minde.

Again he opened magnificently:

> I wonder by my troth, what thou, and I
> Did, till we lov'd? were we not wean'd till then?
> But suck'd on countrey pleasures, childishly?

Here inspiration faded and he resorted to artifice:

> Or snorted we in the seaven sleepers' den?
> T'was so; But this, all pleasures fancies bee.
> If ever any beauty I did see,
> Which I desir'd, and got, t'was but a dreame of thee.

Donne is adept at keeping the ball in the air, but he deceives us here by changing the ball. Coleridge often does the same thing, for example when he fakes a sequel to the inspired opening passage of *Christabel*—but he handles the ball so clumsily that we are seldom deceived.

It is unprofessional conduct to say: 'When next I write a poem I shall use the sonnet form'—because the theme is by definition unforeseeable, and theme chooses metre. A poet should not be conscious of the metrical pattern of a poem he is writing until the first three or four lines have appeared; he may even find himself in the eleventh line of fourteen before realizing that a sonnet is on the way. Besides, metre is only a frame; the atmospheres of two sonnets can be so different that they will not be recognized as having the same form except by a careful count of lines and feet. Theme chooses metre; what is more, theme decides what rhythmic variations should be made on metre. The theory that all poems must be equally rich in sound is an un-English one, borrowed from Virgil. Rainbow-like passages are delightful every now and then, but they match a rare mood of opulence and exaltation which soon fatigues. The riches of *Paradise Lost* fatigue, and even oppress, all but musicians. Rainbows should make their appearances only when the moment has come to disclose the riches of the heart, or soul, or imagination; they testify to passing storms and are short-lived.

Another professional principle is that *mimesis* should be regarded as vulgar. By mimesis I mean such *tours de force* as Virgil's:

> Quadrupedante putrem sonitu quatit ungula campum,

and Tennyson's:

> The moan of doves in immemorial elms,
> The murmur of innumerable bees.

To these I should add the Homeric:

> Autis epeita pedonde cylindeto laäs anaides,

the shameless stone of Sisyphus bounding downhill, if I did not think that this was high-spirited verbal comedy, proclaiming disbelief in the whole theory of divine punishment.

Pope's translation of the Sisyphus passage, by the way, runs:

> With many a weary sigh, and many a groan,
> Up the high hill he heaves a huge round stone...

though the corresponding lines in the *Odyssey* do not mimic Sisyphus's breathlessness. And Pope's concluding couplet is wretchedly incompetent:

> The huge round stone, resulting with a bound
> Thunders impetuous down and smokes along the ground.

The false internal rhymes of *round* and *bound* and the half-rhymes *down* and *ground* effectively act as brakes on the stone's merry progress. As Blake said in one of his Public Addresses: 'I do not condemn Pope or Dryden because they did not understand imagination, but because they did not understand verse'.

One of the most difficult problems is how to use natural speech rhythms as variations on a metrical norm. And here we meet with the heresy of free verse. Until the time of Blake and his oratorical cadences, it was generally agreed that the reader should never be allowed to lose his sense of metrical norm. But Blake, finding the contemporary technique of poetry too cramping, burst it wide open and wrote something that was neither poetry nor prose. Whitman did much the same, though for different reasons: he epitomizes the restless American habit, first noted in the eighteenth century, of moving adventurously west across the trackless prairie, scratch-farming as one goes, instead of clinging to some pleasant Pennsylvanian farm, improving crops and stock by careful husbandry, and building a homestead for one's children and grand-children. All who, like Whitman, choose to dispense with a rhythmical norm are welcome to explore the new country which he opened up, but it now wears rather a dismal look. Robert Frost's poems, which combine traditional metres with intensely personal rhythms, show the advantage of staying put and patiently working at the problem.[2]

A dogma has recently been planted in English schools that the King James version of the Bible is poetry. It is not. The polishing of the English translation was, of course, admirably done by a team of capable University scholars, trained in the oratorical art. Sometimes they even included a perfectly metrical line:

How art thou fallen from Heaven, O Lucifer, son of the morning!

And:

Come down and sit in the dust; O virgin daughter of Babylon,
Sit on the ground. . . .

But one might as well call *The Times* leaders poetry, because they are written by skilled journalists and because they contain a high proportion of blank-verse lines, sometimes as much as 30 percent.

Ben Jonson told Drummond of Hawthornden that 'for not keeping of accent'—that is to say, allowing his readers to lose the sense of metrical norm—'Donne deserved hanging'. Jonson had also said that Donne was 'the first poet in the world in some things', and that he had a few of his early poems by heart. It is difficult to reconcile these statements. But Jonson seems to be referring to the *Satyres,* where Donne at times deliberately changes the metre—as when a competitor in a walking race shamelessly bends his knees and breaks into a short run:

. . . So in immaculate clothes, and Symetrie
Perfect as circles, with such nicetie
As a young Preacher at his first time goes
To preach, he enters, and a Lady, which owes
Him not so much as good will, he arrests,
And unto her protests, protests, protests;
So much as at Rome would serve to have throwne
Ten Cardinalls into the Inquisition;
And whispers by Jesu, so often, that A
Pursevant would have ravish'd him away
For saying of our Ladies psalter. But 'tis fit
That they each other plague, they merit it. . . .

In the same satire, Donne also makes the units of sense play havoc with the units of metre:

> . . . No, no, Thou which since yesterday hast beene
> Almost about the whole world, hast thou seene,
> O Sunne, in all thy journey, Vanitie,
> Such as swells the bladder of our court? I
> Thinke he which made your waxen garden, and
> Transported it from Italy to stand
> With us, at London, flouts our Presence, for
> Just such gay painted things, which nò sappe, nor
> Tast have in them, ours are; And naturall
> Some of the stocks are, their fruits, bastard all.

But let me speak up for Donne. There are, of course, certain familiar proprieties in English poetry. Accent must be kept, which means, as I have shown, that however the metrical norm may be varied, it should stay recognizable—one must not write lines that go off into another metre altogether. Rhyme must be kept within certain decent limits, and the consonantal part of rhyme must be regarded as more important than the vowel. It is, for instance, indecent to rhyme *charm* with *calm*, or (*pace* W. H. Auden) *bore* with *mother-in-law*; though *love* and *prove*, *all* and *usual*, *fly* and *extremity* are traditionally countenanced. Three-syllable rhymes are indecent, so are mixed metaphors, and what Corinna called 'sowing with the sack'—namely over-ornamentation of every kind. Again: an even level of language should be kept: one must decide to what period each poem belongs and not relapse to an earlier, or anticipate a more modern, diction. Thus it is indecent to address *you* and *thee* in the same verse to the same person—even if Pope and Marvell are quoted in justification. And, most important, there should be no discrepancy between the sound and the sense of a poem. It would be difficult, for instance, to quarrel on technical grounds with a simple iambic stanza such as this:

> Mother is dead; my heart to pieces torn,
> I hear my kinsmen weep—
> Uncle, niece, nephew, cousin, who convey her
> Unto her last long sleep.

But turn this into dactyls, and the effect is ludicrous:

> Mother is dead and my heart is in pieces,
>   Hark how the friends of the family weep!
> Cousins and uncles and nephews and nieces
>   Accompany her to her last long sleep.

These are elementary rules, a few chosen at random from what I may call the Common Law of English Verse. But, in English satire, all rules can be deliberately broken. Byron's satiric comment on Keats's death, for example:

> Strange that the soul, that very fiery particle,
> Should let itself be snuffed out by an article . . .

is emphasized by the deliberate use of the three-syllabled rhyme.

And comically inexact rhyme is the strength of Siegfried Sassoon's squib, written in the palmy days of George V, which he has generously allowed me to resurrect:

> Because the Duke is Duke of York,
> The Duke of York has shot a huge rhinoceros;
> Let's hope the Prince of Wales will take a walk
> Through Africa, and make the Empire talk
> By shooting an enormous hippopotamus,
> And let us also hope that Lord Lascelles
> Will shoot *all* beasts from gryphons to gazelles
> And show the world what sterling stuff we've got in us.

The word *satire* is not derived, as most people suppose, from the witty, prick-eared satyrs of the early Greek comedy, but from the Latin phrase *satura lanx,* or 'full platter'. Latin satire was a burlesque performance at a harvest festival, in which full-fed countrymen would improvise obscene topical jokes to a recurrent dance tune—as the islanders of Majorca still do to the *copeo,* at their annual pig-killing. The harvest atmosphere was free and easy; anything went. Urban satire, as Horace, or Juvenal, or Persius wrote it, was quite a different affair: Greek in origin, and bound by the same rules as epic or pastoral verse. Samuel Butler's *Hudibras* is fescennine; so are Donne's satires. Donne, in fact, did not deserve hanging if he failed to keep his accent in the satires; he could plead privilege.

Pope, who modelled himself as a satirist on Horace, thought fit to regularize Donne's lines:

> Thou, who since yesterday hast roll'd o'er all
> The busy, idle blockheads of the ball,
> Hast thou, oh Sun! beheld an emptier sort,
> Than such as swell this bladder of a court? . . .
> Thus finish'd and corrected to a hair,
> They march, to prate their hour before the fair.
> So first to preach a white-glov'd chaplain goes,
> With band of lily, and with cheek of rose,

> Sweeter than Sharon, in immac'late trim,
> Neatness itself impertinent with him. . . .

The difference between these two versions is that Donne's is readable, and Pope's is not; the regularity of the metre defeats its object after the first fifty couplets. Its readers remain unmoved; they sigh, and fall gently asleep. And this suggests another subject.

The Irish and early Welsh bards had made a discovery, which the Greeks and Romans had never made, and which reached England very late; namely, that regular verse, though a wonderful aid to memory, is soporific unless frequent changes occur in the metre; and that though, say, Virgil's *Aeneid* or Homer's *Iliad* may contain numerous poems, the verse which links these poems together, because written in the same metre, robs them of their force. What jeweller would display a pearl, unless perhaps a black one, in mother-of-pearl setting? The Irish bards, while vellum was prohibitively dear, recorded their chronologies, their treatises on geography, husbandry, and so on, in mnemonic rhyme. Yet their tales (of which they had to know nine hundred or more) were prose; and these the poet told in his own way, to keep them fresh, and individual, and up to date; until he reached a dramatic climax, and this was a traditional poem, which he had to know by heart.

Mother-of-pearl, though a noble material for cutting and engraving, is not pearl. The greater part of every long poem, even Spenser's *Faerie Queene,* is necessarily mother-of-pearl. Ben Jonson hinted at this in his *Discoveries.* He wrote:

> Even one alone verse sometimes makes a perfect poem as when Aeneas hangs up and consecrates the Armes of *Abas* with this inscription:
>
> *Aeneas haec de Danais victoribus arma . . .*

and calls it a *Poeme* or *Carmen.*

This drawing of attention to the poems included in a long work written in set stanzas—as Dante enthusiasts point to *The Death of Ugolino* and similar pearls—suggests that the rest is not up to sample. And how can it be, if the same metre is insisted on throughout?

In blank verse drama one can easily mark off the poems from the roughage. Not only is blank verse capable of almost infinite variations, but prose is allowed to supply comic relief or passages which further the plot. Shakespeare, for instance, makes Trinculo and Stephano in *The Tempest* speak familiar quayside prose, which Caliban answers in poems. But it is manifestly impossible that a long narrative poem which contains genealogy, description of scenery, battles, love-passages, laments, and so on, can be reduced to a single metre without dilution of the poetic content. Long poems are like old French or Spanish tapestries: the design and colour and needlework may be charming but there is no sharpness of detail, no personal characterization, no difference in quality or colour between foreground and background.

Are there any anthropologists present? If so, they may recall the giant yam of Abulam. At Abulam in New Guinea, yams for ordinary eating are planted and tended by the women, but every planting season a tense competition arises among the men: who can grow the yam of the year. This is a purely ritualistic yam, like the Harvest Festival marrow in an English village. The winning exhibit is said to be of approximately the size and shape of a bull-hippopotamus (discounting its head and legs) and perfectly inedible. It provides, in fact, an emblem of the literary epic, which was still being cultivated in Victorian days. With the passing of this Epic, followed by the formal Elegy, and the Ode addressed to heedless nightingales, rocking-chairs, abstractions, and noblemen, of what does poetry now consist? It is reduced, at last, to practical poems, namely the lyrical or dramatic highlights of the poet's experiences with the Goddess in her various disguises. The prose setting is withheld; and, because of this, professional standards demand that it should either explain itself fully, or present a note, as schoolchildren do who arrive late or without some necessary part of their school equipment.

Before closing, I must tell you about a girl who is reading English here under Professor X. I asked her: 'What poems do you enjoy most?' and she answered with dignity: 'Poems are not meant to be enjoyed; they are meant to be analysed'. I hope you do not think that I subscribe to this heresy.

NOTES

[1.] Mēlŏs rhyming with cōelŏs.

[2.] Mr. Eliot has written about free verse: 'It is not defined by non-existence of metre, since even the worst verse can be scanned.' This is to beg the question. In so far as verse can be scanned, it is not freed of metre. He has also written:

> But the most interesting verse which has yet been written is our language has been done [sic] either by taking a very simple form, like the iambic pentameter, and constantly withdrawing from it, or taking no form at all, and continually approximating to a very simple one. It is this contrast between fixity and flux, this unperceived evasion of monotony, which is the very life of verse.

Interesting to some, embarrassing to others, like a jaunt in a car after mixing a little water with the petrol to make it go by fits and starts. I was never interested in that sort of experiment; I expect verse to be verse, and prose to be prose.

PAUL FUSSELL

The Historical Dimension

Paul Fussell gives us a concise account of English prosody, from its Old English origins to the twentieth century. He makes it clear that English has no single prosody: "for historically considered the phenomena of English versification are too complex and multifold to harbor in any one single system of explanation or description." The prosody of a particular age is closely linked to the history of the language; thus the attempt to revive Old English metric in our time is a species of charming antiquarianism, an "excessively self-conscious experience for both writer and reader."

While no one prosodic principle dominates the history of English verse, "we perceive even through the philological upheavals a recurring pattern." English verse has displayed, in somewhat dialectical fashion, a struggle between freedom and restraint. The metrical ideal of the eighteenth century, incarnated in the tightly regulated heroic couplet, gave way in the nineteenth century to a return to accentualism, and, with Whitman and Hopkins, the development of free verse and sprung rhythm. Professor Fussell points out that the dialectic of prosody, unlike Hegel's dialectic of history, reveals no eschatological tendency toward ultimate freedom. Indeed, he makes it explicit that "'freedom' is not a virtue in meter—expressiveness is." Professor Fussell notes that poets will continue to experiment with free verse; they will also return to the traditional syllable-stress metric for significant utterances. The metric is rooted in the structure of Modern English, and "essential changes in the structure of the English language cannot be willed."

Before we can proceed to our main business with meter, namely the use of metrical analysis as a tool of critical judgment, we must explore one more prosodic dimension, the historical. We must develop an awareness of large metrical contexts, traditions, and conventions, the kinds of contexts which we find firmly rooted in historical usage. One way to begin attaining this awareness is to consider the various kinds of prosodies or theoretical systems of meter which have prevailed during the history of the English language.

It is more accurate to speak of the history of English prosodies than of one English prosody, for historically considered the phenomena of English versification are too complex and multifold to harbor in any one single system of explanation or description. Indeed, if we had to construct some generalizations that might hold true for all English poetry from, say, "The Battle of Maldon" in the tenth century to *Four Quartets* in the twentieth, it is doubtful that we could set forth more than the following three:

1. Because English is a much more accentual language than, for example, the Romance tongues, stress has generally played a more significant part in the structure of English verse than it has in many continental poetries.

2. The English language appears most naturally to organize its rhythms in ascending patterns: that is, the main instinct in English poetry is for iambic or occasionally anapestic movements rather than for trochaic or dactylic.

3. Most English poetry seems to shape itself in lines of moderate length, lines with a strong propensity toward an uneven number of distinguishable time-units (i.e., five feet per line). We should not miss the suggestions of a norm which are implied by the fact that about three-quarters of all English poetry is in blank verse. It seems characteristic of the ear trained to Anglo-Saxon usages that, presented with a series of six- or seven-foot lines, it tends to break them down into smaller and presumably more manageable units (two threes; or fours and threes, as in ballad stanza). A long series of hexameters is significantly the metrical mode of the French, rather than the English, drama.

Other than sharing these three common characteristics, English poetries of various historical ages manifest few prosodic similarities. The distinguishing characteristics and conventions of the English prosodies are best seen if we consider them philologically, that is, according to the state of the English language in various periods of its history.

OLD ENGLISH (*c*. A.D. *500–c. 110*): The powerful Germanic accents of the Old English language provide a natural basis for a very heavily accentual prosody in which sense rhythm rather than any abstract metrical imperative tends to supply the meter. The standard poetic line in Old English consists of four strongly stressed syllables arranged, together with any number of unstressed syllables, in two hemistichs (or half-lines) of two stresses each. Stressed syllables frequently alliterate, and the alliteration tends to emphasize even further the force of the accent that resides in them. The over-all organization of materials tends to be stichic rather than strophic—that is, we find an accumulation of lines in additive sequence rather than an organization of lines into short stanzas of significant shape. The two hemistichs which comprise the line are separated by an invariable medial caesura. A sort of gesture toward counterpoint or syncopation is accomplished by occasional "rests" and by the occasional omission of one of the four stressed syllables, especially in the second hemistich.

The following passage from *Beowulf* (lines 4–7) exemplifies the "normal" line structure (lines 1 and 2) and the possibilities for variation through rest and the omission of stress (lines 3 and 4):

Oft Scýld Scéfing	scéaþena þréatum,
mónegum máegþum	méodsetla oftéah,
égsode eórlas	syþþan áerest wearþ
féasceaft fúnden	he þaes frófre gebad. . . .

[Often Scyld, the son of Sceaf, seized the mead-halls of many tribes, even though he had originally been discovered in a wretched state—he lived to find solace for that.]

John Collins Pope has conjectured that, in recitation, the normal position of the four stresses per line was signaled by a chord struck on a harp: this constant underlying beat would provide a sort of metrical underpinning against which the variations dictated by rhetorical emphasis would be counterpointed.

Old English versification presents a delusive air of simplicity: actually it is a metrical system of very subtle expressiveness, for its departures from the ideal meter and its often delightfully coy returns to it give the rhythm a constantly shifting surface bespeaking a high degree of sophistication. If, as Wimsatt and Beardsley find, Old English accentual meter has only a limited capacity for "interplay," most of the poets who have written in it have worked so skillfully that we hardly notice the limitations of the metrical system.

Some modern metrical critics and theorists have suggested that even beneath the iambic pentameter line of modern blank verse or of the heroic couplet we still catch a faint echo of the four-stress Old English line. And some have suggested that what we are talking about when we speak of "metrical variations" is really the line's apparent indecision about whether to adopt a four- or a five-stress structure—an indecision, we might say, about whether to "grow up" historically. As Joseph Malof says, "There is a significant tendency in the [iambic pentameter] line to lead a double life, to qualify for strict iambic pentameter through such devices as 'promotion' of a medial stress to the rank of a full one, and yet to assert beneath the surface the four strong beats of our native meter." But there is one difficulty with such theories—they tend to neglect the fact that, in the Old English line, structural alliteration and strong medial caesura are characteristics which are as strong as its four stresses: Modern English poetry has had no difficulty in casting off these other equally powerful characteristics of Old English verse without the encumbrance of any lurking residue.

Whatever the degree to which the modern iambic pentameter line "remembers" the stress scheme of Old English versification, these essentials of structural alliteration and invariable medial caesura pose problems to contemporary poets who now and then choose to exercise themselves in something like a reminiscence of the Old English mode. Most of W. H. Auden's *The Age of Anxiety* is written in a verse closely resembling the Old English accentual system, and now and then very pleasantly anachronistic effects result:

> . . . lightning at noonday
> Swiftly stooping to the summer-house
> Engraves its disgust on engrossed flesh,
> And at tea-times through tall french windows
> Hurtle anonymous hostile stones.
> No soul is safe. Let slight infection
> Disturb a trifle some tiny gland,
> And Caustic Keith grows kind and silly
> Or Dainty Daisy dirties herself.

It is all a very amusing but perhaps excessively self-conscious experience for both writer and reader.

A more successful suggestion of the tonality of Old English versification is possible when the poetic subject seems more appropriate. Richard Wilbur's "Junk," like Ezra Pound's "translations" from Old English, gives a contemporary twist to a favorite Old English subject, the power of good

workmanship, and we end with a feeling that the spirits of two distinct ages
have momentarily almost been joined:

> An axe angles
> > from my neighbor's ashcan;
> It is hell's handiwork,
> > the wood not hickory,
> The flow of the grain
> > not faithfully followed: . . .
> > > . . . The heart winces
> For junk and gimcrack,
> > for jerrybuilt things
> And the men who make them
> > for a little money . . .
> They shall waste in the weather
> > towards what they were.
> The sun shall glory
> > in the glitter of glass-chips,
> Foreseeing the salvage
> > of the prisoned sand,
> And the blistering paint
> > peel off in patches,
> That the good grain
> > be discovered again.
> Then burnt, bulldozed,
> > they shall all be buried
> To the depth of diamonds,
> > in the making dark
> Where halt Hephaestus
> > keeps his hammer
> And Wayland's work
> > is worn away.

But ultimately we must conclude that, although Old English versification
can be imitated, nothing really like it can be recovered: the language has
changed, and each significant philological change projects us into an altered
metrical world in which the meters of the past can be understood and
appreciated but never again practiced.

MIDDLE ENGLISH (c. 1100–c.1500): After the Norman Conquest, the rapid
changes in the language (loss of inflection, multiplication of dialects, Romance accretions to what had been primarily a Germanic vocabulary) quickly

complicated and diversified what had been a stable and unitary prosody. Although it persisted for a time in the greatly changed language of Middle English, the old four-stress accentual line, with its varying number of unstressed syllables, was gradually abandoned in favor of a line in which, for the first time in English, syllabic numeration becomes an important structural criterion. The two hemistichs of the Old English line seem finally to metamorphose themselves into the alternating four- and three-stress lines of the medieval ballad stanza. Strophic construction begins to compete with stichic as a way of organizing poetic materials. The strongly Germanic accentual quality of the language seems to weaken slightly, and instead of a prosody based on emphatic pressures at equal times we find one expressive of a new consciousness of the qualitative similarities between stressed and unstressed syllables.

The linguistic complexities of the Middle Ages created a situation in which several unique prosodies co-existed simultaneously. Thus we find, as if competing for pre-eminence:

1. A continuation of the Old English four-stress accentual prosody adapted (often by the addition of assonance and rhyme, and by the rejection of the strong medial caesura) to the requirements of an increasingly uninflected language. Thus *Sir Gawain and the Green Knight:*

> After, the sesoun of somer with the soft windes,
> When Zeferus sifles himself on sedes and erbes;
> Wela-winne is the wort that waxes theroute,
> When the donkande dewe dropes of the leves. . . .

2. Accentual-syllabic rhyming verse in lines of four stresses, gradually lengthening to approximate the heroic couplets of Chaucer and Lydgate. An example is Chaucer's early "Romance of the Rose":

> Ful gay was al the ground, and queint,
> And powdred, as men had it peint,
> With many a fressh and sondry flowr,
> That casten up ful good savour.

3. A highly accentual lyric prosody—sometimes overstressed until it approaches sprung rhythm—found especially in songs and other pieces set to music. An example is the anonymous fifteenth century "I Sing of a Maiden":

> I sing of a maiden
> That is makeles;
> King of alle kinges
> To here sone che ches.

> [I sing of a maiden
>   Who knows no equal;
> The King of all Kings
>   For her son she chose.]

> He cam so stille,
>   There his moder was,
> As dew in Aprille
>   That fallith on the gras. . . .

Out of all this prosodic complication and variety, one tradition did gradually succeed in establishing pre-eminence: the accentual-syllabic. With the final relative stabilization of language and dialects long after the initial linguistic shock of the Conquest, the five-stress, decasyllabic line of Chaucer emerged: it is this line—the line that Chaucer can be said to have discovered for English poetry—which furnishes the base for Renaissance and later developments in Modern English.

MODERN ENGLISH (*c.1500–*): *Sixteenth and Seventeenth Centuries:* Three facts are important in Renaissance prosody: (1) the language attained a condition of relative stability; (2) the widespread admiration of the classics of antiquity invited imitation, and imitation served to expose the apparent coarseness of the English metric of preceding ages; and (3) rhetorical and metrical criticism, in the manner of the ancients, began to be written and to be read. There resulted a stream of systematic—and very often prescriptive—prosodic commentary which has continued without intermission to our own age.

The Renaissance admiration for Greek meters impelled one school of prosodists and poets to import Greek quantitative usages into English practice, and theorists, dilettantes, and poets like Ascham, Sidney, Spenser, and Campion labored, with varying seriousness and success, to imitate in English the classical heroic hexameter or the Greek lyric measures. But since the would-be quantitative poet was obliged to remember constantly the arbitrarily assigned "quantities" of the English syllables he chose to use, quantitative composition was a laborious academic-theoretical business, like all such nonempirical enterprises more gratifying to the self-congratulating practitioner than to the perplexed reader.

Along with this impulse to "refine" English verse by making it mimic classical rhythms went the development of the Chaucerian accentual-syllabic pentameter line as a vehicle for narrative and dramatic expression. The initial impulse was to urge the line toward a new mechanical regularity, as Surrey and Sackville did, but soon a more civilized instinct for expressive variations made itself felt. Ironically, the regularists, by mistaking the whole aesthetic premise of meter, made their own unwitting contribution to the great English tradition of expressive metrical variations. As Joseph Malof has said, "The monotonously regular rhythms of the mid-sixteenth century were prerequisite to [the development of a feel for metrical variations] because they offered for the first time, in Tottel and in Gascoigne, the concept of a clear, workable metrical norm from which later poets were to make their prosperous departures." Among the most distinguished of those who soon mastered the art of "prosperous departures" were Marlowe and Shakespeare. Both use the accentual-syllabic pentameter with a consummate sensitivity, calmly inventing new tonalities when they have tired of the challenges of the old. And even the lesser dramatists of the age reveal, through their instinctive comfort within it, that the iambic pentameter is going to become, for whatever ultimate reason, the staple line of the Modern English period.

In lyric verse the song writers, obliged often to fit words to pre-existing airs, produced free accentual lines, and lyric practitioners like Donne, Crashaw, Herbert, and Marvell make of the iambic tetrameter or pentameter line a vehicle for wit, shock, and ecstasy by a bold shifting or addition of stresses.

And yet in the midst of all this happy inventiveness and flexibility we find already planted the seeds of an impulse toward greater prosodic regulation and predictability. Samuel Daniel's *Defense of Rhyme* (1603?) is a conservative prosodic document which anticipates and even invites the practice of such late-seventeenth-century masters of the closed heroic couplet as Denham and Waller. In *Paradise Lost* Milton adheres quite consciously to a fixed decasyllabic limitation. The end of the Renaissance is thus coincident with a reaction against the metrical spontaneity of the Elizabethans: in both theory and practice, prosody is now moving toward an ideal of strict syllabic limitation in the line and even a relative predictability of stress positions.

Eighteenth Century: Prosody after the Restoration betrays a strong French syllabic influence: for a time, indeed, the essential criterion of the English poetic line ceases to be the number of either stresses or feet and becomes the number of syllables. Metrical theorists and dogmatists like Edward Bysshe, Richard Bentley, and Henry Pemberton advocated a rigid regularity in the heroic line, and minor poets like Richard Glover responded by composing as far as they were able in a strictly regular accentual-syllabic verse without any expressive variations. This lust for regularity—"smoothness," the age was pleased to call it—seems to constitute one expression of the orderly and rationalistic impulses of the period. Although the best poets of the early eighteenth century (poets like Dryden, Prior, Gay, Swift, and Pope) largely maintained the Renaissance tradition of expressive variations, even they could not help responding to the regularistic climate: they carefully observed a uniformity in the number of syllables per line—that is, they were careful to use in substitution duple feet only—and they generally rejected the enjambed line in favor of a strict line integrity.

We can see what was happening if we compare a passage from Donne's "Fourth Satire" with a passage of what Pope called his "versification" of it. Donne speaks of a courtier thus:

> Therefore I suffer'd this; Towards me did run
> A thing more strange, than on Nile's slime, the Sun
> E'er bred, or all which into Noah's Ark came:
> A thing which would have pos'd Adam to name:

Notable in Pope's version is an impulse toward both stress regularity and great line integrity: substitution, where it does occur, is permitted only at some distance from the line endings, which are reserved for strictly iambic assertions of the prevailing regularity:

> Scarce was I enter'd, when behold! there came
> A Thing which Adam had been pos'd to name;
> Noah had refus'd it lodging in his Ark,
> Where all the Race of Reptiles might embark.

Soon after 1740, however, another reaction set in: now it was a reaction against the very metrical neatness that Pope and his school had labored to refine. The reaction expressed itself in the prosodic writings of Samuel Say, John Mason, and Joshua Steele, who pointed out that monotony might easily be the cost of iambic lines long continued without trisyllabic substitution, and who emphasized that bold shifting and omission of stress are expressive techniques which the poet aspiring to exploit all the resources of metrical language cannot do without. The arguments of these critics of metrical regularity issue from a new and revolutionary aesthetic, one favoring impulse, spontaneity, and surprise rather than the Augustan values of stability, predictability and quietude. Especially by opposing the poetic contractions necessitated by a strict accentual-syllabism, the late-eighteenth-century metrical revolutionaries advocated an "expandable" line which could swell or diminish expressively according to the dynamics of the rhetorical pressures within it.

Unlike the prosodic theorizing and speculation of the Renaissance, which is still rather sparse, that of the eighteenth century is copious; it is also

systematic, and, under the influence of the empiricism of John Locke, remarkably "psychological." Throughout the century the practice of the poets
substantially follows the urgings of the conservative metrical theorists: although masters like Pope and Johnson shift stresses freely and instinctively,
even they never violate the strict syllabic limitation—which means that they
are careful to eschew trisyllabic substitution—and the lines of many lesser
writers in the heroic couplet will be found to be strikingly regular in the
alternate disposition of stressed and unstressed syllables.

Nineteenth Century: The great phenomenon in nineteenth-century English
versification is the rejection of strict accentual-syllabism in favor of accentualism. This is to say that the use of trisyllabic substitution in duple
metrical contexts becomes the technical hallmark of the age, just as the
careful avoidance of trisyllabic substitution had been the rhythmical sign
of eighteenth-century poetry. In his "Christabel" Coleridge publicly
practiced—and for a wide audience—the principles of trisyllabic substitution
advocated a half-century earlier by Say, Mason, and Steele. As a result of this
new aspiration toward accentualism, the English pentameter line tends to
lose its Augustan formal and oratorical tone and to assume an air of an almost
colloquial intimacy, varying from the sober sincerity of the verse of *The
Prelude* to the racy energy of the verse of "Fra Lippo Lippi." In prosodic theorizing, the impulse toward accentualism manifests itself in the development of
musical analogies to verse and in musical methods of scansion: Sidney Lanier
is a pioneer in this work. And the cause of accentualism was bolstered by the
rise to academic fashion of Germanic philology, which served to remind both
prosodists and poets that English was solidly a Germanic tongue whose
metrical basis must be primarily some arrangement of strong accents. Indeed, the transfer of British intellectual allegiance from France to Germany
during the nineteenth century can be deduced in part from the British
discovery of the charms of accentual versification. But an impatience with
inherited metrical restraints is probably the clearest motive underlying the
metrical behavior of nineteenth-century poets: surely the development of
"free verse" around the middle of the century was conceived by many—and
may be conceived by us—as an expression of nineteenth-century liberalism or
of the primitivist strain of romanticism. Another unique nineteenth-century
prosodic phenomenon is the attempt to enlist triple-based rhythms in support
of nonfrivolous subjects, as Longfellow, Poe, and Swinburne tried to do.

But despite the general atmosphere of mild experimentation, many of
the most prominent practitioners, like Tennyson and Arnold, continued to
work in what is fundamentally the accentual-syllabic line bequeathed them

by the Augustans, with its strict syllabic limitation and its conservative placement of stresses. At the close of the century, it is true, W. J. Stone tried to urge the more academic spirits toward quantitative prosody once more, but the gradual decay of classical learning and enthusiasm—and the increasing association of classical learning with mere gentility—practically guaranteed a tiny and ineffective audience for such Alexandrian pursuits. It was at this time that Hopkins was moved to experiment with his technique of overstressing, which reveals its full parochialism once we perceive how intimately it partakes in the prevailing accentual rhythmical climate and even in the widespread Victorian admiration for all things Germanic.

The main nineteenth-century divagation from accentual-syllabism and the air of genteel quest and experimentation suggest also a current of dissatisfaction with the sound of conservative verse, and this dissatisfaction may have some philological cause. For example, the gradual secession of the American from the British dialects may be connected with the simultaneous British search for new metrical tonalities. The gradual replacement of classical by modern-language studies in schools and universities may also bespeak a subtle alteration in linguistic habits and rhythmical tastes. Whatever the causes and the meaning of the metrical restlessness of many nineteenth-century poets, the restlessness is clearly one expression of their lust for liberal reform and their commitment to the idea of progress.

Twentieth Century: Brooding over the metrical history of our time is the spirit of one of the greatest of traditional accentual-syllabic metrists, William Butler Yeats. It is the force of his example as a poet of rich traditional metrical usages that, time and time again, has brought contemporary poets back to the practice of accentual-syllabism after experimental excursions in other prosodic systems, or after vacations in none at all. Most of the temporary prosodic mutations which have taken place in the twentieth century have been associated with the United States rather than with Britain: perhaps one reason is the greater accessibility to American poets of the fructifying, revolutionary example of Whitman. During the 1920's and 1930's, Ezra Pound and William Carlos Williams tightened the freely cadenced long line of Whitman and made of it a witty, informal instrument for registering the rhythms of actual American speech. T. S. Eliot's poetic dramas have shown what can still be done with a quiet, subtle accentualism, and W. H. Auden has written accentual, accentual-syllabic, and syllabic verse with equal facility. But even such engaging American experiments as the "spatial cadences" of E. E. Cummings and the cadenced syllabism of Marianne Moore have stimulated no great horde of followers and exploiters. Or to put it more accurately: their followers have conspicuously lacked the metrical learning and inventiveness of the American masters of the 1920's and 1930's. The best contemporary American and British poets, after canvassing the possibilities of an apparently "freer" metric, have returned to a more or less stable sort of Yeatsian accentual-syllabism: Frost, the Stevens of "Sunday Morning," Robert Graves, Robert Lowell, Richard Wilbur, Randall Jarrell, and W. D. Snodgrass have all turned from the metrical radicalism of the 1920's, a radicalism which looks every day more naïve aesthetically, and have gravitated toward the system of accentual-syllabism which, for over four centuries, has been found to be the staple system for poetry in Modern English. How closely this return to "the tradition" in metrics is connected with a similar movement in general intellectual taste it would be hard to say. It will be obvious, however, to those who can see in history the very intimate alliance between metrics and the larger intellectual and emotional conventions of an age that no prosodic phenomenon is devoid of wider meaning if only we read it correctly.

When we stand well back and survey the whole history of English versification over almost fifteen centuries, we perceive even through the philological upheavals a recurring pattern. The pattern described by metrical history is similar, perhaps, to the general shape of political history in that it consists of oscillations now toward ideals of tight control and unitary domination and now toward a relaxation of such control and domination. But metrical history differs from political history in one profoundly important way: while political history can be shown to involve a very gradual total tendency toward, say, ideals of egalitarianism or public philanthropy, metrical history exhibits no such long-term "progressive" tendency, and it is the great mistake of the aesthetically naïve to imagine that it ought to. Meter has not become "freer" over the centuries, and indeed "freedom" is not a virtue in meter—expressiveness is. The metrical imperative underlying the words that Yeats arranges is hardly less rigid and "perfect" than that underlying Chaucer's poetic discourse; and each invisible framework is equally distant from such a simplistic scheme as *vers libre*.

We can be certain of only one thing about the future: we can be sure that both poets and readers will someday tire of our current calm accentual-syllabism and will assert again an impulse toward the old, recurrent ideal of "metrical freedom." There will always be those to say with Jane Heap, one of the editors of the *Little Review* between the two World Wars, "A new age has created a new kind of beauty," and who will imagine that the essential conventions of a given art can "progress" or even change drastically as if in response to technological change. But the problem is knowing when a really new age, rather than an apparently new one, has dawned. A "new age" for metrics is a new philological age, not a new technological one: essential changes in the structure of the English language cannot be willed, and it is such essential changes that a new metrical system tends to reflect.

Artistic progressives like Jane Heap seem always destined for defeat in the long run by two facts of life: (1) Modern English is Modern English and not, philologically, something else; and (2) the modern reader of poetry in English, despite his vast difference in extrinsic and learned attitudes from, say, his Elizabethan counterpart, has still the same kind of physique and personal physiological rhythms as his forebears. These will still seem to seek satisfaction and delight in ways which accord with the experienced rhythmic traditions of Modern English. If these traditions should ever become totally irrecoverable, it would not be pleasant to calculate what will be lost forever.

ROBERT BRIDGES

A Letter to a Musician on English Prosody

Robert Bridges maintained a lifelong interest in the principles of English versification. He experimented with meters of his own invention; his scholarship on prosody has permanent value. No student should fail to consult his *Milton's Prosody* (1901, 1921): the most complete analysis of iambic structure ever undertaken. His knowledge was derived not only from his command of Latin and Greek, but also from insights gained as a craftsman in English verse. It is worth noting that Bridges served as mentor and metrical conscience for his fellow experimenter, Gerard Manley Hopkins.

Bridges sees the clear differences among the European metrical systems. The principal systems are the quantitative or classical, the stress, and the syllabic. A confusion in terminology blurs the clarity of these distinctions: what Bridges calls 'syllabic verse' is more accurately described as syllable-stress.

Bridges's classical bias leads him to an unwarranted skepticism about the syllable-stress system, the traditional metric of English poetry. Bridges finds the syllabic system a "wretched skeleton" on which to hang a prosody; yet despite the poverty of this system, its supposed lack of precise rules and its rhetorical freedom, Bridges does observe "the extreme beauty to which verse has attained under the syllabic system." We should point out that modern linguistic inquiry—from Jespersen to Halle and Keyser—has discovered the 'rules' for syllable-stress verse. These are not as

From Robert Bridges, *Collected Essays,* Vol. II. Reprinted by permission of Oxford University Press.

complex or as binding as the rules for classical versification, but they give English poetry "marked and definite rhythms."

My dear—, when lately you asked me to recommend you a book on English Prosody, and I said that I was unable to do so, I had some scruples of conscience, because, as a matter of fact, I have never myself read any of the treatises, though I have looked into many of them, and from that, and from the report of students and reviewers, I think that I know pretty well the nature of their contents; so that your further inquiries come to me as a challenge to explain myself, which if I could not do, I should be in a contemptible position. I embrace the opportunity the more willingly because you are a musician. If my notions are reasonable you will understand them; if you do not, you may conclude that they are not worthy of your attention.

Preliminary

It is impossible, however one might desire it, to set out with satisfactory definitions of *Prosody* and *Poetic rhythm,* for the latter term especially is difficult to fix: and it will be best to examine perfected poetry and see what it is that we have to deal with.

If we take verses by Virgil, Dante or Milton, who were all of them artistic geniuses, we find that their elaborate rhythms are a compound, arrived at by a conflict between two separate factors, which we may call the *speech-rhythm* and the *metric-rhythm.* Take an example from Virgil,

Fluminaque antíquos subterlabentia muros.[1]

I have no doubt that I enjoy this rhythm as Virgil intended it, for I read it in measured longs and shorts, and I find that the speech-accent on *antíquos,* contradicting the metrical ictus, enhances the beauty, and joins on smoothly to the long level *subterlabentia,* with its two little gliding syllables at the end of quiet motion against the solid *muros.* There is no room for difference of opinion; and the same phenomenon meets us everywhere. The poetic rhythm derives its beauty from the conflict between a (prosodial) metre, which makes us more or less expect a certain regular rhythm of accent corresponding with the typical metric structure, and, on the other hand, a speech-rhythm which gives it all manner of variety by overriding it. In the above instance, though the essence of the metre is the sequence of long and short syllables, we yet regard the hexameter as a typically falling rhythm, *i.e.* with its main accents on the initial syllables of the constituent feet, which would give *ántíquós;* and the beauty of Virgil's line contains the contradiction or dislocation of those accents.

Moreover, if we were unacquainted with hexameter verse (*i.e.* with the

Prosody), the line quoted would seem a line of prose, in prose-rhythm, and it would be in itself no less beautiful than it is. Only the knowledge that it is an hexameter adds to our satisfaction; the definition of the value of the syllables and the recognition of the verse-form give us pleasure, and especially because it is one of many varieties of a most skillfully invented form, which by their accumulation make pleasing poems. But this reflection may also convince us of the subjective nature of the quality of poetic rhythm, and consequently how it must defy exhaustive analysis, although it may allow of the analytical separation of its components.

And since we can imagine that the hexameter had never been invented, and yet that these words might still have been written, it will follow that poetic rhythm may be regarded as common speech-rhythm subjected to certain definitions and limitations: and the laws of these will no doubt be the Prosody.

Let us for the moment suppose that there is no such thing as Prosody, and inquire into the elements or factors of speech-rhythm.

The Vocal Factors of Speech-Rhythm

Now if you read English verse aloud, your main endeavor is to express the rhythm. You know what you mean by this, and you are aware whether you are successful or not.

Supposing that you express the rhythm as you wish, you will find that you have freely used the only three means which are at your disposal. First, you will have distinguished some syllables by their comparative length and brevity. Secondly, you will have varied the pitch of your voice. Thirdly, you will have varied the strength of your voice, enforcing some syllables with greater loudness; and you will have freely combined these different components of rhythm. There is nothing else that you can do towards expressing the rhythm, except that (and especially in elaborately written verse) you will have relied a great deal on pauses or silences of suitable duration. These pauses are essential to good reading, but they are not essential to our present consideration. First there are the *metric* pauses, which merely isolate balancing sections of verse-rhythm. Then there are the *grammatical* pauses or stops: these are interruptions of the metric rhythm, which are either condoned for the sake of the sense, or are observed to indicate and separate the ever-varying sections of the speech-rhythm (being thus to speech-rhythm what metric pauses are to the metre). Now the grammatical pause is a physical necessity, as the breath-place, and it must of course be a true "rest" of actual time-value. But its time-value in poetry is indefinite, and it has therefore no rhythmical significance except as the sign of the break in the grammar. If these pauses be all excluded, you will find so few true *intra-rhythmical* pauses left, *i.e.* time-rests within a section of rhythm and essential to its expression, that we may consider them as belonging to a more advanced treatment of the subject, and confine ourselves to the active varieties of vocal effect, namely, Quantity, Pitch, and Loudness.[2]

Of these three you will find on examination that the first, that is difference of quantity, is the only one which will give rhythm without the aid of either of the others. It is well to make this quite clear, and musical examples are the simplest.

Let us, to begin with, take an example where all three are present, the slow movement of an orchestral symphony. When this is performed by the orchestra we hear different time-values of the notes, their differences of pitch, and actual enforcements of loudness, and all of these seem to be essential to the rhythmic effect.

But now if we take the same *Andante* and perform it on the choir-organ, the conditions of which preclude the differences of loud and soft, we find that, though the effect is generally poorer than in the orchestral performance, yet the rhythm is unaffected. We have here then an example of an elaborate rhythm expressed without variations of loudness.

Now to exclude Pitch. The commonest example that I can think of is the monotoning of the prayers in a cathedral service. Here varieties of pitch are of course absent, but you may generally detect the quantities to be complicated by some variation of loudness. In proportion, however, as mono-toning is well done the sound is level in force. Perhaps you will ask, where is the rhythm? I was once induced to establish a choir in a country church, and among my first tasks I had to train the boys in choral monotone. They were naturally without any notion of educated speech-rhythms. But there is no difficulty in teaching boys anything that you yourself understand; they can imitate anything, and love to do it. I had therefore only to offer the correct rhythms to their ears, and they adopted them at once. When we had got the vowels and consonants right, both to spare my own voice, and also because I preferred a model which could not suggest stress to them, I made the organ set the rhythms, and pulling out the great diapason I beat on it the syllables of the Lord's Prayer for the boys to pick up. This was of course nothing but boo, boo, boo, only the boos were of different durations: yet the rhythm was so distinct, it was so evident that the organ was saying the Lord's Prayer, that I was at first rather shocked, and it seemed that I was doing something profane; for it was comic to the boys as well as to me; but the absurdity soon wore off. Now here was rhythm without loudness or pitch.

If you should still ask what I mean by saying that this was rhythm, you need to extend your notion of speech-rhythm to include every recognizable motion of speech in time. The Lord's Prayer is not in poetic rhythm, but if it had been, then the organ would have expressed it even more plainly, and there is no line to be drawn in speech-rhythms between those that are proper verse-rhythms and those that are only possible in prose: there is really no good speech-rhythm which might not be transferred from prose into a poetry that had a sufficiently elaborated prosody, with this proviso only, that it must be a short member; for good prose constructs and combines its rhythms so that in their extension they do not make or suggest verse.

Since we see, then, that rhythm may be expressed by quantity alone, we have to examine whether either *pitch* or *loudness* are sufficient in themselves to give rhythm.

Let us first take Pitch. A common hymn-tune of equal notes would seem to be the most promising example, and to fulfill the conditions, but it does not. It is a melody, and that implies rhythm, but in so far as it has rhythm it is dependent on its *metre,* which exists only by virtue of certain pauses or rests which its subdivision into short sections determines. Now, given these sections, they discover initial and other stresses which are enforced by the words or the metre or the harmony, or by all three, and without these aids and interpretations the structure is arhythmic, and it can be read in many different ways.

It remains only to consider Loudness, which may here be described as accent without pitch or quantity. Now if we take a succession of perfectly equal notes, differing only in that some of them (any that you may choose) are louder than the others, the experiment will suggest only the simple skeletons of the most monotonous rhythms, and if one of these declare itself, such as a succession of threes or fours, you will probably be unconsciously led to reinforce it with some device of quantitive phrasing. To compare such a result with the experiment of beating the Lord's Prayer on the organ is to compare something too elementary to be of any value with something that is too complex and extensive to define.

The Office of Prosody

My examples will have sufficiently illustrated my meaning; your conviction will depend on your own consideration of the matter. On the supposition that you agree we can take an important step, and say that, looking at the question from the point of view of speech-rhythm, it would seem that it is the addition of Prosody to speech-rhythm which determines it to be poetic

rhythm or verse. What, then, exactly is Prosody? Our English word is not
carried over from the Greek word, with its uncertain and various meaning,
but it must have come with the French word through the scholastic Latin;
and like the French term it primarily denotes the rules for the treatment of
syllables in verse, whether they are to be considered as long or short, accented
or unaccented, elideable or not, etc., etc. The syllables, which are the *units* of
rhythmic speech, are by nature of so indefinite a quality and capable of such
different vocal expression, that apart from the desire which every artist must
feel to have his work consistent in itself, his appeal to an audience would
convince him that there is no chance of his elaborate rhythms being rightly
interpreted unless his treatment of syllables is understood. Rules must
therefore arise and be agreed upon for the treatment of syllables, and this is
the first indispensable office of Prosody. Then, the syllables being fixed,
their commonest combinations (which are practically commensurate with
word-units) are defined and named; and these are called *feet*. And after this
the third step of Prosody is to prescribe metres, that is to register the main
systems of feet which poets have invented to make verses and stanzas. Thus
the Alcaic stanza is:

$$- - \cup - - \mid - \cup \cup - \cup \cup$$
$$- - \cup - - \mid - \cup \cup - \cup \cup$$
$$- - \cup - - \mid - \cup - -$$
$$- \cup \cup - \cup \cup \mid - \cup - -$$

and in tabulating metres Prosody is at once involved in rhythm, for we may
say generally that every metre has a typical accentual rhythm of its own—
which was presumably the motive of its invention—though it may be in
some cases difficult to fix on one to the exclusion of all others; certainly (to
take easy examples) we may regard the hexameter as a typically falling
rhythm, and the iambic as a rising rhythm. The force of this prosodial
rhythm will vary in different metres, and with different readers; but one
thing stands out very prominently, namely, that in the essential scheme of
the Greek metre which I have tabulated above it is the quantities only that
are prescribed and fixed, while the accents or stresses are not prescribed, so
that any speech-rhythm which had a corresponding sequence of those quantities would fit the scheme;[3] whereas, if the metre had been an accentual
scheme, that is, if the syllabic signs had been indeterminate with respect to
quantity (instead of being longs and shorts), but marked with prescribed
accents in certain places, then the quantities would have been free, and any
speech-rhythm with a corresponding sequence of accents would have fitted
the form, independently of the length or shortness of any one particular

accented or unaccented syllable. There could thus be two quite distinct systems of Prosody, according as the metres were ruled by one or other of these different factors of speech-rhythm.

Three Kinds of Prosody

Now the history of European verse shows us three distinct systems of Prosody, which can be named:

1. The Quantitive system
2. The Syllabic system
3. The Stress system

I will give a short account of each of these.

1. *Quantitive.* The system of the Greeks was scientifically founded on quantity, because they knew that to be the only one of the three distinctions of spoken syllables which will give rhythm by itself. But the speech-quantities of their syllables being as indeterminate as ours are, the Greeks devised a convention by which their syllables were separated into two classes, one of long syllables, the other of short, the long being twice the duration of the short, as a minim to a crotchet; and this artificial distinction of the syllables was the foundation of their Prosody. The convention was absolutely enforced, even in their prose oratory, and their verse cannot be understood unless it is strictly observed. For the result which they obtained was this: the quantities gave such marked and definite rhythms that these held their own in spite of the various speech-accents which overlaid them. The Latins copying their method arrived at a like result.

2. *Syllabic.* The syllabic system, which has prevailed in various developments throughout Europe from the decay of the Greek system up to the present time, had no more scientific basis than the imitation of the Latin poetry by writers who did not understand it. But I believe that in such matters the final cause is the efficient cause, and that it was therefore the possibility of the results which we have witnessed that led them on their pathless experiments. Criticism discovers two weaknesses in the system: one, the absence of any definite prosodial principle, the other, which follows from the first, the tendency for different and incompatible principles to assert themselves, indiscriminately overriding each other's authority, until the house is so divided against itself that it falls into anarchy.

I will shortly illustrate one or two points. First, my statement that this syllabic system arose from writing quantitive verse without the quantities. The octosyllabic church-hymns give a good example, and for all that I know they may have actually been the first step. The earliest of these hymns were composed in correct iambic metre, *e.g.* (fourth century):

> Splendor paternae gloriae
> De luce lucem proferens
> Lux lucis et fons luminis
> Dies dierum illuminans.

Compare with this what writers wrote who did not know the classic rules, *e.g.*:

> 1. Ad coenam Agni prouidi
>   Et stolis albis candidi
>   Post transitum maris rubri
>   Christo canamus principi.
>
> 2. Ne grauis somnus irruat
>   Nec hostis nos surripiat
>   Nec caro illi consentiens
>   Nos tibi reos statuat.

Such stanzas virtually contain the whole of European syllabic Prosody;[4] though as a matter of fact the rule of elision, which these writers often neglected, was preserved. Since these hymns were intended to be sung to tunes that were generally of equal notes with tendency to alternate accent, the quantities did not signify, and there was a *tendency to alternate stress,* which came to be the norm and bane of syllabic verse;[5] and this leads to another somewhat curious observation, namely, that these writers of non-quantitive iambics were withheld from the natural tendency to write merely in alternate stress to suit their tunes (see ex. 2 above) by their familiarity with the free rhythms of the older well-loved hymns;[6] and since those broken rhythms had been originally occasioned by the unalterable overruling features of the language, they were almost as difficult to avoid as they were easy to imitate. It is pretty certain that the frequency of inversion of the first foot in all English syllabic (iambic) verse is an unbroken tradition from the Latin; the convenience of allowing a disyllable at the beginning of the line being conveyed and encouraged by precedent.

The "prosody" of European syllabic verse may be roughly set out as follows:

> 1. There must be so many syllables in the verse.
> 2. Any extra syllables must be accounted for by elision.

3. Any syllable may be long or short.
4. There is a tendency to alternate stress.

This is honestly the wretched skeleton[7] (indeed, in Milton's perfected "iambics" we may add that any syllable may be accented or unaccented), and no amount of development can rebuild its hybrid construction.[8] For our present consideration of the rules of Prosody the bare skeleton will serve; but to the description we may add that the history of its development shows that it determined its metrical forms mainly by rhyme, and that "stress," there being nothing of equal force to oppose it, gradually predominated, invading and practically ruling syllabic verse long before it was openly recognized, or any hint was given of formulating its principles, or constructing a Prosody of it, the principles of which are irreconcilable with the syllabic system, and which I will now describe.

3. *Stress-Prosody.* In this system the natural accentual speech-rhythms come to the front, and are the determining factor of the verse, overruling the syllabic determination. These speech-rhythms were always present; they constituted in the classical verse the main variety of effects within the different metres, but they were *counterpointed,* so to speak, on a quantitive rhythm, that is, on a framework of strict (unaccented) time, which not only imposed necessary limitations but, certainly in Latin, to a great extent determined their forms. In the syllabic Prosody, in which the prosodial rules were so much relaxed, these speech-rhythms came in the best writers to be of first importance, and in Milton (for example) we can see that they are only withheld from absolute authority and liberty by the observance of a conservative syllabic fiction, which is so featureless that it needs to be explained why Milton should have thought it of any value. For all Milton's free-speech rhythms, which are the characteristic beauty of his verse, and by their boldness make his originality as a rhythmist, are confined by a strict syllabic limitation, viz. that the syllables which compose them must still keep the first two rules of the syllabic Prosody, and be resoluble into so many "iambs." But these so-called iambs are themselves now degraded to nothing, for the disyllabic unit which still preserves that old name has no definition: it has lost its quantities, nor are its lost quantities always indicated by accent or stress; its disyllabic quality, too, is resoluble by the old law of Latin elision (which Milton extended to liquids, reducing Chaucer's practice to certain fixed rules) into trisyllabic forms, so that *either* or *both* of the syllables of the fictive iamb may be long or short, accented or unaccented, while the whole may be a trisyllabic foot of many varieties. Yet in his carefully composed later poetry Milton kept strictly to the syllabic rules, and never allowed himself

any rhythm which could not be prosodially interpreted in this fictitious fashion—"counted on the fingers." Now the stress-system merely casts off this fiction of Milton's, and it dismisses it the more readily because no one except one or two scholars has ever understood it.

Stress being admitted to rule, it follows that the stress-rhythms are, up to a certain point, identical with modern music, wherein every bar is an accent followed by its complement: and there is no rhythm of modern music which is not also a possible and proper rhythm of stress-prosody; and the recognition of pure stress-prosody was no doubt mainly influenced by the successes of contemporary music. But poetry is not bound, as our music is, to have equal bars; so that its rhythmic field is indefinitely wider. To understand the speech-rhythms of poetry a musician must realize from what an enormous field of rhythm he is excluded by his rule of equal bars. Musicians, however, do not nowadays need to be informed of this; for, having executed all the motions that their chains allowed them, they are already beginning to regret their bonds, and tax their ingenuity to escape from them, as the frequent syncopations and change of time-signature in their music testify.

What rules this new stress-prosody will set to govern its rhythms one cannot foresee, and there is as yet no recognized Prosody of stress-verse. I have experimented with it, and tried to determine what those rules must be; and there is little doubt that the perfected Prosody will pay great attention to the quantitive value of syllables, though not on the classical system.[9] Here, however, I wish only to differentiate that system from the others, and what I have said shows this conclusion:

Summary

1. In the Greek system the Prosody is quantitive.
2. In the syllabic system it is "syllabic" (as described).
3. In the stress-system it is accentual.

And while in the classical Prosody the quantities were the main prosodial basis, first ordered and laid down, with the speech-rhythms counterpointed upon it, in the stress-system, on the other hand, it is the speech-rhythms which are the basis, and their quantitive syllables will be so ordered as to enforce them, and their varieties will be practically similar to the varieties of modern music with its minims, crotchets, quavers, dotted notes, etc., etc.

These things being so, it would seem to me indispensable that any treatise on Prosody should recognize these three different systems: indeed, a Prosody which does not recognize them is to me unintelligible. Before my few final remarks you will expect me to say something about rime.

Rime

Rules for rime are strictly a part of Prosody within my definition of the term, but they call for no discussion here. It is, however, well to understand the relation in which rime scientifically stands to poetry. The main thing in poetry must be the ideas which the words carry; its most important factors are the aesthetic and intellectual form, and the quality of the diction in which the ideas are conveyed; with none of these things are we concerned, but supposing these at their best, with the rhythms suitable and the Prosody also sufficient, the poet will still find that his material is often insurmountably refractory in the matter of syllabic euphony. His wish is that the sounds should always be beautiful or agreeable, and this is impossible, for language was not invented with this aim, and it almost always falls short of what is desirable (the history of English accidence is a disgrace to the aesthetic faculties of the nation); there is, in fact, a constant irremedial deficiency in this merely phonetic beauty, and it is reasonable that extraneous artifices should have been devised to supply it. Alliteration, assonance, and rime are all contrivances of this sort; they are in their nature beautifications of the language independent of the ideas, and of the rhythm, and of the diction, and intended to supply by their artificial correspondences the want of natural beauty in the garment of language. But it must not be overlooked that they were also well nigh necessitated by the unscientific character of the syllabic Prosody, which having in ignorance discarded the scientific Prosody of the poetry which it imitated, had to devise new rules for itself experimentally as it grew up, and eagerly seized on such external artifices of speech to dress out its wavering forms, just as an architecture which has lost its living traditions of fine form will seek to face itself with superficial ornament. Alliteration in early English Poetry was a main feature of structure. It has perished as a metrical scheme, but it is freely used in all poetry, and it is so natural to language that it finds a place in the commonest as well as the most elaborated speech of all kinds. Rime has had a long reign, and still flourishes, and it is in English one of the chief metrical factors. Like a low-born upstart it has even sought to establish its kinship with the ancient family of rhythm by incorporating the aristocratic *h* and *y* into its name. As it distinguishes verses that have no other distinction, its disposition determines stanza-forms, etc.; and for this reason it usurps a prominence for which it is ill-suited. Dryden, indeed, and others have ridiculed the notion of "unrimed" verse in English ; and their opinion is a fair consequence of the poverty of their Prosody. Milton's later poems were an attempt so to strengthen English Prosody as to render it independent of rime. In my opinion he saw exactly what was needed, and it would have been strange if he had not seen. Rime is so trammelling, its effects so cloying, and its worthiest resources are so quickly exhausted,[10] and often of such conspicuous artificiality, that a Prosody which was good enough to do without it would immediately discard it, in spite of its almost unparalleled achievements.

Remarks

I. If these three systems are to be treated of together as one system, it is necessary to find a common-measure of them, and the science of rhythm is at present inadequate to the task.

II. The confusing of them is so universal as to have acquired a sort of authority; and the confusion has discredited the whole subject.

III. The main source of error is the wrong way in which classical scholars read classical verse, and the teaching of their misinterpretations in our schools. Classical poetry being on a quantitive system of longs and shorts, it must be read, not as we read our syllabic verse, but in longs and shorts as it was composed, and if it is not so read it is misunderstood. If it is read in longs and shorts, then the quantitive rhythms appear, and the speech-accents give no difficulty.

IV. To give one all-convincing example of what classical scholars actually do, by treating the different systems as equivalent, the hexameter will serve. This, as Professor Mackail once complained to me, is read by them as AN ACCENTUAL RHYTHM IN THE TRIPLE TIME OF MODERN MUSIC, that is, made up of tribrachs and trochees all stressed on the first syllable. It is of course patent that if the hexameter were in a time of modern music it would be a duple and not a triple time; but it has absolutely nothing in common with the stress-rhythms of modern music.

V. A difficulty is naturally felt in the unlikelihood that such a consensus of learned opinion, from the confident multiscience of Goethe to the equally confident fastidiousness of Matthew Arnold, should be open to such a monstrous reproach of elementary incompetence. But the explanation is not difficult, if the whole blunder is perceived as the misrepresentation of quantity by accent. English people all think that an accent (or stress) makes a syllable long, whereas many of our words are accented as independently of their quantities as the Greek words were, e.g. magistrate, prolific: and all our pyrrhic words (= ∪ ∪) like habit, very, silly, solid, scurry, are accented, like the Latin, on the first syllable, and some very strongly, and this of course absolutely explodes the vulgar notion that accented syllables can be reckoned always as long: besides, you may see that this accent in some cases actually *shortens the syllable* further, as in the word *báttle*; for in the older form *battail*, in which the first syllable had not this decided accent, you will not pronounce it so short, but immediately that you strengthen its accent, as in our *battle* (= bát'l) the *t* closes up the *a* much more quickly and perceptibly shortens it.

VI. To call Milton's blank verse "iambic," as he himself called it, is reasonable enough, and in the absence of a modern terminology[11] it serves well to distinguish it from the hexametric epic verse, and it describes its disyllabic basis, and suggests its rising rhythm (which may rightly be considered as the typical iambic stress, such as we see in Catullus's carefully accentual verse, "Phaséllus ílle quém vidétis hóspites," etc.): moreover, our disyllabic verse is the direct descendant of and substitute for the classic iambic. But a scientific treatise on Prosody cannot afford to use analogical terms.

VII. I should confidently guess that the five-foot metres of our blank verse, etc., came from the Sapphic line.[12] This was always familiar and was very early reduced by musical settings to an accentual scheme, which still obtains in common settings of decasyllabic "iambic" lines in church hymns, and occurs frequently in all our blank verse. I open Wordsworth at hazard in *The Borderers* and find:

> Here at my breast and ask me where I bought it.
> I love her though I dare not call her daughter.
> Oh the poor tenant of that ragged homestead.
> Justice had been most cruelly defrauded.

These lines would be quite comfortable in the notorious *Needy Knife-Grinder,* which was a skit on the accentual Sapphic, though it is often taken seriously. . . .

XI. The use of the Greek quantitive terminology in explaining syllabic or stress-verse implies that the terms are equivalent in the different systems, or requires that they should be plainly differentiated. It is demonstrable that they are not equivalent, and if they are differentiated the absurdity of applying the Greek notions to English poetry is patent. Try the inverse experiment of writing Greek verse with the "syllabic" definition of the classic feet.

XII. The syllabic system attained its results by learned elaboration; and in blank verse this elaboration evolved so many forms of the line (as we see in Milton) that almost any prose, which maintained a fair sprinkling of alternate accents, could be read as blank verse; the puerile degradation of the haphazard decasyllabic rhythm satisfied the verse-maker, and equally beguiled the writer of prose, who sought after rhythmical effect. A clergyman once sympathetically confessed to me that he was himself by nature some-thing of a poet, and that the conviction had on one occasion been strangely forced upon him. For after preaching his first sermon his rector said to him in the vestry, "Do you know that your sermon was all in blank verse?" "And, by George, it was" (he said with some pride); "I looked at it, and it was!" This man had the usual long classical training, and was a fellow of his college.

XIII. To judge from one or two examples I should be tempted to say that the qualification of an English prosodist might be (1) the educated misunderstanding of Greek and Latin verse; (2) a smattering of modern musical rhythm. His method (1) to satisfy himself in the choice of a few barrel-organ rhythms, and (2) to exert his ingenuity in finding them everywhere. The result is not likely to be recommendable to a student.

NOTES

[1.] The line scans: F̄lu m̆i n̆a | quēan t̄i | quōs s̄ub | tēr l̄a | bēn t̆i ă | m̄u r̄os (Ed. note).

[2.] Loudness. I use this word and not "stress," because, though some authorities still maintain that stress is only loudness, I need the word *stress* to indicate a condition which is much more elaborate, and induced very variously. (a) I should admit that loudness may give stress, but (b) I hold that it is more frequently and more effectually given by tonal accent, in which case it is (for our purpose) included under Pitch. (c) It is also sometimes determined by Quantity, and (d) sometimes by Position; as in the last place of our decasyllabic verses where that lacks true accentual stress. When therefore I confine my third voice-effect to loudness, and pretend that my classification is exhaustive, I leave a small flaw in my demonstration: but you will perceive that it does not materially invalidate the argument, because position is the only condition which escapes; and that plainly belongs to a much more elaborate scale of treatment, wherein metres would be analyzed and the effects of the combinations of the different factors would also be shown. For instance, a concurrence of length, high pitch, loudness, and position gives an overwhelming stress, and all possible combinations among all four of the them may occur, and the first three of them are all very variable in degree. It is no wonder that it is difficult to define *stress*.

[3.] Not always making good verse; but the details of that are omitted as not affecting the argument: their varieties often cancel each other.

[4.] My necessary brevity confines me to consideration of the disyllabic metres; but this is justified by their overruling historical importance, and their overwhelming preponderance in European syllabic verse.

[5.] In the absence of a philosophic grammar of rhythm one can only offer opinions as guesses, but it would seem to me that alternate stress can only be of rhythmic value in poetry as the firmest basis for the freest elaboration. One's memory hardly reaches back to the time when it could satisfy one. The force of it always remains as one of the most powerful resources of effect, but its unrelieved monotony is to an educated ear more likely to madden than to lull. (See Remark No. XII.)

[6.] And 'Turcos oppressi et barbaras gentes excussi' is in this category.

[7.] Try the experiment of supplying lacunae. Suppose four syllables to be missing from the middles, respectively, of a Greek iambic, a Latin hexameter, and an English blank verse. In the two former cases the prosodial limitations include many desirable words; in the syllabic scheme almost any words will fit.

[8.] I would not wish to seem to underestimate the extreme beauty to which verse has attained under the syllabic system. Shakespeare and Milton have passages of blank verse as fine as poetry can be. I would make three remarks here. (1) A free and simple basis (such as the syllabic system has) probably offers the best opportunity for elaboration. (2) It is probable that no verse has ever been subject to such various elaboration as the European syllabic verse; the question is rather whether any further development on the same lines is possible. (3) On the simplest syllabic scheme it is impossible in English to write two verses exactly alike and equivalent, because of the infinite variety of the syllabic unit and its combinations: and these natural and subtle differences of value, though common to all systems of prosody, are perhaps of greater rhythmical effect in the syllabic than in the quantitive system.

9·Indifference to quantity is the strangest phenomenon in English verse. Our language contains syllables as long as syllables can be, and others as short as syllables can be, and yet the two extremes are very commonly treated as rhythmically equivalent. A sort of rhythmical patter of stress is set up, and MISPRONUNCIATION IS RELIED ON to overcome any "false quantities." *This was taught me at school,* *e.g.* the Greek word γλῠκύς was pronounced as a spondee of the heaviest class accented strongly on the first syllable, and then had to be read in such a verse as this (corresponding to the *tia* of the line quoted from Virgil):

τοῦτ' ἄρα δεύτατον εἶπεν ἔπος, ὅτε οἱ γλυκὺς ὕπνος.

It is really difficult to get an average classical scholar, who has been educated as I was, to see that there is any absurdity here. On the other hand, an average educated lady will not believe that the scholars can be guilty of an absurdity so manifest. (See Remark V below.)

10·If you observe the rimes to *knight* in Spenser's *Faerie Queene,* you will find the poem considerably damaged thereby.

11·The absence of terminology is evidence of the unscientific character of the system as I have described it.

12·The scheme of the Sapphic line was:

$$— \smile — \smile — \smile \smile — \smile — \smile$$

(Ed. note)

I. A. RICHARDS

Rhythm and Metre

The interests of Professor Richards reside in the "regime of consciousness" and in the mind's response to the stimulus of rhythm and meter. His approach, then, is psychological and even neurological; the mind's feelings of "expectancy . . . must be thought of as a very complex tide of neural settings. . . ." Professor Richards differentiates between rhythm and meter, the latter "the specialised form" of the former. It is the larger movement, the rhythm, which weaves the whole "texture of expectations, satisfactions, disappointments, surprisals." Meter, on the other hand, focuses our response; through it we become "patterned ourselves." Meter functions to articulate the parts of the poem, and in doing so aids memory. Meter, as Coleridge and Yeats have testified, also affects the mind as a hypnotic agent as well as an agent of hyperaesthesia—it both lulls consciousness and sharpens our powers to experience sensation.

Professor Richards is the thorough contextualist; no rhythmical or metrical effect can "be separated from its contemporaneous other effects." He acknowledges the complexity of the sound-sense relationship; the rhythm may qualify, embellish, or comment on the meaning of the words. The more specific function of meter is to produce "the frame effect, isolating the poetic experience from the accidents and irrelevancies of everyday existence." Meter acts as the agent of aesthetic distance; in the

From *Principles of Literary Criticism* by I. A. Richards. Reprinted by permission of Harcourt Brace Jovanovich, Inc.

words of Donald Justice, "The meters signify . . . that we are at that remove from life which traditionally we have called art."

> . . . when it approaches with a divine hopping.
>
> *The Joyful Wisdom*

Rhythm and its specialised form, metre, depend upon repetition, and expectancy. Equally where what is expected recurs and where it fails, all rhythmical and metrical effects spring from anticipation. As a rule this anticipation is unconscious. Sequences of syllables both as sounds and as images of speech-movements leave the mind ready for certain further sequences rather than for others. Our momentary organisation is adapted to one range of possible stimuli rather than to another. Just as the eye reading print unconsciously expects the spelling to be as usual, and the fount of type to remain the same, so the mind after reading a line or two of verse, or half a sentence of prose, prepares itself ahead for any one of a number of possible sequences, at the same time negatively incapacitating itself for others. The effect produced by what actually follows depends very closely upon this unconscious preparation and consists largely of the further twist which it gives to expectancy. It is in terms of the variation in these twists that rhythm is to be described. Both prose and verse vary immensely in the extent to which they excite this 'getting ready' process, and in the narrowness of the anticipation which is formed. Prose on the whole, with the rare exceptions of a Landor, a De Quincey, or a Ruskin, is accompanied by a very much vaguer and more indeterminate expectancy than verse. In such prose as this page, for example, little more than a preparedness for further words not all exactly alike in sound and with abstract polysyllables preponderating is all that arises. In short, the sensory or formal effect of words has very little play in the literature of analysis and exposition. But as soon as prose becomes more emotive than scientific, the formal side becomes prominent.

Let us take Landor's description [1] of a lioness suckling her young:

> On perceiving the countryman, she drew up her feet gently, and squared her mouth, and rounded her eyes, slumberous with content; and they looked, he said, like sea-grottoes, obscurely green, interminably deep, at once awakening fear and stilling and suppressing it.

After 'obscurely green' would it be possible (quite apart from sense) to have 'deeply dark' or 'impenetrably gloomy'? Why, apart from sense, can so few of the syllables be changed in vowel sound, in emphasis, in duration or otherwise, without disaster to the total effect? As with all such questions about sensory form and its effects, only an incomplete answer can be given. The expectancy caused by what has gone before, a thing which must be thought of as a very complex tide of neural settings, lowering the threshold for some kinds of stimuli and raising it for others, and the character of the stimulus which does actually come, both play their part.

Even the most highly organised lyrical or 'polyphonic' prose raises as it advances only a very ambiguous expectation. Until the final words of the passage, there are always a great number of different sequences which would equally well fit in, which would satisfy the expectancy so far as that is merely due to *habit,* to the *routine of sensory stimulation.* What is expected in fact is not this sound or that sound, not even this kind of sound or that kind of sound, but some one of a certain thousand kinds of sounds. It is much more a negative thing than a positive. As in the case of many social conventions it is easier to say what disqualifies than to say what is required.

Into this very indeterminate expectancy the new element comes with its own range of possible effects. There is, of course, no such thing as *the* effect of a word or a sound. There is no one effect which belongs to it. Words have no intrinsic literary characters. None are either ugly or beautiful, intrinsically displeasing or delightful. Every word has instead a range of possible effects, varying with the conditions into which it is received. All that we can say as to the sorting out of words, whether into the 'combed' and 'slippery', the 'shaggy' and 'rumpled' as with Dante, or in any other manner, is that some, through long use, have narrower ranges than others and require more extraordinary conditions if they are to change their 'character'. What effect the word has is a compromise between some one of its possible effects and the special conditions into which it comes. Thus in Shakespeare hardly any word ever looks odd until we consider it; whereas even in Keats the 'cold mushrooms' in the *Satyrs' Song* give the mind a shock of astonishment, an astonishment which is full of delight, but none the less is a shock.

But with this example we have broken down the limitation to the mere sound, to the strictly formal or sensory aspect of word sequences, and in fact the limitation is useless. For the effect of a word as sound cannot be separated from its contemporaneous other effects. They become inextricably mingled at once.

The sound gets its character by compromise with what is going on already. The preceding agitation of the mind selects from a range of possible characters which the word might present that one which best suits with what is happening. There are no gloomy and no gay vowels or syllables, and the army of critics who have attempted to analyse the effects of passages into vowel and consonantal collocations have, in fact, been merely amusing themselves. The way in which the sound of a word is taken varies with the emotion already in being. But, further, it varies with the sense. For the anticipation of the sound due to habit, to the routine of sensation, is merely a part of the general expectancy. Grammatical regularities, the necessity for completing the thought, the reader's state of conjecture as to what is being said, his apprehension in dramatic literature of the action, of the intention, situation, state of mind generally, of the speaker, all these and many other things intervene. The way the sound is taken is much less determined by the sound itself than by the conditions into which it enters. All these anticipations form a very closely woven network and the word which can satisfy them all simultaneously may well seem triumphant. But we should not attribute to the sound alone virtues which involve so many other factors. To say this is not in the least to belittle the importance of the sound; in most cases it is the key to the effects of poetry.

This texture of expectations, satisfactions, disappointments, surprisals, which the sequence of syllables brings about, is rhythm. And the sound of words comes to its full power only through rhythm. Evidently there can be no surprise and no disappointment unless there is expectation, and most rhythms perhaps are made up as much of disappointments and postponements and surprises and betrayals as of simple, straightforward satisfactions. Hence the rapidity with which too simple rhythms, those which are too easily 'seen through', grow cloying or insipid unless hypnoidal states intervene, as with much primitive music and dancing and often with metre.

The same definition of rhythm may be extended to the plastic arts and to architecture. Temporal sequence is not strictly necessary for rhythm, though in the vast majority of cases it is involved. The attention usually passes successively from one complex to another, the expectations, the readiness to perceive this rather than that, aroused by the one, being either satisfied or surprised by the other. Surprise plays an equally important part here; and the difference in detail between a surprising and delightful variation and one which merely irritates and breaks down the rhythm, as we say, is here, as elsewhere, a matter of the combination and resolution of impulses too subtle for our present means of investigation. All depends upon whether what comes can be an ingredient in the further response, or whether the mind must, as it were, start anew; in more ordinary language, upon whether there is any 'connection' between the parts of the whole.

But the rhythmic elements in a picture or a building may be not successive but simultaneous. A quick reader who sees a word as a whole commonly overlooks misprints because the general form of the word is such that he is only able at that instant to perceive one particular letter in a particular place and so overlooks what is discrepant. The parts of a visual field exert what amounts to a simultaneous influence over one another. More strictly what is discrepant does not get through to more central regions. Similarly, with those far more intricate wholes, made up of all kinds of imagery and incipient action of which works of art consist. The parts of a growing response mutually modify one another and this is all that is required for rhythm to be possible.

We may turn now to that more complex and more specialised form of temporal rhythmic sequence which is known as metre. This is the means by which words may be made to influence one another to the greatest possible extent. In metrical reading the narrowness and definiteness of expectancy, as much unconscious as ever in most cases, is very greatly increased, reaching in some cases, if rime also is used, almost exact precision. Furthermore, what is anticipated becomes through the regularity of the time intervals in metre virtually dated. This is no mere matter of more or less perfect correspondence with the beating of some internal metronome. The whole conception of metre as *'uniformity* in variety', a kind of mental drill in which words, those erratic and varied things, do their best to behave as though they were all the same, with certain concessions, licences and equivalences allowed, should nowadays be obsolete. It is a survivor which is still able to do a great deal of harm to the uninitiated, however, and although it has been knocked on the head vigorously enough by Professor Saintsbury and others, it is as difficult to kill as Punch. Most treatises on the subject, with their talk of feet and of stresses, unfortunately tend to encourage it, however little this may be the aim of the authors.

As with rhythm so with metre, we must not think of it as in the words themselves or in the thumping of the drum. It is not *in* the stimulation, it is in our response. Metre adds to all the variously fated expectancies which make of rhythm a definite temporal pattern and its effect is not due to our perceiving a pattern in something outside us, but to our becoming patterned ·rselves. With every beat of the metre a tide of anticipation in us turns and ɔwings, setting up as it does so extraordinarily extensive sympathetic reverberations. We shall never understand metre so long as we ask, 'Why does temporal pattern so excite us?' and fail to realise that the pattern itself is a vast cyclic agitation spreading all over the body, a tide of excitement pouring through the channels of the mind.

The notion that there is any virtue in regularity or in variety, or in any other formal feature, apart from its effects upon us, must be discarded before any metrical problem can be understood. The regularity to which metre tends acts through the definiteness of the anticipations which are thereby aroused. It is through these that it gets such a hold upon the mind. Once again, here too, the failure of our expectations is often more important than success. Verse in which we constantly get exactly what we are ready for and no more, instead of something which we can and must take up and incorporate as another stage in a total developing response, is merely toilsome and tedious. In prose, the influence of past words extends only a little way ahead. In verse, especially when stanza-form and rime co-operate to give a larger unit than the line, it may extend far ahead. It is this knitting together of the parts of the poem which explains the mnemonic power of verse, the first of the suggestions as to the origin of metre to be found in the Fourteenth Chapter of *Biographia Literaria,* that lumber-room of neglected wisdom which contains more hints towards a theory of poetry than all the rest ever written upon the subject.

We do great violence to the facts if we suppose the expectations excited as we read verse to be concerned only with the stress, emphasis, length, foot structure and so forth of the syllables which follow. Even in this respect the custom of marking syllables in two degrees only, long and short, light and full, etc., is inadequate, although doubtless forced upon metrists by practical considerations. The mind in the poetic experience responds to subtler niceties than these. When not in that experience but coldly considering their several qualities as sounds by the ear alone, it may well find two degrees all that are necessary. The obvious comparison with the difference between what even musical notation can record in music and the player's interpretation can usefully be made here.

A more serious omission is the neglect by the majority of metrists of the pitch relations of syllables. The reading of poetry is of course not a monotonous and subdued form of singing. There is no question of definite pitches at which the syllables must be taken, nor perhaps of definite harmonic relations between different sounds. But that a rise and fall of pitch is involved in metre and is as much part of the poet's technique as any other feature of verse, as much under his control also, is indisputable. Anyone who is not clear upon this point may compare as a striking instance Milton's *Hymn on the Morning of Christ's Nativity* with Collins' *Ode to Simplicity.* Due allowances made for the natural peculiarities of different readers, the scheme of pitch relations, in their contexts, of

> That on the bitter cross
> Must redeem our loss;

and of

> But com'st a decent maid,
> In Attic robe array'd,

are clearly different. There is nothing arbitrary or out of the poet's control in this, as there is nothing arbitrary or out of his control in the way in which an adequate reader will stress particular syllables. He brings both about by the same means, the modification of the reader's impulses by what has gone before. It is true that some words resist emphasis far more than perhaps any resist change of pitch, yet this difference is merely one of degree. It is as natural to lower the pitch in reading the word 'loss' as it is to emphasise it as compared with 'our' in the same context.

Here again we see how impossible it is to consider rhythm or metre as though it were purely an affair of the sensory aspect of syllables and could be dissociated from their sense and from the emotional effects which come about through their sense. One principle may, however, be hazarded. As in the case of painting the more direct means are preferable to the less direct, so in poetry. What can be done by sound should not be done otherwise or in violation of the natural effects of sound. Violations of the natural emphases and tones of speech brought about for the sake of the further effects due to thought and feeling are perilous, though, on occasion, they may be valuable devices. The use of italics in *Cain* to straighten out the blank verse is as glaring an instance as any. But more liberties are justified in dramatic writing than elsewhere, and poetry is full of exceptions to such principles,[2] We must not forget that Milton did not disdain to use special spelling, 'mee', for example, in place of 'me', in order to suggest additional emphasis when he feared that the reader might be careless.

So far we have been concerned with metre only as a specialised form of rhythm, giving an increased interconnection between words through an increased control of anticipation. But it has other, in some cases even more important powers. Its use as an hypnotic agent is probably very ancient. Coleridge once again drops his incidental remark, just beside yet extremely close to the point. "It tends to increase the vivacity and susceptibility both of the general feelings and of the attention. This effect it produces by the continued excitement of surprise, and by the quick reciprocations of curiosity still gratified and still re-excited, which are too slight indeed to be at any moment objects of distinct consciousness, yet become considerable in their aggregate influence. As a medicated atmosphere, or as wine during animated conversation, they act powerfully, though themselves unnoticed." (*Biographia Literaria*, Chap. XVIII.) Mr. Yeats, when he speaks of the function of metre being to "lull the mind into a waking trance," is describing the same effect, however strange his conception of this trance may be.

That certain metres, or rather that a certain handling of metre, should produce in a slight degree a hypnoidal state is not surprising. But it does so not, as Coleridge suggests, through the surprise element in metrical effects, but through the absence of surprise, through the lulling effects more than through the awakening. Many of the most characteristic symptoms of incipient hypnosis are present in a slight degree. Among these susceptibility and vivacity of emotion, suggestibility, limitations of the field of attention, marked differences in the incidence of belief-feelings closely analogous to those which alcohol and nitrous oxide can induce, and some degree of hyperaesthesia (increased power of discriminating sensations) may be noted. We need not boggle at the word 'hypnosis'. It is sufficient to say, borrowing a phrase from M. Jules Romains, that there is a change in the regime of consciousness, which is directly due to the metre, and that to this regime the above-mentioned characteristics attach. As regards the hyperaesthesia, there may be several ways of interpreting what can be observed. All that matters here is that syllables, which in prose or in *vers libre* sound thin, tinny and flat, often gain an astonishing sonority and fullness even in verse which seems to possess no very subtle metrical structure.

Metre has another mode of action not hitherto mentioned. There can be little doubt that historically it has been closely associated with dancing, and that the connections of the two still hold. This is true at least of some 'measures'. Either motor images, images of the sensations of dancing, or, more probably, imaginal and incipient movements follow the syllables and make up their 'movement'. Once the metre has begun to 'catch on' they are almost as closely bound up with the sequence of the words as the tied 'verbal' images themselves.

The extension of this 'movement' of the verse from dance forms to more general movements is natural and inevitable. That there is a very close connection between the sense and the metrical movement of

> And now the numerous tramplings quiver lightly
> Along a huge cloud's ridge; and now with sprightly
> Wheel downward come they into fresher skies,

cannot be doubted whatever we may think of the rime.

It is not less clear in

> Where beyond the extreme sea wall, and between the
> remote sea gates,

> Waste water washes, and tall ships founder, and deep
> death waits,

or in

> Ran on embattell'd Armies clad in Iron,

than it is in

> We sweetly curtsied each to each
> And deftly danced a saraband.

Nor is it always the case that the movement takes its cue from the sense. It is often a commentary on the sense and sometimes may qualify it, as when the resistless strength of Coriolanus in battle is given an appearance of dreadful ease by the leisureliness of the description,

> Death, that dark spirit, in's nervy arm doth lie
> Which being advanc'd declines, and then men die.

Movement in poetry deserves at least as much study as onomatopoeia.

This account, of course, by no means covers all the ways by which metre takes effect in poetry. The fact that we appropriately use such words as 'lulling', 'stirring', 'solemn', 'pensive', 'gay' in describing metres is an indication of their power more directly to control emotion. But the more general effects are more important. Through its very appearance of artificiality metre produces in the highest degree the 'frame' effect, isolating the poetic experience from the accidents and irrelevancies of everyday existence. We have seen how necessary this isolation is and how easily it may be mistaken for a difference in kind. Much which in prose would be too personal or too insistent, which might awaken irrelevant conjectures or might 'overstep itself', is managed without disaster in verse. There are, it is true, equivalent resources in prose—irony, for example, very frequently has this effect—but their scope is far more limited. Metre for the most difficult and most delicate utterances is the all but inevitable means.

NOTES

[1] *Works,* II, 171.

[2] It is worth remarking that any application of critical principles must be indirect. They are not any the less useful because this is so. Misunderstanding on this point has often led artists to accuse critics of wishing to make art a matter of rules, and their objection to any such attempt is entirely justified.

JOHN HOLLANDER

The Metrical Frame

Vision and Resonance, from which this essay is taken, reveals a poet's
sensibility, a theorist's powers of analysis and discrimination, and a historian's contextual depth. While acknowledging the importance of linguistics to prosodic study, Professor Hollander raises some cogent objections.
Many linguists proceed to metrical analysis with an aggressively synchronic orientation: "most linguistic models of the production or the
reading of English verse seem to have propounded a maker or a reader with
no memory and no range of reading, a world of poetic language sacred to
motherless Muses." Professor Hollander reminds us that rhythms and
meters operate in historical contexts, that a poet chooses his metrical or
non-metrical mode within historically determined conventions and contingencies. A particular metrical form can assume the authority of a period
style; in the eighteenth century the "metrical emblem," the heroic couplet, "had the fundamental work of *defining* the utterance as a literary
event." Dr. Johnson, a man in so many ways at one with his age, had ears
so conditioned by the period style that he could not hear the strangely
proportioned music of *Lycidas*. (In our own time poets compose metered
verse with the faint sense that they are betraying the *Zeitgeist*: they should
be writing in Absolute Rhythm, Projective Verse, or in W. C. Williams'
"variable feet.")

Poetic rhythms echo down the corridors of literary history, "beyond

the boundaries of the poem itself. . . ." Milton recalls Spenser, Wordsworth recalls Milton, Wallace Stevens recalls Wordsworth and Milton. It
is the task of criticism to chart metrical modes, to "trace [a meter's] family
tree by appeal to those resemblances which connect it, in some ways with
one, in some ways with another kind of poem that may, historically,
precede or follow it."

<h1 style="text-align:center">I</h1>

Fifty years ago, I. A. Richards distinguished between two functions of poetic meter. After acknowledging its primary domain of interest for poets
from Wordsworth and Coleridge on ("The fact that we appropriately use such
words as 'lulling,' 'stirring,' 'solemn,' 'pensive,' 'gay,' in describing metres is
an indication of their power more directly to control emotion."), he turned
away from this formulation of the "music" of verse to "more general effects,"
as he called them. "Through its very appearance of artificiality metre produces in the highest degree the 'frame' effect, isolating the poetic experience
from the accidents and irrelevancies of everyday existence."[1] The relation
between the music, as it were, and the frame, as it were: the way the second
affects us both independently and by the ways in which the first of them is
contingent upon it—this is the subject of the study of form that has proved
most tantalizing in recent decades.

Aside from their use in Classical and Modern musical theory, the words
"meter" and "rhythm" might be conveniently applied along the line of
demarcation drawn by Richards so long ago. The word of flow, "rhythm,"
characterizes the series of actual effects upon our consciousness of a line or
passage of verse: it is the road along which we read. The meter, then, would
apply to whatever it was that might constitute the framing, the isolating; its
presence we infer from our scanning. The distinction is rather useful because so many other sets of opposed linguistic and literary dimensions seem
to be comprehended by it: design and particular; norm and instance; spatial,
or at least schematic, and temporal; singing or speaking and writing; and
ultimately, in the matter of the angles of vision of linguistic theory itself,
synchronic and diachronic, phenomenological and historical.

These distinctions have come to be disregarded in recent work on
prosody not because the terms "meter" and "rhythm" continue to be used
interchangeably, but largely because of the primarily synchronic orientation
of most linguists who have turned their attention to problems of poetic
structure. Whether concerned with the phonemic actualities of the poem as
an act of speech, or, more recently, with the idea of a metrical scheme as a set
of rules for generating lines of verse (each, be it said, with its unique set of

characteristics which might be called rhythmic), most linguistic models of the production or the reading of English verse seem to have propounded a maker or a reader with no memory and no range of reading, a world of poetic language sacred to motherless Muses. Nevertheless, their contributions have been of great use and interest, both in sweeping away useless and inoperative critical apparatus, and in lighting up some dusty corners.

II

"Meaning," "significance," "function," "relevance," on the one hand, then; on the other, "meter," "prosody," "music," "form." To connect the terms of the first group with those of the second; to distinguish between the terms in each group and to account for and prevent their frequent confusion; and, finally, to justify the lines along which these distinctions are drawn, have come more and more in recent years to engage the fullest concerns of poetics. The more specifically instrumental roles played by structural linguistics in this engagement were considerable. Many of its basic principles were brought to bear by Richards upon the clichés and mystiques that, accumulating over two centuries of poetic theory, had blurred the boundaries and overlappings of these analytic concepts. In addressing itself to the problem of sound, pattern, and sense, recent inquiry has been particularly successful in clearing away a compost heap of conflicting, often self-inconsistent traditional prosodical theory, increased in the past hundred years by ritually sustained errors and, even more, by an inability to confront what it actually was that contemporary poets were doing. Thomas Hardy was possibly the last major poet to write in a long tradition of English versifying whose founding we might assign to Ben Jonson on the grounds that he confessed to writing all his verses "first in prose." And yet one of Hardy's chief difficulties as a poet resided in his latent uneasiness with a tradition for which he invokes the authority of Wordsworth: "It is supposed that by the act of writing in verse an author makes a formal engagement that he will gratify certain known habits of association." It is possible, that is, to speak of Hardy's *choice of meter* in a way that we would be reluctant to in the case of Hopkins, Eliot, Pound, or Yeats, and, even more, to pass judgment on that choice by designating it an arbitrary one. For it is the poet's own sense of the function of the verse itself which changes from one literary epoch to another, and recent critical methods which treat poems like objects, like artifacts such as vases or sculptures, or even like organisms with souls, all answer in some measure the requests of modern poems to be treated as just that.

Traditional prosodical analysis, whether carried on for polemical or avowedly speculative reasons, was still a little too much like cataloguing styles in clothing to be able to deal effectively with a body of new poetry with the form of cloth puppets or sea animals whose garments were their bodies or shells themselves. In such a world of organistic, post-symbolist poetry and criticism it was the particular utility of structural linguistics to take us back to taxonomy, to encourage us in the use of biological categories that help us to classify, sort, dissect, and anatomize the natural history of verse. English poetry since Hardy has cried out for such murder, if murder it be. The study of literary history itself may be seen to have profited from it, if only because it revealed the long record of prosodical inquiry itself as a history of ideology and of taste in analytic methods.

The uses of linguistics as a tool have actually extended beyond the clearing away of traditional confusions, and the resolving of questions like that of quantitative verse in English by undermining the bases of traditional arguments about them. A general program of making more public, of verifying, the private insights of the ear of a sensitive reader, for example, has proved a hopeful one. Particularly in the case of those poets, such as Wyatt, Shakespeare, and Jacobean tragedians, Donne, Yeats, and Frost, whose formal diction is always informed by the syntactic and emphatic stress patterns of colloquial speech, have the suppositions, if not the methods, of modern linguistics been helpful.

By an examination of contemporary poetry in which a purely graphic scheme of line arrangement can operate in open conflict with equally prominent phonemic ones, almost any reader can come to understand how aural and visual entities merge in status when they operate as metrical segments. And here a more general application of linguistic theory to poetics presents itself. For just as the conceptual distinction between the phonetic and the phonemic is crucial if one is to talk about the elements of a particular language, so is a clear distinction between the phonetic and the metric basic to a consideration of the role of sound in the game of poetic sense. In short, it is as a heuristic model that phonemics might have been most useful to poetic theory, rather than merely as an implement for the treatment of a poem as a spoken utterance.

There is good reason, I think, in the light of recent work and old warnings both, for drawing this distinction. In the first place, although poems are neither purely spoken utterances nor inscriptions, their peculiar status, straddling the two, seems to lose itself under certain kinds of analysis that start out with putting the poem into phonemic transcription. The poem becomes the phonetic parts of its texture, really, while metrical conventions, the whole substance of traditional prosodic theory, are ignored or treated at best as an unexamined *donnée*, a given condition rather like the fact that the poem is in English, but in no way as binding on the interpretation of discrete signals. It may be that the influence of recent statistical approaches has generated the view that signals with a low probability of occurrence must necessarily have an increased *importance*. Within the framework of information theory, it is certainly true that the more surprising event is the more significant one, for the only kind of significance is defined as a function of the reciprocal of the probability of occurrence. But to equate "information" with "significance" in a non-rigorous sense may not be possible. In many cases, something like the opposite would appear to be true. The extremely high redundancy of capital letters at the beginning of lines of printed verse, for example, renders their informative value, in the above sense, trivial. But their actual role is of considerable importance, being one of definition, or of labeling the utterance in question as a poem. Their significance for the statistical analyst lies in the fact that they set up a prior expectation that will itself affect the relationship between the "surprise value" (for the reader) and the probability of occurrence (for the post-mortem analyst). Information theory must necessarily take the highly probable event more or less for granted. But in the analysis of a poem as a work of literature, these conventional events are of major importance.[2]

It has been rather to the structure of self-contained poetic texts, than to the metrical conventions governing many such texts, that linguistic analysis has been devoted. But the literary critic, or even the well-informed reader, tends to think in terms of both what he is reading and how what he is reading resembles other things that he has read, of the poem as a thing in itself, and as an example of a literary form. The reader of any subtlety at all will often talk about a poem as if he felt that there were two sequences of events going on at once. The literary critic (who may have helped train the reader to talk in this way) will distinguish "meter" from "rhythm," assumed norm from actual instance, and perhaps resort to Gerard Manley Hopkins's rich, but misleading notion of "counterpoint" to describe their relation. The greatest temptation to employ this notion arises when one occurrence in a poem seems to be part of two different schemes simultaneously. . . .

In the most general sense, an enjambment is any lack of alignment between syntax and line structure, but it is usually considered in the cases where a normal correspondence between the two is violated. Textual analysis treats enjambments not only in terms of their effects upon the poem's "flow of movement," but for their direct semantic operation. The most obvious cases of this occur when a compound is broken up between two lines, suddenly revealing, in a startling way, that the whole, rather than the separable part, is to be employed:

> And one can have a savory or a sweet
> Potato after dinner, if he chooses.

Another example might be that of the covert allusion for which only a line division seems to provide optimum syntactic ambiguity:

> Under a soupy tree
> Mopes Daphnis, joined by all
> The brown, surrounding landscape:
>
> Even in Arcady
> Ego must needs spoil
> Such a beautiful friendship!

Here the rhymes and the sense (depending on a modern colloquial use of "ego" or *amour-propre*) as well as the line structure force a separation of the two words which, when juxtaposed, recall the famous *memento mori* in the paintings of Guercino and Poussin, *Et in Arcadia Ego,* with the exception here that vanity, rather than death as the speaker, is made the ubiquitous subject. T. S. Eliot's notorious

> Princess Volupine extends
> A meagre, blue-nailed, phthisic hand
> To climb the waterstair. Lights, lights,
> She entertains Sir Ferdinand
>
> Klein. Who clipped the lion's wings
> And flea'd his rump and pared his paws?

makes the name straddle two stanzas as well as two lines, but the abruptly turned to question nevertheless claims, by its alliterating "clipped," a line kinship with what is nastily being treated as the offending patronymic particle.

It is to a case which may have actually influenced Eliot in this poem which I should now like to turn. Ben Jonson's ode *To the Memory and Friendship of that Noble Pair, Sir Lucius Cary and Sir H. Morison* is, from the point of view of metrical conventions, not only an extremely programmatic poem, but a didactic one as well. It is the second purported but first actually imitative "Pindaric" ode in English, written in couplets of varying line length to suggest Pindaric irregularity, pedantically labeling each triad strophe, antistrophe, and epode as "The Turne," "The Counter-Turne," and "The Stand," respectively.[3] The poem mourns and moralizes upon, in an appropriately public way, the separation of a pair of close friends brought about by the death of the younger of them. Cary and Morison were both public men as well as members of Jonson's coterie. Jonson's stanzaic form keeps to the pattern of the Pindaric ode, *aab,* with two stanzas identical in structure, the third slightly different in its pattern of line length and rhyme. Although the stanza headings serve more as glosses than as discrete titles, the stanzas are self-contained and end-stopped. When an occasional enjambment does occur, it is of the common type that realigns itself in the very next line, creating no effect of surprise. But in Jonson's eighth stanza an enjambment even more startling in some ways than Eliot's occurs:

> The Counter-Turne
> Call, noble *Lucius,* then for wine,
> And let thy lookes with gladnesse shine:
> Accept this garland, plant it on thy head,
> And thinke, now know, thy Morison's not dead.
> Hee leap'd the present age,
> Possesst with holy rage,
> To see that bright eternall Day:
> Of which we *Priests* and *Poets* say
> Such truths, as we expect for happy men,
> And there he lives with memories; and *Ben*
>
> The Stand
>
> *Jonson,* who sung this of him, e're he went
> Himselfe to rest.

This is again a kind of pun by discovery. Just as "Sir Ferdinand" is a perfectly proper appellation, abruptly qualified by the enjambed remainder, the *contre-rejet,* so the line

> And there he lives with memories; and *Ben*

is complete in itself, ending its stanza like the others on a full stop (the seventeenth-century punctuation often uses colons and semicolons where we would employ commas). Just "Ben" may appear overfamiliar; but for the living Cary and the late Morison, as well as the close-knit coterie of friends who called themselves "The Tribe of Ben," "Ben" alone was as frequently employed in dedicatory poems as in conversation. The line ending *"Ben,"* then, is for a coterie reader; with the addition of the *contre-rejet,* it becomes

more properly public. But Jonson continues his ninth stanza through an even
more grotesque example:

> Or taste a part of that full joy he meant
> To have exprest,
> In this bright *Asterisme:*
> Where it were friendships schisme,
> (Were not his *Lucius* long with us to tarry)
> To separate these twi-
> Lights, the *Dioscuri;*
> And keepe the one halfe from his *Harry.*

Even more grotesque, perhaps, although some readers might rush through
the hyphenation unperturbed, and with some reason to which I shall turn in
a moment. But those readers who do dwell over the hyphenation will be
following Jonson's conceit of the Greek twins Castor and Pollux being separated by death (this grows into the splitting of the constellation Gemini);
they will read the "twi-" of "twi-/ lights" as both root and prefix. "To
separate these two (or twin) lights" is itself "separated" quite literally; the
name, in an almost schematic logical trick, is treated *qua* object in the same
way that its metaphorical bearer (the pair of Cary and Morison) is thereby
reported to be treated. An effective device, this is not an unusual sort of
thing in the Renaissance, being commonly used in polyphonic songs (*cf.*
John Wilbye's madrigal "Sweet Honey-Sucking Bees": "For if one flaming
dart come from her eye,/Was never dart so sharp, ah, then you die!," where
on the last line, the upper soprano part moves to an f# on the word
"sharp"). [4]

But the impulse of many readers to carry along through the break, to
treat this as the common kind of flowing, non-ironic enjambment, is also of
interest. The hyphenated enjambment is rare, but not in the least capricious,
in the poetry of Jonson's age; it was used in English verse that was consciously attempting to model itself on certain Greek meters. Thomas Campion's polemical *Observations in the Art of English Poesie* (1602), a metrical
study that urges the abandonment of all rhyme and stressed scansion by
English verse in favor of an adopted quantitative system making even less
phonemic sense than it may have for Latin, contains an example of hyphenation in one of the model poems therein set forth:

> Like cleare springs renu'd by flowing,
> Ever perfet, ever in them-
> selves eternall.

The *locus classicus* for this is in Greek choric meters, in Pindar, and in Sappho; Catullus and Horace (I think only once) so hyphenate in their Latin Sapphics. Its justification in Jonson's ode must be ascribed to a purpose akin in some ways to Campion's, and although he eschewed the latter's prosodic theories, his commitment to Classical models was very strong. Any reader in any way aware of the models, either through direct knowledge or through other adaptations, will to some degree recognize the device. Like Campion's and others' quantitative experiments it is a purely graphic convention (it was on the basis of letters, rather than phonemes, that syllables were assigned their weight); but in the case of both of Jonson's enjambments the separation engages the phonemic junctures of English.

I should like to cite a final case in which a less startling but equally effective enjambment produces [a] quasi-metaphorical kind of effect. . . . The second stanza of Keats's ode *To Autumn* invokes the personified season in an idle moment, after the images of harvest in the first stanza, and proceeds through indolent play, winnowing, and reaping. Keats says to her:

> And sometimes like a gleaner thou dost keep
> Steady thy laden head across a brook.

F. R. Leavis remarks of these lines that "As we pass the line-division from 'keep' to 'steady' we are made to enact, analogically, the upright steadying carriage from one stone to the next. And such an enactment seems to me properly brought under the head of 'image.'"[5] I dislike intensely this way of putting it. Such a notion of analogical enactment is being used in a kind of magical way; this is really nothing more than a little poem of Dr. Leavis's about what is going on in Keats's lines. Actually, all we are being made to enact here is all that lines of poetry ever make us enact: an act of speech. But to say this is not so trivial as one might think. Certainly the enjambment is an effective one, especially in a poem whose norm is more in the direction of being end-stopped. And certainly we do have a feeling of a heavy bale of grain balanced on Autumn's head as she picks her way through the waters of a stream or across stepping stones.

But there need be no mystery in explaining the way that Keats's metrical device works. In ordinary speech the English phrase "keep steady" is accented (*keep steady*); that is, the first monosyllable abandoning principal stress to the first syllable of the second word. But here, the word "keep" is in a stressed position in the first line, as if it were to be followed by something like

> And sometimes like a gleaner thou dost keep
> A bale of grain against the winter's blast. . . .

Here there is no surprise at the enjambment, for "keep" is both transitive and primary, and the line break follows a subject-predicate boundary. But Keats's "keep" is tinged with an auxiliary quality—it is almost as if it were a Greek middle, say; the verb is "keep steady," and the cut between the words points this up. Again,

> And sometimes like a gleaner thou dost keep
> Thy laden head steady across a brook

would remove the effect, while setting up a more Miltonic ambiguity of reference of the "steady." The Keatsian arrangement forces us to read a stress pattern of " ′ / ′ · " , which in ordinary speech would be given to the phrase used in a musical way to assist verbally someone who was indeed balancing something and nervous about it. In short, it is quasi-imperative, something uttered by an onlooker who tries to assist with verbal magic, with incantatory body english.

But it is to Ben Jonson's enjambments, and particularly to his second one, that I should like to return. There seem to be two different *sorts* of significance at work here. The first is semantic; the second, more purely formal, in this case, graphic or what we might call *literal*. We have already observed that Jonson's intention throughout the ode seems to be referential; it might be suggested that the overhangs, and particularly the hyphenated one, were consonant, if not actually cooperative, with the strophic titles. It is the fact of their appearance, however, and their role once they have appeared in the texture of the poem, that I wish to contrast here. The significance of the elements of Neoclassic "form" in Jonson's ode is quite simply a historical significance; while the ironic and quasi-self-descriptive effects of the two might more properly be considered as showing up under the application of some poetic analogue of a synchronic analysis. (Of course, our knowledge about the "tribe of Ben," the frequent use of the Christian name alone in verse, etc., are historical facts themselves. But invoking them, one is simply giving the meaning of the word "Ben" in Jacobean and Caroline poems).

Now even if we want to reject the notion that either or both of these effects of the enjambments are, properly speaking, significances; and especially if we wish to follow a by now proverbial philosopher's guide, "Don't look for the meaning; look for the use," we may observe that their *functions* are clearly different, the uses to which they are put are as divergent as any verbal acts, such as admonishing, deceiving or requesting, can be. The workings of the formal, *metrical* effect are somehow prior to those of *rhythmic* (and since English has phonemic stress, *semantic*) processes; the former set up contingencies affecting the latter. The problem of accounting for and charting these contingencies actually underlies some of the most dubious enterprises of traditional prosody, placing much weight on graphic conventions or choices of form, perhaps (as if there were several possible outfits for the same poem, albeit one proper one) without really knowing why they might be important.

III

Let us look at some of the operations of poetic rhythm as it works within the contingencies established by the poet's chosen, normative meter. I say "chosen" not because I wish to imply that the actual effects of linguistic sound which occur within the poem itself are forced upon the poet; or necessarily unconsciously selected; or revealed to him by an incontrovertible muse. Even in the case of the most complicated and apparently "free" rhythmic schemes, the actual composition of lines within the pattern seems to result from a different order of decision-making than does the selection of the scheme to begin with. Whether willing or not, poets are capable of discussing their choice of meter, while rarely would we trust their analyses of their rhythmic invention. It seems possible to show that in some cases the over-all poetic form, metrical scheme, etc., may result from a bit of *"donnée,"* given, material, whether a phrase, an image, a word, a rhythmic effect of some kind. In this case, the metrical choice will depend on finding the meter in which a rhythmic event will be utilized, as well as on the possibilities afforded by convention. The famous so-called *vers donné* from Racine's *Phèdre,* for example, has for generations been held out to French schoolboys as the triumph of pure poetry over the absence of rhythmic effect, imagery, and poetic diction. Bloch, in *Swann's Way,* introduces it to Marcel, with an air of hermetic confidence, as a line which "says absolutely nothing": *"La fille de Minos et de Pasiphaë."* The line was praised because only a great poet could have characterized his heroine in so bare a way, the truest poetry, according to this doctrine at least, being the least feigning. It appears that Racine may have taken the line from a handbook of mythology; here we have a case of the poetic act consisting not of writing the line, but of seeing it (1) as an Alexandrine, (2) as the conclusion of the couplet, and (3) as being able to carry the weight of a meaning of monstrosity; born by historical reference alone. A similar example in English is Yeats's great line in "A Long-Legged Fly":

> There on that scaffolding reclines
> Michael Angelo.

Here it is a matter, again, of seeing the name as one of the three-beat lines of the poem; of the name carrying great weight after the subject of the first stanza of the poem (Caesar) has been mentioned in epithet ("Our master Caesar"), of the second only by "she"; and finally of the fragmentation of the name into what looks like a name and an epithet again.

The choices governing rhythmic execution are as complex and elusive of analysis as are the elements of our response to rhythmic events. There exists a celebrated pyrotechnical display of such execution that is all the more of a triumph because it sets out to brandish its machinery, and must stand or fall by how well it really works. It is even more interesting for our purposes because, as a rhythmic display, it is set off within the confines of a meter so formal and confining that Matthew Arnold could think of it only as a kind of mechanical jingle which was overlaid on prose. In Book II of Pope's *An Essay on Criticism,* he puts forth the thoroughly Hobbesian notion that "Imagination is the dress of thought"; that the relation of poetic invention to poetic *sentence* or meaning is like the relation of clothes to a body, a mechanistic version of the Platonistic relation of body to soul. The passage I wish to discuss starts out with an attack on those bad critics who reject the true notion that *le style,* so to speak, *c'est l'homme,* in favor of the fashionable error that, figuratively speaking, clothes make the man:

> But most by Numbers judge a Poet's song;
> And smooth or rough, with them, is right or wrong:
> In the bright Muse tho' thousand charms conspire,
> Her Voice is all these tuneful fools admire;
> Who haunt Parnassus but to please their ear,
> Not mend their minds; as some to Church repair,
> Not for the doctrine, but the music there.
> These equal syllables alone require,
> Tho' oft the ear the open vowels tire;
> While expletives their feeble aid do join;
> And ten low words oft creep in one dull line:
> While they ring round the same unvary'd chimes,
> With sure returns of still expected rhymes.
> Where-e'er you find "the cooling western breeze,"
> In the next line, it "whispers thro' the trees";
> If crystal streams "with pleasing murmurs creep,"
> The reader's threaten'd (not in vain) with "sleep."
> Then, at the last and only couplet fraught
> With some unmeaning thing they call a thought,

A needless Alexandrine ends the song,
That, like a wounded snake, drags its slow length along.

An Essay on Criticism, II, 337–57

The denunciation here is of what Empson once called the "cult of pure sound," which, he remarked, always struck him as being rather like Darwin playing the trombone to his French beans. Dryden had voiced the basic sentiment earlier, when he wrote of John Oldham, "But satire needs not these and wit will shine / Through the harsh cadence of a rugged line," but he was helping to initiate the metrical form in which Pope was to succeed so brilliantly, and he could not go so far with it as could his successor, particularly in playing tricks with it. The eighteenth-century metricians who demanded that accentual weight be equalized were ruling out the possibility of effective rhythmic writing by loving unwisely and too well what they thought to be a basis of musical rhythm itself. Yet Pope puts them down by a stroke of syntactic genius: the line about the open syllables would not work so well if the word order were "Though oft the open vowels tire the ear"—it depends on the triad of "Tho' oft," "the ear," "the open," and, of course, on neglecting the elision rules which Pope himself normally uses but which, if employed here, would give a tetrameter line "Tho' oft th'ear th'open vowels tire." Again, the line with all the monosyllables in it is a dull one because (1) he tells us it is and (2) he makes it dull by repeating the rhythmic pattern "ten low words"—"one dull line": the two phrases have the identical stress contour in speech. In addition, he makes things harder by following up "And ten low words" with a great density of prominent syllables. Were he to have written "And ten low words are all a man can bear," there would have been a dip in prominence of the following syllables: a stickler for *phonetic* rather than metrical stress here would say that in Pope's line there were eight stresses rather than five, whereas in my revision there were at any rate only five, although grouped [·′′′·· ·′·′].

As we go on through the lines, we find that all the effects are accountable for along two axes, the phonetic and the contextually semantic. These lines are aimed at those who prefer sound to sense, and the lines themselves are all self-descriptive. In formal logic, self-descriptiveness leads to pure and empty paradox; here, they lead to a kind of poetic meaninglessness. What they are about is how bad they are. The ways in which they are bad result from the manipulation of phonetic and morphophonemic material in patterns that are too regular at one level, while they strain and distort the regularity of another kind that constitutes the essence of smoothness for Pope.

The joke about the rhymes, for example, momentarily aligns these two axes. The alliteration in the line centers on the "ring-round" nucleus. After we have been put off by not getting the word "rhymes" but instead a non-alliterating word that makes us realize our loss by rhyming with the withheld word, the additional "r" sounds in "unvary'd," "sure," and "returns" make us realize that not only have we not been expecting the word when it does come in the second couplet, but that we have, like Pavlov's dog, been slavering for it. And finally, we realize that the trouble with rhyming can be that the word which names a unit of it rhymes, itself, with "chimes." There is, of course, the logical play here with a thing and its name. A full-blown use of the logical trap of confusing use and mention (such as, for example, in the innocent remark that "there's spaghetti on the menu") comes in the line about the sleep that crowns the short list of clichés that also rhyme.

In the lines about the Alexandrine, we get a much subtler use of the phonetic-semantic interplay. In the first two lines, the same progression is repeated: [some unmeaning thing thought] and [needless Alexandrine ends]. In each case, the subject ("thing" and "Alexandrine") is connected to an epithet and a logical predicate by means of some sound association. And the Alexandrine itself, conventional in a closed-couplet style when used at the end of some kind of rhetorical period (although its use in triads was much abused between the stylistic peaks of Dryden and Pope), commits all the faults of a bad one. Its split in the middle into two trimeters is underlined by the unusually sharp syntactic break of the caesura. The second half-line seems even slower than the first, because the consonantal clusters and piled-up stresses of "drags its slow length" end up with a pun on "along," conditioned by the noun preceding it.

But after this demolition job, Pope goes on to reconstruct, and, like Amphion playing on his lyre and causing the walls of Thebes to build themselves, he sings the elements of a style back into their proper place.

> Leave such to tune their own dull rhymes, and know
> What's roundly smooth, or languishingly slow;
> And praise the easy vigour of a line,
> Where Denham's strength, and Waller's sweetness join.
> True ease in writing comes from art, not chance,
> As those move easiest who have learn'd to dance.
> 'Tis not enough no harshness gives offence,
> The sound must seem an Echo to the sense:
> Soft is the strain when Zephyr gently blows,
> And the smooth stream in smoother numbers flows;

But when loud surges lash the sounding shore,
The hoarse, rough verse should like the torrent roar:
When Ajax strives some rock's vast weight to throw,
The line too labours, and the words move slow;
Not so, when swift Camilla scours the plain,
Flies o'er th' unbending corn, and skims along the main.

The sound effects here differ from those in the first part of the passage by reason of the fact that these are "good" lines, rather than examples of "bad" ones, and that they all have a fine, straightforward, pseudo-Classical subject matter. They are all about the great, model subject, rather than, as in the earlier ones, about their own ineptitude.

The couplet about the smoothness, for example, employs not only the device of phonetic linking which connects the core attributive word, "soft," with "strain" and eventually with "Zephyr gently," which two words finally give us the "f" and "t" phonemes of "soft" in the proper order. In the second line of the couplet, the image which gives the line its weight of content engages a powerful allusion to the canonical emblem of the kind of style which Pope's age takes for granted. The idea that lines of verse should move like flowing water is embodied in a text that was almost scriptural for the Augustan age. In Denham's *Cooper's Hill* the poet, surveying the beneficent prospect of the Thames from his visionary eminence, concludes a passage of moralized topography with the proto-Augustan hope, couched in full-blown Augustan sincerity, neatness, and aptness of thought:

O could I flow like thee, and make thy stream
My great example, as it is my theme!
Though deep, yet clear, though gentle, yet not dull,
Strong without rage, without o'erflowing, full.

What Pope referred to a few lines earlier as "Denham's strength" was thought to be expressed here as a program for the Augustan use of the heroic couplet. The "smooth stream" in Pope's line is, of course, some stream being described in the line, not improbably Skamander; but by a conventional image, it is also the line itself. There is the further implementation of the phonetic linkings of [*smooth-stream*] and [*smoother-numbers*]. Then again, there is the final clinching of the implicit argument that art often more obviously conforms to the mechanical rules of created order than does nature (although, with Pope, "to copy nature" was "to copy them"). This is done by the rhythmic contrast between the first half-line [··′′] ("And the smooth stream") and the second, which is absolutely canonical in its distribution of stresses: "in smoother numbers flows" [· ′· ′· ′], where the phonetic linkings of the subjects and the smoothness attributed to them are disposed first in a less, then in a more regular way.

"When Ajax strives," we strive, too, not to produce a string of words like "When Ajax drives": the enunciation forced upon us by the consonantal cluster, and the realization that it is intentional is forced upon us by the growing realization that his rock is, symbolically, the remainder of the line. In a trivial phonetic sense, *the words move slow,* despite the tendency in spoken English time units in actual utterances to dispose themselves into syntactic paradigms. Thus, in the following sequence of utterances, the durations of enunciation increase much less rapidly than the increasing amount of linguistic material crowded into the same sentence matrix would lead one to conclude:

> "I'm going on Tuesday."
> "I'm going home on Tuesday."
> "I'm going home to Indianapolis on Tuesday."

Pope must slow up his words by setting up a parallel rhythmic package at the beginning and end of this line, reinforced by the syntax of "the line, too, labours" as well as by the symmetry of the assonance of "too" and "move," which pins the rhythmic structure together: phonetically, we have a pattern like this:

· ′ ′ ′ · The line, too, labours	· · ′ ′ ′ and the words move slow
syntax forces a juncture	*parallelism dictates one here*

rhyme (assonance)
enforces parallelism

Here, as always, it is a sound pattern working with semantic and syntactic ones which gains the desired effect.

So, too, in the case of the quickly moving lines. Notice that swift Camilla flies along in an Alexandrine, but by no means a slow one; this is an added bit of virtuosity, for in the context of the previous section, Pope has almost made us feel that it is the essence of Alexandrines to be too long. Here again, too, it is Cam*i*lla who is chosen to be the sw*i*ft one, because of the linking assonance, and here, too, we have the association of [*scours the plain*] (′ · ′) and (*skims along the main*) [′(··)· ′]: the extra two syllables in the second line become less prominent when we view the phrase in the rhythmic matrix set up by the first, and the Alexandrine seems to contract.

This is indeed a virtuoso rhythmic performance. It is conducted within the confines of a rigorous metrical scheme, one which allows less displacement of alternation of stressed syllables, on the whole, than Milton's iambic pentameter, or Keats's or Wordsworth's. And yet the effects are profound, and the moral pointed. We cannot, in studying the effects of rhythm or of its associated phenomena, ignore the interaction of the rhythmic groupings and patterns with lexical and syntactic elements. Any general theory of metaphor in poetry must deal with the notion of non-literalness of meaning, with transfer, or distortion or reshaping of reference. But the way in which, as Pope puts it, the sound can "seem an Echo to the sense" is effected only by means of associations between words which rub off, somehow, onto their designata: it is something like the metaphorical process, but it operates somehow at a different level. By and large, the so-called imitative effects of poetic rhythm will be seen to work in two ways: through those devices which associate words or parts of words, and through those which enforce re-groupings of them by more subtle means than simply those of connection. The use in Latin poetry of *intralinear juxtaposition* as allowed by flexible syntax, for example, allows us to discern discrete semantic packets within the line, where the sense of a word is transferred to an adjacent one without being syntactically connected with it at all. Rhyme links not only lines, but words; whether used as end rhymes or as interior ones, rhyming syllables have an increased prominence, no matter what their metrical role, and play an important part in associating the words that contain them. Assonance and alliteration link parts of words, as well as syllables, and their operation is through what a linguist would call a morphophonemic medium, creating momentary fictions about the association of sound and sense in the language. The effects of onomatopoeia in general can all be traced to these devices.

All of these methods may be employed either metrically or rhythmically. They may play only a structural role in defining the schematic form of the poem or its lines. Or they may be used for the kind of expressive effects we have been considering. For example, alliteration occurs prominently in Old Germanic verse, in Spenser, in the Shakespeare sonnets, and in Hopkins. And yet we would want to characterize its roles very differently in the four cases. In the first instance, the alliteration is a necessary feature of the meter, and while it tends to produce a little poetic package in the first half-line consisting of two words linked by the alliteration, its frequency of occurrence tends to depress its significance for expressive purposes. Not so in Spenser, where its relatively high frequency of occurrence in *The Faerie Queene* is nevertheless a matter of rhythmic texture rather than of metrical form. Still, Spenser's alliterations tend to produce a decorative surface rather than a metaphoric connection. In the opening line of *F.Q.*: "A gentle knight was

pricking on the plain" we have a typical instance of its use to link parts of a
predicate, although the noun-adjective pair is even more common. At times,
the rate of alliteration per line will go up in passages describing an excited
encounter or a lush display, but the higher rate will simply add up to a
slightly more ornate linguistic surface. In the Shakespeare sonnets, however,
the alliteration functions in several ways. Occasionally it will be in the
Elizabethan, Spenserian "decorative manner," but often it will be used expressively, to echo sense.

For example, sonnet 116:

> Love's not Time's fool, though rosy lips and cheeks
> Within his bending sickle's compass come.

The naïve observation would be that we seem to hear the sound of the blade
mowing the grass to which the implicitly invoked scriptural text likens all
flesh. The effect depends upon several rhythmic events. In the first place,
there is, as Empson has observed, the grammatical ambiguity of *bending:* it
means both "bent" and "causing to bend," and these two meanings help to
establish a frame within which we recall the lines we have just heard. Then
there is the core word for the alliterating sequence, "sickle." Its first syllable
suggests words like "Click," "pick," "flick," "nick," etc.; we half expect the
following sequence "compass," "come" to finish up with "cut." The iteration
of the hard "k" sound carries through the core association of "sickle" and
suggests the repeating blows that we know a reaping blade to give.

A similar analysis of the associative effects of expressive alliteration
might be given for the more famous "When to the sessions of sweet, silent
thought / I summon up remembrance of things past," where the two core
words are "sessions" and "silent," both employing initial "s" and final nasal,
but with only the latter containing a "t." They are further distinguished by
the fact that "sessions" manifestly establishes the vehicle of the law court
conceit and "silent" the tenor of it, the mood of moral meditation. Only the
final phrase, "things past," contains both nasal and "t" elements and encompasses both levels of the conceit.

As with alliteration, so with assonance. We can have purely decorative
patternings, as in the phonetic chiasmus of Coleridge's "In Xanadu did
Kubla Khan." It is more frequently used expressively, often with reinforcing
alliteration, as, again from Pope, this time of unrelenting old harridans: "A
fop their passion, but their prize a sot; / Alive, ridiculous, and dead, forgot."

The assimilation of these devices into generalized onomatopoeic musi-
cality is frequent in Spenser, Keats, and Tennyson.[6] Onomatopoeia, as I. A.

Richards has observed, must be divided into two sorts, which we might differentiate by applying the distinction that Greek philosophers used, illusory as it was, when considering etymology: *physei,* or natural, and *nomo,* or by convention. Certain primary onomatopoetic representations of non-linguistic sounds, such as the characteristic noises of animals, become morphemes of a language quite early in its development; the result is that they seem "natural" to it. Thus, "meeow," "tick-tock," "ding-dong," "baa-baa," "cock-a-doodle-doo" are common English patterns, showing either reduplication or a front-back alternation of vowel. Secondary, or conventional, onomatopoeia is the kind we find used in verse, or in jokes like the proverbial "The pig is rightly so-called." In it, words are made to sound not like the noises of nature or of physical processes, but like other words. Some core word, often itself designating something about sound, may be associated with others. Occasionally a word not itself specified may be echoed by other ones: the classic case is the song about fancy in *The Merchant of Venice,* where the rhymes on "bred," "head," "nourishëd" all call to mind the lead casket which we know must be chosen if all is to end well.

There are also the famous, lush lines from Tennyson that are always extolled to school children:

> The moan of doves in immemorial elms
> And murmuring of innumerable bees.

In cases like this, we must first rule out the operation of those minimal sound clusters which seem to act like ghosts of morphemes: on the surface, it would appear that words like "slide," "slip," "slick," "slink," "slim," "slop," "slope," and others are associated, through their initial cluster, with a general connotation of smoothness. But such cases are too rare to allow us to assume that onomatopoeia operates in any other way than to associate words already given us with others having common sounds. Assonance, alliteration, and even rhyme do some of the work of metaphor by associating words through their sounds alone, and by thus juxtaposing them with some of the same strength as an actual image. Thus, in the lines from Tennyson, the alliterating words are "moan," "immemorial," "elms," "murmuring," and "innumerable" with "bees" being related to the last syllable of "innumerable" and the phrase "of doves" being linked by a rhyme. Clearly the *core word* for these alliterations is "murmuring," and we associate with it all the connected words. But it is flatly misleading to tell a student that the "m" sounds have any meaning or evocative power, apart from words they connect. I realize that such assertions are frequent, and some appreciators of poetry

like Dame Edith Sitwell carried this method to a comical extreme. Clearly
Tennyson's lines have a suggestive musical richness. But just as clearly, this
is a music of words, not of extrapolated sounds.

"Imitative movement" of words can, of course, really only imitate the
sounds of other words or sounds. Some of the finest examples of it occur when
a semantic relation is reinforced by a rhythmic parallel between words or
phrases, and when we are almost tempted to say that the designatum of the
phrase is being represented by that movement rather than the phrase itself.
Thus in Florizel's great speech to Perdita in *The Winter's Tale* (IV, iv)

> When you do dance, I wish you
> A wave o' the sea, that you might ever do
> Nothing but that; move still still so. . .

the description of the girl's imitative dance doesn't "sound like the sea," but
rather follows the rhythm of the phrase "a wave o' the sea." Also, in Yeats's
"Sailing to Byzantium," the "Monuments of unaging intellect" at the end of
stanza I are echoed in a later line invoking singing schools that all study
"Monuments of their own magnificence." Here, again, the repetition of the
word "monuments" is reinforced by the symmetrical alliterating rhythm of
the final word in the line: the whole line, so to speak, looks into a mirror and
gazes at itself.

Something more might be said here about echoic patterns in general.
There are echoes which operate beyond the boundaries of the poem itself, and
those which work purely within it. Examples of the first abound, whether in
open or hidden form. There is no difficulty with the relation between (again,
from "Sailing to Byzantium") "Those dying generations" and Keats's hungry
ones in the Nightingale ode. Sir Richard Fanshawe's translation of the famous chorus on the golden age from Guarini's *Il Pastor Fido,* which is itself
full of material from Tasso, Ovid, and Horace, works in a specific little
Catullan allusion of his own, by echoing Ben Jonson's adaptation of *"Vivamus
mea Lesbia, atque amemus"* ("'Tis no sin love's fruit to steal, / But the sweet
theft to reveal") in his own heroic couplet: "Nor think'st it any fault love's
sweets to steal, / So from the world thou canst the theft reveal." Less public,
avowed, or even, perhaps, conscious are echoes which allude to words, structures, rhythms, rather than quoting or re-framing, like the above. Thus, for
example, there is the delicate echo of Spenser at the end of Milton's *On the
Morning of Christ's Nativity:* "And all about the Courtly Stable / Bright
harnest Angels sit in order serviceable." In this most Spenserian poem,
Milton sinks at the end into a cushion of borrowed music; in Calidore's vision
of the ring of damsels in *F.Q.,* VI, x, the thirteenth stanza concludes with

the setting into heaven of the constellation Corona: "And is unto the stars an ornament, / Which round about her move in order excellent." It is not merely the specific phrase inverted pattern of "—in order (adjective)" which came to mind (or should we say, to ear?). It occurs in Spenser in a terminal position in a stanza, in the propounding of a complex and central image in what is hardly an obscure region of *The Faerie Queene,* and ends in an Alexandrine. Milton was echoing a whole movement.

Again, Wallace Stevens can echo Milton in equally subtle ways. There is the allusive Miltonic movement, transmuted from one kind of blank verse, through Wordsworth's, to another in the flight of the Canon Aspirin in *Notes Toward a Supreme Fiction:* "Descending to the children's bed, on which / / They lay. Forth then with huge pathetic force / Straight to the utmost crown of night he flew." But the echo of *Il Penseroso,* II. 73-75, in "Moving across wide water, without sound" from "Sunday Morning" is more like the Milton-Spenser case mentioned above. The source goes:

> I hear the far-off Curfew sound,
> Over some wide-water'd shore. . . .

Stevens's *La Penserosa,* turning away from one sort of conventional meditation (in church) toward her own questionings, heeds but rejects the call not of a curfew, but a Sunday church bell.[7] This sort of echoing is not allusive, is not a public signal but rather a kind of private one for the poet himself.

So, I should think, would be the internal echo, the muted half-refrain of Keats's Grecian Urn ode, save that here it sets up an interesting grammatical ambiguity. The relation is between the second line: "Thou foster-child of silence and slow time" and the much later one: "Pipe to the spirit ditties of no tone," the echo being located in the final spondee. The problem is that, once heard, the echo tends to make "spirit" in the second line adjectival, so that instead of meaning "pipe toneless ditties to the spirit" it suggests "pipe to the tune of those spiritual, silent ditties." It is not so much that the second reading is probably incorrect, but that Keats's metrical, rhythmical, and grammatical styles do indeed allow for it.

We have been examining a wide range of "musical" or attention-shaping effects of poetic rhythms operating within, in these instances, accentual-syllabic English verse. It is clear that many of them depend upon the very contingencies set up by the metrical choice for their ability to function. But the framing, defining, conventional aspect of the metrical choice with which this essay commenced must not in any sense be thought of as submerged or effaced by the occasionally prominent ways in which they can affect the ear. Let us return for a moment to this title or rubric-like function of metrical form, to the way in which style and genre are intertwined, to the ways in which a verse form may set up referential or allusive ground-rules for the poem and the reader, as well as serving to mark, diagram, underline, or gloss the language organized within it.

IV

Behind so much Western aesthetics since Classical antiquity lies a nostalgia for what was believed quite naïvely to have been a perfect, mystical marriage, in Attic times, of musical mode and ethos, of form and the effect upon human behavior proper to that form; a nostalgia for what was thought to have been a perfect music-poetry that made of human sense an instrument whose own sound was human feeling. The myth of such a golden age in which communication was immediate, and guided only by the channel of suitable form, became in the Renaissance a myth of literature itself. Like the musical modality that many Greek writers themselves appear to us to misunderstand, meters and verse schemes have seemed to widely differing ages to possess inherent, psychologically affective qualities, and seemed to be measurable by decorum, in that any breach of this in their use would reveal itself upon comparing the nature and function of a mode, form, or style. This is a little like the way we *feel,* and have been rightly chastised for thinking, about onomatopoeia, sound symbolism and the like. (It may be worth noting here that the important classic parables of decorum for Neoclassic ages included that of Terpander, who was punished for adding an extra string to his lyre, and of Marsyas, who was flayed for playing the wild, passionate *aulos* which the goddess of reason had disgustedly cast aside—in both cases, the breach consisted in strengthening or widening the effectiveness of the music.)

This musical metaphor that underlies the history of literary notions about literary form was such a convenient one for poetic theory, and for so long, precisely because it could accommodate both the notions of formal significance under consideration here. In the whole Classical doctrine of form and ethos there lay resolved what later ages came to feel as a dialectic of conventional and instant form, revealed in the struggle for authority of schematic and pathetic accounts of the workings of music and poetry. In antiquity, the only "formal" elements were of the first type, the *metrical* type (although *meter* and *rhythm* had clearly opposed and also several confused sets of meanings in Greek times); any particular work was distinguishable only cognitively ("rationally") from other works in the same convention. The rationalistic treatment of music by Greek theorists made this possible by ignoring all textless music for theoretical purposes; *song* was always the subject under discussion. A conceptual distinction between "music" and "poetry" of the kind that has been made since the Renaissance was impossible; and there was no need to create musical metaphors to aid in describing the ethos of any particular poetic utterance.

This whole paradise of communication was originally a quasi-mythical account of the power of literature (as opposed to persuasive speech: it was only the later Renaissance that sought metaphorically to identify music and rhetoric). But its power as an ideal account of the less obvious workings of carefully planned utterances held poetic theory in subjection for ages. For an empirical world view that demands much more of its accounts of things, such a myth is hardly even heuristically useful. The ethos of a passage of poetry or of a segment of that passage is to be understood as operating linguistically, that is, in that domain of shared experience of sound that connects a speaker and his hearer. And if there were no such thing as *literature,* but only *poetry;* that is, if all poems were utterances whose structure was as significant as their assertions, making no attempt to share or imitate structures, but only to generate novel ones, then the whole problem of the two kinds of significance would vanish. There would remain only the "rhythm" of poems; there would be no such thing as "meter," for there would be no common scheme, no redundant elements, nothing "given."

But this is not the case. Poets continue to believe in modal myths long after they abandon other creeds. They continue to think in terms of "choosing" a meter even though, in stylistically eclectic ages like our own, they may resurrect, adapt, or newly forge their stylistic patterns. And poems continue to be literary events, which is also to say that it may be misleading to consider them as existing in any but a rather peculiar dialect of the language in which they are written. Their literary status in no way obliterates their linguistic status; it qualifies it only. Neither does the classification of a shouted "Go to the devil!" as a curse prevent it from remaining an utterance nevertheless; it merely specifies a rhetorical context. Now "meter" traditionally considered as arising from the literary classification and analysis of poems, jumps into prominence as a result of the historical mapping of several kinds of utterances in their historical contexts. The "rhythm," the flow of the poem in passage (aural or visual), the stream of effect upon the reader are all just as much the special concern, it is true, of the linguistically oriented poetic analyst as is the "meter" the concern of the historian or of the apologist for a style. To analyze the meter of a poem is not so much to scan it as to show with what other poems its less significant (linguistically speaking) formal elements associate it; to chart out its mode; to trace its family tree by appeal to those resemblances which connect it, in some ways with one, in some ways with another kind of poem that may, historically, precede or follow it.

But we have seen how in one case metrical qualities may coincide, coexist in the same element, with rhythmical ones. This may occur with respect to rhymes, stress patterns, syllabic arrangements, or even larger forms. The sonnet form functions, apparently, in two ways at once. By setting up certain canons of line length, rhyme scheme, etc., and by tending to limit larger syntactical patterns (in the case of a Shakespearean sonnet, by tending to set up an arrangement of a clause with two dependent clauses and a final sentence), the sonnet is spoken of as demanding a certain kind of logical form. On the other hand, the sonnet form itself is like a title, in that it serves to set up a literary context around the utterance, directing the reader to give to it a certain kind of attention just as the frame around a picture can urge a viewer to look at the picture in a particular way. Thus, to talk about the sonnet form of any poem may be to comment on either its "rhythm" or "meter" or both; about the particular role that it announces for itself, on the one hand, or about its actual movements on stage, so to speak, on the other.

Now this titling, framing (or, as we might call it, *emblematic* or *badge-like*) function of meter is no less a linguistic operation than are those of smaller elements of the poem. To qualify the study of that function as macro-linguistic, or to confine it to a diachronic domain, may be a strategy necessary to the organization of a whole empirical pursuit. But there seems to be no reason for trying to separate the literary from the over-all linguistic in any metaphysical way (perhaps by insisting that there is "something more" to works of literature than the language they are composed of).

Whatever may have been accomplished by traditional metrical studies in the way of dissecting out and displaying this emblematic function of meter may have to be done over again without recourse to beliefs that poems were somehow beyond language, or to methods of analysis that barely hid their function of stylistic prescription. It has always been literary critics per se, arbiters, stylistic apologists, and makers of judgments who have directed most attention to the metrical emblem and its framing, self-titling function. In connection with this, it should also be observed that the metrical emblem operates differently under different stylistic climates: an epoch like the Augustan age in England, for example, marked by a canonical style like that of the heroic couplet; or a "pre-literary" or "folk" period in which there may be single authoritative styles, not strictly canonical in the sense that they are ruled into usage so as to exclude certain others, but retaining status because there is little or no contact with foreign or past forms and styles; and finally, an eclectic, history-ridden age like the present one in which such stylistic anarchy prevails that one almost feels that a poem need be defined as any utterance that purports to be one. In the first two cases, the badge of meter has the fundamental work of *defining* the utterance as a literary event (Dr. Johnson could hardly consider Christopher Smart's rich, mad *Jubilate Agno* as a poem; but an age that includes *The Cantos* among its monuments must surely value highly the fragments that Smart in the eighteenth century "shored against his ruin"). But in the last case, that of the eclectic age in which competing styles war for a lost authority, the meter becomes more than Wordsworth's "formal engagement"; it becomes almost a stipulation of what a poem ought to be. The frame begins to recommend, so to speak. And the emblem starts to take on a moral.

But the urging of a work of literature, perhaps accomplished by its formal frame, is no less an act of urging than any other kind of exhortation. The analysis of urging and exhorting can no longer be properly linguistic. And, finally, it is *as such* that it lies outside the realm of poetics.

NOTES

1. I. A. Richards, *Principles of Literary Criticism* (London, 1925), p. 145.

2. When this essay was originally conceived, information theory appeared to be of some interest for formalist poetics; see the statements by René Wellek and myself in *Style and Language*, ed. Thomas A. Sebeok (Cambridge, Mass., 1960), pp. 396–419. The relation between critical and linguistic approaches to problems of form has been rather complex, even during the past two decades. For a sophisticated and most useful account of this with an excellent selected bibliography, see Seymour Chatman and Samuel R. Levin, "Linguistics and Literature," in *Current Trends in Linguistics*, 10 (The Hague, 1973), 250–94.

3. Carol Madison, *Apollo and the Nine* (Baltimore, 1960), p. 301, suggests that Jonson may have borrowed the terms from Antonio Sebastiano Minturno's *volta, rivolta,* and *stanza* in two odes published in 1535.

4. There is a further complication with the Dioscuri, though; Jonson knows well the etymology of the word from *dios + kouroi* ("two boys"), but because of his pun on the "twi-lights," he seems to pretend that the etymology is Italianate (*di* or *duo + oscuro*)—the twin darks, the setting suns, stars, or Sons, of a world made less perfect by their setting.

5. F. R. Leavis, *Revaluation* (New York, 1947), pp. 263–64.

6. One would, for example, analyze the "mimetic" effectiveness of the wonderful line from Keats's "The Eve of St. Agnes"—"The hare limped trembling through the frozen grass"—in the same manner as Pope's line about Ajax. The common ground is the iambic metrical framework and the role of the consonantal clusters. On the other hand, the celebrated mimetic lines from Tennyson's *Idylls of the King* (e.g., "First as in fear, step after step she stole / Down the long tower-stairs hesitating"—a kind of scazon) depend, as one might expect in a more Miltonic poetry, upon syntactical as well as accentual arrangements.

7. But see the discussion of other Stevensian echoes, and the claim that the source is Tennysonian, in Robert Buttel, *The Making of Harmonium* (Princeton, 1967), p. 223. If there is indeed a Tennysonian echo in "Sunday Morning," it is probably of "The earliest pipe of half-awakened birds" from "Tears, Idle Tears."

PART TWO

Theories of Meter

OTTO JESPERSEN

Notes on Metre

Otto Jespersen was perhaps the most prodigiously talented of modern linguists. No writer on the subject of language displayed such vast knowledge, theoretical subtlety, and logical clarity. Gifted with a fabulously sensitive ear that could discern any variety of stress and pause, he was uniquely equipped to hear the meters of English poetry.

In this brief essay—almost schematic in its organization—Jespersen establishes the rules of English iambic meter. These rules also operate in the iambic verse of German and Scandinavian poets. He clears away the numerous fallacies and lays the "conceptual ghosts" (John Hollander's phrase) that have prevented any accurate understanding of the structural principles of English meter. He discards the inappropriate terminology of longs and shorts, and the macron (—) and breve (◡) of classical prosody; he points out that we will understand "the chief irregularities of blank verse" only if we speak of "positions" rather than feet; and, in anticipation of Trager and Smith, suggests that while "in reality there are infinite gradations of stress," for the purposes of metrical analysis we need only recognize four degrees. 'Metricality' is a function of the relative stress between syllables; corollary to this principle is "that syllables which ought

Reprinted from *Linguistica* (Copenhagen: Levin & Munksgaard, 1933). Copyright 1933 by Otto Jespersen. Used by permission of the publishers, Munksgaard International Publishers Ltd.

Read in Danish in the "Kgl. danske videnskabernes selskab" on 16 Nov. 1900, printed as "Den psykologiske grund til nogle metriske faenomener" in *Oversigt* (1900), p. 487. Here translated with a few rearrangements and many omissions, chiefly with regard to Danish and German examples and the refutation of the views of the Danish metrist E.v.d. Recke.

seemingly to be strong are weakened if occurring between strong syllables, and naturally weak syllables gain in strength if placed between weak syllables."

We can hear the operation of the rule of relative stress in this line:

The course of true love never did run smooth.

Because *love* is positioned between two strongly stressed syllables (*true* and *nev-*), it loses strength and becomes metrically weak. "It is the relative stress that counts."

Jespersen proposes a notation of scansion that is adopted by Halle and Keyser (q.v.). The paradigm for the iambic line may be illustrated by the "symbol string"

aB aB aB aB aB (a).

This becomes Halle and Keyser's

WS WS WS WS WS WS (W).

A. Walter Bernhart notes ("Generative Metrics," *Poetics* 12, April 1974), "as studies in modern linguistics tend ultimately to go back to Saussure, studies in modern metrics are generally based on Jespersen. . . ."

1. The iambic pentameter may without any exaggeration be termed the most important metre of all in the literatures of the North-European world. Since Chaucer used it in its rimed form (the heroic line) and especially since Marlowe made it popular in the drama in its unrimed form (blank verse), it has been employed by Shakespeare, Milton, Dryden, Pope, Thomson, Cowper, Wordsworth, Byron, Shelley, Tennyson, by Lessing, Goethe, and Schiller, as well as by numerous Scandinavian poets, in a great many of their most important works. I shall here try to analyse some peculiarities of this metre, but my remarks are directly applicable to other metres as well and indirectly should bear on the whole metrical science, which, if I am right in the theories advanced below, would seem to require a fundamental revision of its principles, system of notation, and nomenclature.

According to the traditional notation the metre mentioned above consists of five iambi with or without an eleventh weak syllable:

$\smile - | \smile - | \smile - | \smile - | \smile - | (\smile)$

Her eyes,	her haire,	her cheeke,	her gate,	her voice.	(1)
Give ev'	ry man	thine ear',	but few	thy voyce:	(2)
Take each	mans cen	sure, but	reserve	thy judg'	ment. (3)
Ein un	nütz Le	ben ist	ein früh	er Tod.	(4)
Zufrie	den wär'	ich, wenn	mein Volk	mich rühm	te.[1] (5)

2. But pretty often we find deviations from this scheme, a "trochee" being substituted for an "iambus". This phenomenon, which may be called briefly inversion, is especially frequent in the first foot, as in

$$— \ \smile \quad \smile \ — \quad \smile \ — \quad \smile \ — \quad \smile \ — \quad \smile$$

Told by | an id | iot, full | of sound | and fu | ry.　　　　　(1)

Even two "trochees" may be found in the same line, as in

$$— \ \smile \quad \smile \ — \quad — \ \smile \quad \smile \ — \quad \smile \ — \quad \smile$$

Tyrants | themselves | wept when | it was | report | ed　　　　(2)
Ihn freu | et der | Besitz; | ihn krönt | der Sieg (*ihn* emphatic).　(3)

Why, now, are such inversions allowed? How is it that the listener's sense of rhythm is not offended by the fact that once or even twice in the same line he hears the very opposite movement of the one he expected, a "trochee" instead of an "iambus"? He expects a certain pattern, a regular alternation in one particular way of ten syllables, and his disappointment at encountering one trochee can be mathematically expressed as affecting two-tenths of the whole line; in the case of two trochees his disappointment is one of four-tenths or two-fifths; and yet he has nothing like the feeling of displeasure or disharmony which would seize him if in a so-called hexameter like

Strongly it bears us along in swelling and limitless billows

an "anapaest" were substituted for a "dactylus":

It is strong, bears us along in swelling and limitless billows

or if in

Jack is a poor widow's heir, but he lives as a drone in a beehive

we substituted an "amphibrach":

Behold a poor widow's heir, but he lives as a drone in a beehive.

Naturally science cannot rest contented by calling deviations "poetical licences" or by saying that the whole thing depends on individual fancy or habit: as poets in many countries, however different their verse is in various other respects, follow very nearly the same rules, and to a great extent followed these before they were established by theorists, there must be some common basis for these rules, and it will be our task to find out what that basis is.

3. The permissibility of a trochee in an iambic metre is very often justified by the assertion that purely iambic lines following one another

without intermission would be intolerably monotonous and that therefore a trochee here and there serves to introduce the pleasing effect of variety.[2] But there are several objections to this view. In the first place even a long series of perfectly regular lines is not disagreeably monotonous if written by a real poet. In one of Shakespeare's finest scenes we find in the first hundred lines not more than four inversions (*As You Like It,* II, 7); it can hardly be those four lines which make the whole scene so pleasing to the ear. In Valborg's speech in Oehlenschläger's *Axel og Valborg,* III, 69, we have twenty-eight beautiful lines without a single deviation from the iambic scheme.

Secondly, if harmony were due to such irregularities, it would be natural to expect the same effect from similar deviations in trochaic and other metres. The reader of Longfellow's *Hiawatha* no doubt feels its metre as much more monotonous than the five-foot iambus, yet here no deviations would be tolerated; an iambus in a trochaic metre is an unwelcome intruder, while a trochee in an iambic line is hailed as a friendly guest.

Thirdly, the theory gives no explanation of the fact that the use of trochees is subject to some limitations; if the only purpose were to relieve monotony, one would expect trochees to be equally welcome everywhere in iambic verses, but that is very far from being the case. True, the rare occurrence of trochees in the fifth foot is explained by saying that deviations from the ordinary pattern are always best tolerated in the beginning of the verse, because then there is still time to return to the regular movement. But if this were the only reason, we should expect trochees to tend to decrease as we approached the end of the line, the second foot presenting more instances than the third, and the third than the fourth; but this again does not tally with the actual facts, for the second foot has fewer inversions than any other foot except the fifth. König gives the following numbers for Shakespeare:

first foot more than	3000
second foot only	34
third foot more than	500
fourth foot more than	400.[3]

4. If we are to arrive at a real understanding of the metre in question and of modern metre in general, it will be necessary to revise many of the current ideas which may be traced back to ancient metrists, and to look at the facts as they present themselves to the unsophisticated ears of modern poets and modern readers. The chief fallacies that it is to my mind important to get rid of are the following:

(1) *The fallacy of longs and shorts.* Modern verses are based primarily not on length (duration), but on stress (intensity). In analysing them we should

therefore avoid such signs as — and ᴗ, and further get rid of such terms as iambus (ᴗ —), trochee (— ᴗ), dactylus (— ᴗ ᴗ), anapaest (ᴗ ᴗ —), pyrrhic (ᴗ ᴗ), choriamb (— ᴗ ᴗ —), etc. To speak of an iambus and interpret the term as a foot consisting of one weak and one strong syllable is not quite so harmless a thing as to speak of consuls and mean something different from the old Roman consules. It is not merely a question of nomenclature: the old names will tend to make us take over more than the terms of the old metrists. There are other misleading terms: what some call "arsis" is by others termed "thesis", and inversely.

(2) *The fallacy of the foot,* i.e. the analysis of a line as consisting of parts divided off by means of perpendicular straight lines ᴗ — | ᴗ — | ᴗ — | etc. Such signs of separation can only delude the reader into "scanning" lines with artificial pauses between the feet—often in the middle of words and in other most unnatural places. On the other hand a natural pause, occasioned by a break in the meaning, may be found in the middle of a foot as well as between metrical feet. It is also often arbitrary where we put the division-mark: Are we to scan Tennyson's line

> The de | light of | happy | laughter

or

> The delight | of hap | py laugh | ter?

The line mentioned above (1, 1) is analysed by E. K. (now Sir Edmund) Chambers in his Warwick edition of *Macbeth* as having "the stress inverted in every foot" and a dactylus in the first:

> Told′by an | i′ diot, | full′of | sound′and | fu′ry.

Some metrists (Bayfield among them) even incline to treat such lines as 1.3 as "trochaic" with an anacrusis:

> Take | each mans | censure, | but re | serve thy | judg'ment.

In such cases it would almost seem as if the vertical stroke were used as the bar in music, to indicate where the strong note or stress begins, though most metrists would deny the legitimacy of that analogy.

We shall see below that the abolition of the fallacy of the foot will assist us in understanding the chief irregularities of blank verse.

(3) *The fallacy of two grades.* The ancients recognized only longs and shorts though there are really many gradations of length of syllables. In the same way most of the moderns, while recognizing that stress is the most important thing in modern metres, speak of two grades only, calling every-

thing weak that is not strong. But in reality there are infinite gradations of stress, from the most penetrating scream to the faintest whisper; but in most instances it will be sufficient for our purposes to recognize four degrees which we may simply designate by the first four numbers:

4 strong
3 half-strong
2 half-weak
1 weak.

It is not always easy to apply these numbers to actually occurring syllables, and it is particularly difficult in many instances to distinguish between 3 and 2. Unfortunately we have no means of measuring stress objectively by instruments; we have nothing to go by except our ears; but then it is a kind of consolation that the poets themselves, whose lines we try to analyse, have been guided by nothing else but *their* ears—and after all, the human ear is a wonderfully delicate apparatus.

5. Verse rhythm is based on the same alternation between stronger and weaker syllables as that found in natural everyday speech. Even in the most prosaic speech, which is in no way dictated by artistic feeling, this alternation is not completely irregular: everywhere we observe a natural tendency towards making a weak syllable follow after a strong one and inversely. Rhythm very often makes itself felt in spite of what might be expected from the natural (logical or emotional) value of the words. Thus syllables which ought seemingly to be strong are weakened if occurring between strong syllables, and naturally weak syllables gain in strength if placed between weak syllables. *Uphill* is 24 in *to walk uphill,* but 42 in *an uphill walk.* *Good-natured* is 44, but becomes 43 or 42 in *a good-natured man.* The last syllable of *afternoon* is strong (4) in *this afternoon,* but weaker (2 or 3) in *afternoon tea. Back* is weaker in *he came back tired* than in *he came back with sore feet,* etc.

Illustrations of this principle are found in the following verse lines in which the middle one of the three italicized syllables is weakened, giving 434 (or 424) instead of 444:

But *poore old man,* thou prun'st a rotten tree.	(1)
The course of *true love never* did run smooth.	(2)
Oh that his *too too sol*id flesh would melt.	(3)
You are my ghests: do me no *foule play, friends.*	(4)
The *still sad mus*ic of humanity.	(5)

A *long street climbs* to *one tall-tow*er'd mill.   (6)
Doch sein geschwungner *Arm traf ih*re Brust (*ihre* emphatic).(7)

6. Of two successive weak syllables that one is the relatively stronger which is the further removed from the strongly stressed syllable; consequently we have the formula 412 in *happily, gossiping, lexicon, apricot, Socrates,* etc., and the inverse 214 (or 314) in *condescend, supersede, disinter;* 2141 in *collocation, expectation, intermixture,* 21412 in *conversational, international, regularity.*

The effect of surroundings is seen clearly in the following line, where *when one* is 23 after the strong *know,* and 32 before the strong *lives:*

I know when one is dead, and when one lives. (1)

Other examples (*I, and, when*—now "weak", now "strong" without regard to meaning) are found in the passage analysed below in 24. *It is* according to circumstances may be 12 or 21, and the same is true of *into* in Shakespeare and other poets. *Is* is "strong", i.e. 2, between two weak syllables (1) in

A thing of beauty is a joy for ever—

and any page of poetry affords examples of the same phenomenon.

7. Our ear does not really perceive stress relations with any degree of certainty except when the syllables concerned are contiguous. If two syllables are separated by a series of other syllables, it is extremely difficult even for the expert to tell which of them is the stronger, as one will feel when comparing the syllables of such a long word as *incomprehensibility: bil* is the strongest, *hen* is stronger than both *pre* and *si,* but what is the relation between *hen* and *com?* or between *in* and *ty?* Another similar word is *irresponsibility,* only here the first syllable is stronger than the second. What is decisive when words have to be used in verse is everywhere the surroundings: the metrical value of a syllable depends on what comes before and what follows after it.

Even more important is the fact that we have to do with *relative degrees of force only:* a sequence of syllables, a verse line may produce exactly the same metrical impression whether I pronounce it so softly that it can scarcely be heard at two feet's distance, or shout it so loudly that it can be distinctly perceived by everyone in a large theatre; but the strongest syllables in the former case may have been weaker than the very weakest ones in the latter case.

8. This leads us to another important principle: the effect of a *pause:* If I hear a syllable after a pause it is absolutely impossible for me to know

whether it is meant by the speaker as a strong or as a weak syllable: I have
nothing to compare it with till I hear what follows. And it is extremely
difficult to say with any degree of certainty what is the reciprocal relation
between two syllables separated by a not too short pause.

9. Let us now try to apply these principles to the "iambic pentameter."
The pattern expected by the hearer is a sequence of ten syllables (which may
be followed by an eleventh, weak syllable), arranged in such a way that the
syllables occupying the even places are raised by their force above the sur-
rounding syllables. It is not possible to say that the scheme is

$$1\,4 \quad 1\,4 \quad 1\,4 \quad 1\,4 \quad 1\,4 \quad (1)$$

for this is a rare and not particularly admired form, as in

> Her eyes, her haire, her cheeke, her gate, her voice.   (1)
> Of hairs, or straws, or dirt, or grubs, or worms.   (2)

Lines of that type were pretty numerous in the earliest days of blank
verse, in Gorboduc and in Peele. But it was soon felt that it was much more
satisfactory to make the difference in force between the strong and the weak
elements of the line less than that between 1 and 4 and at the same time less
uniform, for the only thing required by the ear is an upward and a downward
movement, a rise and a fall, an ascent and a descent, at fixed places, whereas
it is of no importance whatever how great is the ascent or the descent. It is
therefore possible to arrange the scheme in this way, denoting the odd
syllables by a and the even ones by b:

$$a \nearrow b \searrow a \nearrow b \searrow a \nearrow b \searrow a \nearrow b \searrow a \nearrow b(\searrow a) \sim$$

or, if we denote relative strength by a capital,

$$a \, B \, a \, B \, a \, B \, a \, B \, a \, B \,(a).$$

10. It is the relative stress that counts. This is shown conclusively when
we find that a syllable with stress-degree 2 counts as strong between two 1s,
though it is in reality weaker than another with degree 3 which fills a weak
place in the same line because it happens to stand between two 4s. This is,
for instance, the case in

> The course of true love never did run smooth.   (1)

did (2) occupies a strong place though no sensible reader would make it as
strong as *love,* which counts as weak in the verse.

In consequence of this relativity it is possible on the one hand to find
lines with many weak syllables, e.g.

It is a nipping and an eager ayre.   (2)

Here *is* and *and* on account of the surroundings are made into 2s; the line contains not a single consonant and only two long vowels.

On the other hand there are lines with many strong and long syllables, such as

And ten low words oft creep in one dull line.   (3)
The long day wanes: the slow moon climbs: the deep
Moans round with many voices.   (4)
Thoughts blacke, hands apt, drugges fit, and time agreeing. (5)
Day, night, houre, tide, time, worke, and play.   (6)
Rocks, caves, lakes, fens, bogs, dens, and shades of death. (7)

In lines like the last two, however, the pauses make the regular alternation of 3 and 4 difficult or even impossible.

With inversion in the beginning we have Browning's dreadfully heavy

Spark-like mid unearthed slope-side figtree-roots.   (8)

A comparison of such extremes of light and heavy lines shows conclusively that *quantity as such has no essential importance in the building up of blank verse*.

The principle of relativity allows an abundance of variety; there are many possible harmonious and easy-flowing verses, with five, or four, or three really strong syllables (degree 4); and the variety can be further increased by means of pauses, which may be found between the lines or at almost any place in the lines themselves, whether between or in the middle of so-called feet.

So much for the normal "iambic pentameter".

11. Let us now analyse a line with inversion, e.g.

Peace, children, peace! the king doth love you well.   (1)

The stress numbers for the first four syllables are 4314 (or possibly 4214, though 3 seems more likely than 2 for the second syllable). Here the ear is not disappointed in the first syllable: after the pause preceding the line one does not know what general level to expect: a syllable which objectively is pretty strong might turn out to be a relatively weak introduction to something still stronger. A mathematician might feel tempted to express this in the following way: the proportion between the 0 of the pause and the 4 of a strong syllable is the same as between 0 and the 1 of a weak syllable.

It is therefore not till this strong syllable is followed by one that is weaker instead of stronger that the ear experiences a disappointment and feels a deviation from the regular pattern. But the transition from the second to the third syllable is a descent in strict conformity with the pattern; and in the same way there is perfect regularity in the relation between the third and the (strong) fourth, and indeed in the whole of the rest of the line. The scheme accordingly is the following:

$$a \backslash b \backslash a \diagup b \backslash a \diagup b \backslash a \diagup b \backslash a \diagup b,$$

which should be compared with the scheme given above, 9, as normal.

This amounts to saying that while according to the traditional way of notation one would think that the departure from the norm concerned two-tenths (one-fifth) of the line if one heard a "trochee" instead of an "iambus", the ear is really disappointed at one only out of ten places. The deviation from the norm is thus reduced to one-tenth—or even less than that, because the descent is only a small one. The greater the descent, the greater also the dissatisfaction, but in the example analysed the descent was only from 4 to 3. A beginning 4114 is comparatively poor, but 4314 or 4214 does not sound bad, for from the second syllable (or from the transition to the third) one has the feeling that everything is all right and the movement is the usual one. In the case of two inversions in the same line we have in two places (not in four!) disappointments, each of them amounting to less than one-tenth, and so far separated from the other that they do not act jointly on the ear.

12. We shall now collect some classified examples which tend to show that poets have instinctively followed this hitherto never formulated principle.

A. First we have instances in which the three syllables concerned belong to the same word. Such words, of the stress-formula 431 or 421, are very frequent in Danish and German; I have therefore been able to find a great many lines like the following:

Sandhedens kilder i dets bund udstrømme.	(1)
Staldbroder! hav tålmodighed med Axel.	(2)
Granvoxne Valborg!—Elskelige svend!	(3)
Kraftvolles mark war seiner söhn' und enkel.	(4)
Unedel sind die waffen eines weibes.	(5)
Hilfreiche götter vom Olympus rufen.	(6)

In English, on the other hand, words of this type are comparatively rare, and in Elizabethan times there was a strong tendency to shift the stress rhythmically so as to have 412 instead of 431 or 421; thus *torchbearer, quicksilver, bedfellow,* etc. But we have 431 in

Sleek-headed men, and such as sleepe a-nights. (7)
Grim-visag'd warre hath smooth'd his wrinkled front. (8)
All-seeing heaven, what a world is this? (9)

13. B. The first two syllables form one word.

Doomesday is neere, dye all, dye merrily. (1)
Welcome, Sir Walter Blunt, and would to God... (2)
England did never owe so sweet a hope. (3)
Something that hath a reference to my state. (4)
Nothing that I respect, my gracious lord. (5)
Ofspring of Heav'n and Earth, and all Earths Lord. (6)
Noontide repast, or Afternoons repose. (7)

This is frequent in Danish:

Valborg skal vorde Axel Thordsøns brud. (8)
Alting er muligt for er trofast hjerte. (9)

14. C. The first word is one syllable, the second two or more.

Urge neither charity nor shame to me. (1)
Dye neyther mother, wife, nor Englands queene! (2)
Peace, master marquesse, you are malapert. (3)
Peace, children, peace! the king doth love you well. (4)
First, madam, I intreate true peace of you. (5)

Danish and German examples:

Tak, høje fader, for din miskundhed! (6)
Spar dine ord! Jeg kender ikke frygt. (7)
Den baere kronen som er kronen voxen. (8)
Frei atmen macht das leben nicht allein. (9)
Sie rettet weder hoffnung, weder furcht. (10)

In cases like the following one may hesitate which of the first two syllables to make 4 and which 3:

Yong, valiant, wise, and (no doubt) right royal. (11)
Friends, Romans, countrymen, lend me your ears. (12)
Foule wrinkled witch, what mak'st thou in my sight? (13)
Ros, rygte, folkesnak i sold den ta'er. (14)
Rat, mässigung und weisheit und geduld. (15)

15. D. Two monosyllables.

Here there will naturally be a great many cases in which the correct distribution of stresses is not self-evident: one reader will stress the first and another the second word. I think, however, that in the following lines most readers will agree with me in stressing 4314 or 4214 (or 5314):

Long may'st thou live, to wayle thy childrens death.	(1)
Greefe fils the roome up of my absent childe.	(2)
God will revenge it. Come, lords, will you go.	(3)
Their woes are parcell'd, mine is generall.	(4)
Sweet are the uses of adversitie.	(5)
Lye there what hidden womans feare there will.	(6)
Cours'd one another downe his innocent nose.	(7)
Knap var det sagt, så stod for dem den tykke.	(8)
Klog mand foragter ej sin staerke fjende.	(9)
Dank habt ihr stets. Doch nicht den reinen dank.	(10)
Wohl dem, der seiner väter gern gedenkt.	(11)

In the middle of a line:

As it is wonne with blood, *lost be it* so.	(12)
Den nordiske natur. *Alt skal du* skue.	(13)
So kehr zurück! *Thu, was dein* Herz dich heisst.	(14)

16. While in the lines examined so far a natural reading will stress the second syllable more than the third, it must be admitted that there are many lines in which the words themselves do not demand this way of stressing. Nevertheless the possibility exists that the poet had it in his mind, and expert elocutionists will often unconsciously give a stronger stress to the second syllable just to minimize the deviation from the scheme and avoid the unpleasant effect of the sequence 4114. I think this is quite natural in cases like the following, in which a proper name or another important word calls for an emphatic enunciation which makes the second syllable stronger than it might have been in easy-going prose:

Clarence still breathes; *Edward* still lives and raignes.	(1)
Never came poyson from so sweet a place.	(2)
Never hung poyson on a fowler toade.	(3)
Tyrants themselves wept when it was reported.	(4)
Hakon er konge, Valborg er en mø.	(5)
Himlen er ej så blå som disse blomster.	(6)

Even in a line like

Cowards dye many times before their deaths   (7)

an actor may feel inclined to express his contempt and to point the contrast to the following words—"The valiant never taste of death but once"—by giving special stress (53 or 54) to *cowards* and by extra stress on *many* to weigh down *die* to something comparatively insignificant, which is all the more natural as the idea of death has been mentioned in the preceding lines, while *cowards* is a new idea: new ideas are well known to attract strong stress. It is worth noting how often the figure is used as a rhetorical device to emphasize a contrast, in exclamations and in personal apostrophe (cf. König, p. 78). It is particularly apt for this use because a forcible attack of the voice after a pause will immediately catch the attention, before the verse settles down in its usual even course.

17. In spite of all this there will remain some instances in which the second syllable cannot easily be made stronger than the third. Metrics is no exact science aiming at finding out natural laws that are valid everywhere. All we can say is that by arranging syllables in such and such a way the poet will produce a pleasing effect; but of course a poet is free to sacrifice euphony if other things appear more important to him—not to mention the possibility that he is momentarily unable to hit upon anything more felicitous.

18. In all the cases dealt with in the preceding paragraphs there was a pause immediately before the strong syllable which had taken the place of a weak. The pause is often, but of course not everywhere, indicated by a full stop or other punctuation mark. A natural explanation of the varying frequency of inversion at different places in the line (see above 3) is found in the fact that a pause is not equally natural at all places. In the vast majority of cases inversion is found at the very beginning of a line, because the end of the preceding line is more often than not marked by a break in the thought, and even where this is not the case a reciter or actor will often make a pause between two lines. Not quite so frequently comes a pause and inversion in the middle of a line, after the second or third "foot". It is necessarily rarer after the first foot, because a division of the line into two such unequal parts (2 + 8 syllables) is not natural: the two syllables are awkwardly isolated and cut off from organic cohesion with the rest. This is even more true of a pause after the eighth syllable: a strong syllable here will not leave us time enough to regain the natural swing of the verse before the line is ended. In such a case as

It is his Highnesse pleasure, that the Queene
Appeare in person here in Court. Silence!   (1)

it would not even be unnatural to shout out the two last syllables as 44 or 45.

19. In yet another way a pause may play an important role in the verse. If we analyse the following lines in the usual way we find that the syllables here italicized form trochees where we should expect iambs, and if we read them without stopping they are felt to be inharmonious:

Like to a step-*dame, or* a dowager.   (1)
Lye at the proud *foote of* a conqueror.   (2)
As wilde-*geese, that* the creeping fowler eye.   (3)
And let the soule *forth that* adoreth thee.   (4)
To bear the file's *tooth and* the hammer's tap.   (5)
John of the Black *Bands with* the upright spear.   (6)
A snow-*flake, and* a scanty couch of snow
Crusted the grass-*walk and* the garden-mould.   (7)
Den, der er blind*født el*ler blind fra barndom.   (8)
Nu, det var smukt *gjort, det* var vel gjort, godt gjort.   (9)
Denn ihr allein *wisst, was* uns frommen kann.   (10)

If, on the other hand, we read these lines with the pause required (or allowed) by the meaning, the ear will not be offended in the least. The line is in perfect order, because in the first place *dame* with its 3 is heard together with *step* (4) and thus shows a descent in the right place, and secondly *or* with its 2 is heard in close connexion with *a* (1), so that we have the required descent between these two syllables. Graphically:

Like to	a step-	dame, or	a dow	ager
. . . . . .	iamb	trochee	iamb	. . . .
. . . . . . 1 4		3 2	1 4	
. . . . . . a ╱ b		╲ a(╲)b╲	a ╱ b	

The descent marked in parenthesis between *dame* and *or* is not heard, and is thus non-existent. Similarly in the other examples.[4]

20. The phenomena dealt with here (in 12 ff. and 19) are singularly fit to demonstrate the shortcomings of traditional metrics (cf. above 4). In the first case (inversion after a pause) we had a "trochee", whose second syllable acts in connexion with the first syllable of the following foot, as if the latter had been the second syllable of an iambus. In the second case (19) we had a "trochee" whose first syllable as a matter of fact will be perceived in the verse as if it were the first part of an iambus, and whose second syllable is similarly playing the role of the latter part of an iambus, and yet it is impossible to call these two successive iambic syllables a real iambus. In both cases the ear thus protests against the paper idea of a "foot". In the former case the perpen-

dicular line | is made to separate the two syllables whose mutual relation is really of great rhythmic importance and which accordingly ought to go together. In the latter case two similar straight lines join together syllables which are not to be heard together, and whose relation to one another is therefore of no consequence, while the syllables that have to be weighed against one another are by the same means separated as if they did not concern one another. Could anything be more absurd?

21. The irregularities in lines like

And they shall be one Flesh, one Heart, one Soule.	(1)
The wretched annimall heav'd forth such groanes	(2)

might be explained by means of a pause after *be* and *animal: shall be* is 12, and *one flesh* 34, and similarly *animal* is 412 and *heav'd forth* 34, but the irregular ascent between 2 and 3 is concealed by the pause:

$$1 \diagup 2 (\diagup) 3 \diagup 4 \text{ or } a \diagup b (\diagup) a \diagup b.$$

This explanation does not, however, hold good for numerous groups of a similar structure, e.g.:

In the sweet pangs of it remember me.	(3)
And the free maides that weave their thred with bones.	(4)
In the deepe bosome of the ocean buried.	(5)
But the queenes kindred and night-walking heralds.	(6)
Of the young prince your sonne: send straight for him.	(7)
I will feede fat the ancient grudge I beare him.	(8)
As his wise mother wrought in his behalfe.	(9)
Of a strange nature is the sute you follow.	(10)
Whose homes *are the dim caves* of human thought.	(11)
The ploughman lost his sweat, *and the greene corne*.	(12)
Did I deserve no more *then a fooles head?*	(13)

This figure is frequent in English verse, but not in other languages. I incline to read it with 1234 and thus to say that the ascent is normal between the first and the second as well as between the third and the fourth syllable, so that there is only the one small anomaly of a slight ascent instead of a descent between the second and the third syllable. It is worth noting how frequently this figure contains an adjective (stressed 3) before a substantive (stressed 4); *fooles* before *head* is equivalent to an adjective.

Some metrists here speak of a double iambus ($\smile \smile — —$). Robert Bridges (*Milton's Prosody*, 1894, p. 56) calls it "a foot of two unstressed short syllables preceding a foot composed of two heavy syllables" and says, "Whatever the account of it is, it is pleasant to the ear even in the smoothest verse, and is so, no doubt, by a kind of compensation in it".

22. The role of a pause which covers and hides away metrical irregularities is seen also in the case of extra-metrical syllables. In Shakespeare these are particularly frequent where a line is distributed between two speakers. The pause makes us forget how far we had come: one speaker's words are heard as the regular beginning, and the next speaker's as the regular ending of a verse, and we do not feel that we have been treated to too much, though this would not pass equally unnoticed if there had been no break. Examples may be found in any book on Shakespeare's verse;[5] one occurs in the passage of Henry IV analysed below (24, line 33). An interesting use of an extra-metrical syllable is made in King Lear IV, 1, 72

> (Let the superfluous . . . man . . . that will not see,)
> Because he do's not feele, feele your power quickly:

the second *feel,* which is necessary for the meaning, is heard as a kind of echo of the first and therefore enters into its place in the line.

23. There is one phenomenon which is even more curious than those mentioned so far, namely that which Abbott has termed *amphibious section.* Recent metrists do not as a rule acknowledge it, but its reality seems indisputable. It will not be found in poets who write for the eye, but Shakespeare was thinking of the stage only and was not interested in the way his plays would look when they were printed. He could therefore indulge in sequences like the following:

> He but usurpt his life. | Beare them from hence. | Our
> present businesse | is generall woe. | Friends of my soule, you
> twaine | Rule in this realme | and the gor'd state sustaine. (1)

This is a sequence of 6 + 4 + 6 + 4 + 6 + 4 + 6 syllables, and in all the places here marked | (except perhaps two) a pause is necessary; after *life* a new speaker begins. The audience will not be able to notice that anything is missing: they will hear the first 6 + 4 as a full line, but the same four syllables go together with the following six to form another full line, and so on. A modern editor is in a difficult dilemma, for whichever way he prints the passage one line is sure to be too short:

> He but usurped his life. Bear them from hence.
> Our present business is general woe.
> Friends of my soul, you twain
> Rule in this realm and the gored state sustain.

Or

> He but usurped his life.
> Bear them from hence. Our present business
> Is general, etc.

A second example is:

> Utter your gravitie ore a gossips bowles,
> For here we need it not. | — You are too hot. | 6 + 4
> Gods bread! it makes me mad. | (2)   6

Or

> For here we need it not.—   6
> You are too hot. Gods bread! it makes me mad.   4 + 6

And a third:

> Who, I, my lord! We know each others faces,
> But for our hearts, | he knowes no more of mine | 4 + 6
> Then I of yours; | 4
> Nor I no more of his,[6] | then you of mine. | 6 + 4
> Lord Hastings, you and he | are neere in love. | (3)   6 + 4

Such passages are thus elaborate acoustic delusions which are not detected on account of the intervening pauses.

24. It may not be amiss here to give the analysis of a connected long
passage according to the principles advocated in this paper. The passage
(*Henry IV,* A, I, 3, 22 ff.) is metrically of unusual interest.

> 29 My liege, I did deny no prisoners.
> 30 But I remember when the fight was done,
>   When I was dry with rage and extreame toyle,
>   Breathlesse and faint, leaning upon my sword,
>   Came there a certain lord, neat and trimly drest,
> 34 Fresh as a bride-groome, and his chin new reapt
>   Shew'd like a stubble land at harvest-home.
>   He was perfumed like a milliner,
>   And 'twixt his finger and his thumbe he held
> 38 A pouncet-box, which ever and anon
>   He gave his nose, and took't away againe:
>   Who therewith angry, when it next came there,
>   Tooke it in snuffe: and still he smil'd and talk'd:

> 42 And as the souldiers bare dead bodies by,
>   He call'd them untaught knaves, unmannerly,
>   To bring a slovenly unhandsome coarse
> 45 Betwixt the wind and his nobility.

Line 29. *I* in weak position, but in 30 and 31 in strong position (2) on account of the surroundings, 9. Similarly *when* strong (2) in line 30, but degree 1 in line 31.

Line 31. *Extreame* with rhythmic stress on *ex-* on account of its position before a strongly stressed word (see A. Schmidt, *Sh-Lex.,* II, p. 1413; my *Modern English Grammar,* I, 5. 53 f.; above 5). In the same way *untaught* line 43, but *unmannerly* and *unhandsome* with weak *un.*

Line 32. Two examples of inversion, 13.

Line 33. Which of the two words, *Came there,* is the stronger may be doubtful, 15. *Neat* an extra-metrical syllable, which is not felt as such on account of the pause, 22.

Line 34. Beginning inversion according to 15. *Groome* 3, *and* 2, with pause between them, 19; *new* 3 between two 4's, 5.

Line 35. *Showed like* inversion, 15.

Line 36. *Was* 2, stronger than *he* and *per-. Perfumed* 141. This is the ordinary stressing of the verb, also in our times; but in *Henry IV,* B, III, 1, 12, we have rhythmic shifting 41 before 4: "Then in the perfum'd chambers of the great". *Like* 2, as in preceding line.

Line 37. First *and* 1, second *and* 2 between weak syllables, 6. The two following *and*s also 2; this is likewise the case with *when* in line 40.

Line 41. Inversion, 17.

Line 42. *As* 2, 6, but *dead* 3 or 2 between strong syllables, 5.

Line 43. *untaught,* see above.

Line 44. *slovenly* 412 or perhaps 413 before *un-,* 6.

Line 45. *his* 2 or 3, probably not emphatic.

25. We have not yet offered an answer to the question raised in 2: why is a trochee among iambs easier to tolerate than inversely an iamb among trochees? But the answer is not difficult on the principles we have followed throughout. Take some trochaic lines, e.g.:

> Tell me not, in mournful numbers,
> Life is but an empty dream

and substitute for the second line something like

> A life's but an empty dream,

or

> To live's but an empty dream.

The rhythm is completely spoilt. Or try instead of

> Then the little Hiawatha
> Learned of every bird its language

to say

> The sweet little Hiawatha
> Acquired every sound and language.

(*Every* of course in two syllables as in Longfellow).

In such cases with 14 instead of 41 we have the disagreeable clash of two strong syllables; further, we have two disappointments per line. It is true that if we pronounced the first strong syllable weaker than the second, thus made the whole 1341, we should have only one disappointment: $a \diagup b \diagup a \diagdown b$ instead of the regular $a \diagdown b \diagup a \diagdown b$; but it will be extremely hard to find examples of the sequence 34 as regularly occurring in any of the cognate languages. We shall see in the next paragraph the reason why 34 is not found within one and the same word; and when a word of the formula 14 is placed before a strongly stressed word, it is not generally reduced to 13, as the ordinary tendency in such cases is rather to substitute for it 31 or 21. See many examples from English in my *Modern English Grammar*, I, 156 ff.: "The other *upon* Saturn's bended neck" (Keats), "Protracted *among* endless solitudes" (Wordsworth), "a spirit *without* spot" (Shelley), "in *forlorn* servitude" (Wordsworth). For Danish examples, see *Modersmålets fonetik*, p. 139. The disinclination to "invert" in trochaic rhythms is thus seen to be deeply rooted in linguistic habits and in the phonetic structure of our languages.

26. What is the essential difference between a rising and a falling rhythm? (Or, in the old terms, between an "iambic" or "anapaestic" rhythm on the one hand and a "trochaic" or "dactylic" rhythm on the other?) Some writers minimize this difference and say that they are virtually identical, as the "anacrusis" has no real importance; instead of the sequence 14 14 14 ... ($\smile - | \smile - | \smile - | \cdots$) they would write 1 41 41 41..., ($\smile | - \smile | - \smile | - \ldots$). According to them the initial weak syllable is just as unimportant as an up-beat (auftakt, mesure d'attaque) is in music.

But is such an up-beat (a note before the first bar begins) really unimportant in music? I have taken a number of music books at random and counted the pieces in which such an up-beat occurs; I found that it was less frequent in pieces with a slow movement (largo, grave, adagio, andante) than in those with a quick movement (allegro, allegretto, rondo, presto, prestissimo, vivace):

Slow	Beethoven	Schubert	Schumann	Sum
with up-beat	5	1	5	11
without up-beat	17	7	7	31
Quick				
with up-beat	31	14	12	57
without up-beat	19	11	10	40

This agrees with the general impression of verse rhythms: a sequence didúm didúm didúm . . . tends to move more rapidly than dúmda dúmda dúmda. . . . I think this depends on a deeply rooted psychological tendency: there is a universal inclination to hurry up to a summit, but once the top is reached one may linger in the descent. This is shown linguistically within each syllable: consonants before the summit of sonority (which in most cases is a vowel) are nearly always short, while consonants after the summit are very often long; cp. thus the two *n*'s of *nun,* the two *t*'s of *tot,* the two *m*'s of *member.* Words of the type 43 with long second syllable are frequent: *football, folklore, cornfield, therefore,* while corresponding words with 34 are rare: they tend to become 24 or even 14: *throughout, therein, austere, naïve, Louise, forgive*—with more or less distinct shortening of the vowel.

In this connexion it is perhaps also worth calling attention to the following fact. As a stressed syllable tends, other things being equal, to be pronounced with higher pitch than weak syllables, a purely "iambic" line will tend towards a higher tone at the end, but according to general phonetic laws this is a sign that something more is to be expected. Consequently it is in iambic verses easy to knit line to line in natural continuation.[7] Inversely the typical pitch movement of a "trochaic" line is towards a descent, which in each line acts as an indication of finality, of finish. If a continuation is wanted, the poet is therefore often obliged to repeat something—a feature which is highly characteristic of such a poem as *Hiawatha,* where each page offers examples like the following:

> *Should you ask* me, *whence* these stories?
> *Whence* these *legends and traditions,*
> *With* the odours of the forest,
> *With* the dew and damp of meadows,
> *With* the curling smoke of wigwams,
> *With* the rushing of great rivers,
> *With* their frequent repetitions, (N.B.)

And their wild reverberations,
As of thunder in the mountains?
I should answer, I should tell you,
From the . . . etc. (*From the* 6 times.)
Should you ask where Nawadaha
Found these songs, so wild and wayward,
Found these *legends and traditions,*
I should answer, I should tell you
In the . . . (*In the* 4 times.)[8]

These, then, seem to be the distinctive features of the two types of metre: rapidity, ease of going on from line to line without a break on the one hand, and on the other slowness, heaviness, a feeling of finality at the end of each line, hence sometimes fatiguing repetitions. Tennyson utilized this contrast in a masterly way in *The Lady of Shalott,* where the greater part of the poem is rising, but where a falling rhythm winds up the whole in the description of her sad swan-song:

Heard a carol, mournful, holy,
Chanted loudly, chanted lowly,
Till her blood was frozen slowly,
And her eyes were darkened wholly,
        Turned to tower'd Camelot.

References for the lines quoted.

Sh = Shakespeare. The titles of plays indicated as in A. Schmidt's Shakespeare-Lexicon. Numbers of act, scene, and line as in the Globe edition.

PL = Milton's *Paradise Lost,* as in Beeching's reprint of the original edition of 1667.

Ø = Øhlenschläger, *Axel og Valborg,* number of page according to A. Boysen's edition of *Poetiske skrifter i udvalg,* III, 1896.

P-M = Paludan-Müller, *Adam Homo,* Anden deel, 1849.

H = Hertz, *Kong Renés datter,* 7de opl., 1893.

G = Goethe, *Iphigenie auf Tauris.* Number of act and line according to Sämtliche werke XI in Cotta's Bibl. d. weltlitt.

  1. 1. Tro. I, 1. 54. — 2, 3. Hml. I. 3. 68, 69. — 4. G I. 115. — 5. G I. 226.

  2. 1. Mcb. V. 5. 27. — 2. R3 I. 3. 185. — 3. G I. 27.

  5. 1. As II. 3. 63. — 2. Mids. I. 1. 134. — 3. Hml. I. 2. 129. — 4. Lr. III. 7. 31. — 5. Wordsw. Tint. Abb. — 6. Tennyson, En. Arden 5. — 7. G III. 317.

  6. 1. Lr. V. 3. 260.

  9. 1. Tro. I. 1. 54. — 2. Pope.

  10. 1. Mids. I. 1. 134. — 2. Hml. I. 4.2.— 3. Pope Ess. Crit. 347. — 4. Tennyson Ulysses. — 5. Pope. — 6. Rom. III. 5. 178. — 7. PL II. 621. — 8. The Ring and the Book I. 6.

  11. 1.R3 II. 2. 17.

  12. 1. P-M 21. — 2. Ø 8. — 3. Ø 23. — 4. G I. 329. — 5. G I. 483. — 6. G III. 242. — 7. Caes. I. 2. 193. — 8. R3 I. 1. 9. — 9. ib. II. 1. 82.

13. 1. H4A IV. 1. 134. — 2. ib. IV. 3. 31. — 3. ib. V. 2. 68. — 4. As I. 3. 129. — 5. R3 I. 3. 295. — 6. PL IX. 273. — 7. ib. IX. 403. — 8. Ø 7. — 9. Ø 21.

14. 1. R3 I. 3. 274. — 2. ib. I. 3. 209. — 3. ib. I. 3. 255. —4. ib. II. 2. 17. — 5. ib. II. 1. 62. — 6. Ø 17. — 7. H 95. — 8. Ø. Hakon Jarl. — 9. G I. 106. — 10. G III. 71. — 11. R3 I. 2. 245. — 12. Caes. III. 2. 78. — 13. R3 I. 3. 164. — 14. P-M 40. — 15. G I. 332.

15. 1. R3 I. 3. 204. — 2. John III. 4. 93. — 3. R3 II. 1. 138. — 4. ib. II. 2. 81. — 5. As II. 1. 12. — 6. ib. I. 3. 121. — 7. ib. II. 1. 39. — 8. P-M 12. — 9. Ø 27. — 10. G I. 93. — 11. G I. 351. — 12. R3 I. 3. 272. — 13. Ø 8. — 14. G I. 463.

16. 1. R3 I. 1. 161. — 2. ib. I. 2. 148. — 3. ib. I. 2. 149. — 4. ib. I. 3. 185. — 5. Ø 15. — 6. Ø 8.

18. 1. Wint. III. 1. 10.

19. 1. Mids. I. 1. 5. — 2. John V. 7. 113. — 3. Mids. III. 2. 20. — 4. R3 I. 2. 177. — 5. The Ring and the Book I. 14. — 6. ib. I. 47. — 7. ib. I. 608-9.

21. 1. PL VIII. 499. — 2. As II. 1. 36. — 3. Tw. II. 4. 16. — 4. ib. II. 4. 46. — 5. R3 I. 1. 4. — 6. ib. I. 1. 72. — 7. ib. II. 2. 97. — 8. Merch. I. 3. 48. — 9. ib. I. 3. 73. — 10. ib. IV. 1. 177. — 11. Shelley Prom. I. 659. — 12. Mids. II. 1. 94. — 13. Merch. II. 9. 59.

22. Hml V. 2. 352. — ib. IV. 7. 80.

23. 1. Lr. V. 3. 317. — 2. Rom. III. 5. 178. — 3. R3 III. 4. 11.

POSTSCRIPT

During the more than thirty years since this paper was first written, I have read many books and papers on metre, but have found nothing to shake my belief in the essential truth of my views, though I have often had occasion to regret that I wrote my paper in Danish and buried it in a place where fellow metrists in other countries were not likely to discover it.

If E. A. Sonnenschein had been alive, I should probably have written some pages in refutation of much in his book *What is Rhythm?* (Oxford, 1925). Now I shall content myself with pointing out how his inclination to find classical metres in English and to attach decisive importance to quantity leads him to such unnatural scannings of perfectly regular lines as

The véry spírit   of Plantágenèt
| ᴗ ᴗ ᴗ | ⌒ ᴗ ᴗ | ⌒ o | ⌒ — | ᴗ ᴗ |

The first foot is an iambus, but as such should contain a long syllable; now both *e* and *r* in *very* are known to Sonnenschein as short; he therefore takes *y* as part of a trisyllabic foot, but it must at the same time be the "fall" of the next foot (his mark for the "protraction" which makes this possible is ⌒); the second iambus again has as its "rise" the two short syllables *spirit,* of which the second again is protracted to form the "fall" of the third foot; but *of* "does not fill up the time of the rise completely, unless it receives a metrical ictus, which would be accompanied by lengthening"—this is marked o. In a similar way are treated

O píty,   píty,   géntle héaven, píty!

| ~ ∪ ∪ | ⌒ ∪ ∪ | ⌒ ~ | ∪ ∪ ∪ | ⌒ ∪ ∪ | ⌒

and the shorter

Apollo's summer look

| ∪ ∪ ∪ ⋮ ∪ ∪ ∪ | ⌒ ~ | (p. 158–59).

We get rid of all such pieces of artificiality by simply admitting that short syllables like *ver-, spir-, pit-, -pol-, sum-* are just as susceptible of verse ictus as long ones.

Unfortunately experimental phonetics gives us very little help in these matters. Sonnenschein and others have used the kymograph for metric purposes, and "the kymograph cannot lie" (Sonnenschein, p. 33): but neither can it tell us anything of what really matters, namely stress, however good it is for length of sounds. The experimentalist Panconcelli-Calzia even goes so far as to deny the reality of syllables, and Scripture finds in his instruments nothing corresponding to the five beats of a blank verse line. So I am afraid poets and metrists must go on depending on their ears only.

English prosodists are apt to forget that the number of syllables is often subject to reduction in cases like *general, murderous, separately, desperate;* compare the treatment of *garden* + *er*, of *person* + *-al* and of *noble* + *ly* as disyllabic *gardener, personal, nobly,* and the change of syllabic *i* before another vowel to non-syllabic [j] as in *Bohemia, cordial, immediate, opinion,* etc., in which Shakespeare and others have sometimes a full vowel, sometimes syllable reduction, the former chiefly at the end of a line, where it is perfectly natural to slow down the speed of pronunciation. Compare the two lines (Ro II. 2. 4 and 7) in which *envious* is first two and then three syllables:

> Arise faire Sun and kill the envious Moone . . .
> Be not her maid since she is envious.

Similarly *many a, many and, worthy a, merry as,* etc., occur in Shakespeare and later poets as two syllables in conformity with a natural everyday pronunciation (my *Modern English Grammar,* I, 278).

I must finally remark that the whole of my paper concerns one type of (modern) metre only, and that there are other types, based wholly or partially on other principles, thus classical Greek and Latin verse. On medieval and to some extent modern versification of a different type much light is shed in various papers by William Ellery Leonard (himself a poet as well as a metrist): "Beowulf and the Nibelungen Couplet"; "The Scansion of Middle English Alliterative Verse" (both in *University of Wisconsin Studies in Language and Literature,* 1918 and 1920), "The Recovery of the Metre of the Cid" (*PMLA,* 1931) and "Four Footnotes to Papers on Germanic Metrics" (in *Studies in Honor of F. Klaeber, 1929).*

NOTES

[1.] The places from which quotations are taken will be indicated at the end of the paper. Quotations from Shakespeare are given in the spelling of the 1623 folio, except that sometimes an apostrophe is substituted for a mute *e,* and that the modern distinction of *u* and *v,* and *i* and *j* is carried through.

[2.] "Their attractiveness may be due precisely to the fact that the accent of the first foot comes as a surprise to the reader", Sonnenschein, *What Is Rhythm?* (Oxford, 1925), p. 105.

[3.] *Der Vers in Shakespeares Dramen* (Strassburg: Quellen und Forschungen, 1888), 61, p. 79, cf. 77. Only "worttrochäen" are here numbered, not "satztrochäen".

[4.] A corresponding interpretation of the metre of Shakespeare's *Lucrece* (1611 and 1612) is found in A. P. van Dam, *W. Shakespeare, Prosody and Text* (Leyden 1900), p. 206.

[5.] But it is necessary to read these writers with a critical mind, for very often lines are given as containing such supernumerary syllables which are perfectly regular in Shakespeare's pronunciation, e.g.

I am more an antique Roman than a Dane (I am = I'm).

The light and careless livery that it wears (livery = livry).

[6.] Folio: Or I of his, my Lord.

[7.] Two rimed lines in succession will, however, produce the impression of finish—a feature that is often found in the Elizabethan drama, more particularly when a scene or a speech ends with a sententious saying.

[8.] These two things, a trochaic metre and constant repetition, are found together in Finnish popular poetry, which Longfellow imitated.

YVOR WINTERS

The Audible Reading of Poetry

Winters 'rediscovers' the principle of relative stress. His scansions as well as his concept of the correct "audible reading of poetry" seem to me unexceptionable. He makes important distinctions between rhetorical and metrical stressing; he points out the difficulties that result if the poet or reader neglects metrical structure and prefers a "conversational" or "dramatic" rendering. He notes the ambiguities of contrastive stress in Keats' line,

> Bright star, would I were steadfast as thou art . . .

and how Keats' "meaning was struggling with the meter."

Winters selects the poems of the Elizabethan songwriters for special metrical analysis, noting the effects achieved by substitution and 'springing.' It is unfortunate that Winters shows no interest in the relationships between words and music, or in the influence of music on the later Elizabethan lyric. A history of English metric that would take into account the relevant developments in music might shed more light than the futile debates between rival prosodists. The Elizabethan and Jacobean songbooks, especially the four great examples of John Dowland, offer a starting point for such a history.

Reprinted from *The Function of Criticism: Problems and Exercises* by Yvor Winters. Copyright © 1957 by Yvor Winters. Used by permission of The Swallow Press, Inc.

My title may seem to have in it something of the jargon of the modern
Educationist; if so, I am sorry, but I mean to indicate something more than
the reading of poetry aloud. I mean to indicate the reading of poetry not
merely for the sensual ear, but for the mind's ear as well; yet the mind's ear
can be trained only by way of the other, and the matter, practically considered, comes inescapably back to the reading of poetry aloud.

It is also important to learn to read prose aloud, and to hear the prose
when one reads it silently. Melville, Gibbon, or Samuel Johnson about
equally will be lost on us if we do not so hear it. Yet the readers are numerous
who hear nothing when they read silently and who are helpless in their efforts
to read aloud: some of them have defective sensibilities; some have merely
never been trained; some have been trained by one or another of our
psychological educationalists to read in this fashion in order that they may
read more rapidly. That they can read more rapidly without hearing, I
believe there is no doubt, especially if the matter with which they are dealing
is trivial. The trouble is that the activity cannot properly be called reading.
Such "readers" are barbarians; literature is closed to them, in spite of the fact
that they may think otherwise. The scholar who appears to have read everything has commonly understood very little, and his failure to hear is one of
the reasons.

My subject may seem a bit precious and tenuous, but it is neither; it is a
matter of the utmost importance to the proper understanding of poetry, a
matter fully as important as the philosophical speculation and learned para-
phrasing of the New Critics, of whom I am sometimes reputed to be one. It
is a matter of which there is almost no understanding at the present time.

Poetry, as nearly as I can understand it, is a statement in words about a
human experience, whether the experience be real or hypothetical, major or
minor; but it is a statement of a particular kind. Words are symbols for
concepts, and the philosopher or scientist endeavors as far as may be to use
them with reference to nothing save their conceptual content. Most words,
however, connote feelings and perceptions, and the poet, like the writer of
imaginative prose, endeavors to use them with reference not only to their
denotations but to their connotations as well. Such writers endeavor to
communicate not only concepts, arranged, presumably, either in rational
order or in an order apprehensible by the rational mind, but the feeling or
emotion which the rational content ought properly to arouse. The poet
differs from the writer of any kind of prose in that he writes in metrical
language. Any good prose is rhythmical up to a certain point: even purely
expository prose should be rhythmical to the point that audible obstructions
are minimized and meanings are emphasized; the prose of such a writer as

Melville is far more elaborately rhythmical than this. But a rhythm which is not controlled by a definite measure will be relatively loose and lacking in subtlety. Poetry and music are based upon definite measure; in this they differ from all other forms of composition.

Rhythm and meter, it should be observed, are quite distinct from each other, in spite of the fact that many critics (myself among them) sometimes use the two words as if they meant the same thing. Meter is the arithmetical norm, the purely theoretic structure of the line; rhythm is controlled departure from that norm. The iambic pentameter norm, for example, proceeds as follows:

One *two,* one *two,* one *two,* one *two,* one *two.*

Yet no other line in the language corresponds exactly to the line just given; and to achieve another as regular one will have to resort to the same repetitive structure with a new pair of syllables. Every other line will depart from this one for these reasons: no two syllables ever have the same degree of accent—that is, so far as versification is concerned there is no such thing as an inherently accented or unaccented syllable, but syllables which count technically as accented can be recognized as such only with reference to the other syllable or syllables within the same foot; secondly, although quantity or syllable-length has no part in the measure, it is, like accent, infinitely variable and it affects the rhythm; and thirdly, feet of other types may be substituted for iambic feet, at least within reason. As I have said, rhythm results from the proper control and manipulation of these sources of variation.

Now rhythm is in a measure expressive of emotion. If the poet, then, is endeavoring to make a statement in which rational understanding and emotion are properly related to each other, metrical language will be of the greatest advantage to him, for it will provide him with a means of qualifying his emotion more precisely than he could otherwise do, of adjusting it more finely to the rational understanding which gives rise to it. The rational and emotional contents of the poem thus exist simultaneously, from moment to moment, in the poem; they are not distinct, but are separable only by analysis; the poet is not writing in language which was first conceptual and then emotionalized, nor in prose which has been metered; he is writing in poetical language. And the rhythm of the poem permeates the entire poem as pervasively as blood permeates the human body: remove it and you have a corpse. It is for this reason that the audible reading of poetry is quite as important as the philosophical understanding of poetry; without audible reading, and adequate audible reading, you simply do not have poetry.

We are thus confronted with the question of what constitutes adequate audible reading. From what I have just said, it should be obvious that adequate audible reading will be reading in which the rhythm of the poem is rendered intact, without the sacrifice of any other element. But what variety of reading will best achieve this end, and what are some of the problems which arise in connection with it?

Since I am defending an unpopular cause, I 'shall not scruple to avail myself of eminent support. In looking over the *Selected Writings* of Paul Valéry recently issued by New Directions, I found Valéry writing as follows:

> . . . in studying a piece of poetry one intends to recite, one should not take as source or point of departure ordinary conversation and common parlance, in order to rise from this level of prose to the desired poetic tone: but, on the contrary, I thought one should take song as a base, and should put oneself in the state of a singer; adjust one's voice to the plenitude of musical sound and from there descend to the somewhat less resonant state suitable to verse. This, it seemed to me, was the only way to preserve the musical essence of poems. Above all, the voice must be placed quite away from prose, and the text studied from the point of view of necessary attack, modulation, sustained tone, little by little, lowering this musical disposition, which in the beginning one has exaggerated, to bring it down to the proportions of poetry . . . above all do not be in a hurry to arrive at the meaning. Approach it without effort and, as it were, insensibly. And only in or by means of the music attain to tenderness or to violence. . . . Remain in this pure musical state until such time as the meaning, appearing little by little, can no longer mar the musical form. You will introduce it at the end as the supreme nuance that will transfigure the passage without altering it.[1]

This appears to be a plea for a restrained but formal chant, in which a sustained tone and movement will serve as an impersonal but definite base for subtle variation. It is only by such a reading, for example, that *Le Cimetière Marin* can be rendered; it is only by a man who so read that such a poem could have been written.

A poem in the very nature of the case is a formal statement; and the reading of a poem is thus a formal occasion. A poem is not conversation; neither is it drama. Conversation is in general the least premeditated and least rhythmical of human utterance; and it depends very heavily upon intonations and even gestures and facial expressions which are not at the disposal of the poet. Dramatic speech is merely more or less formalized conversation. Dramatic poetry, of course, presents a special problem, and one with which I shall not at present concern myself, though it is closer to the kind of poetry with which I am dealing than it is to dramatic prose, and I agree with Valéry that it is commonly botched by the actors. I have never witnessed a performance of Shakespeare without more of pain than of profit or of pleasure. I have been repeatedly reminded of a story told by W. B. Yeats of the great Shakespearian actor of whom it was said that he read Shakespeare so beautifully that no one could tell it was poetry. In general I think the world would be well enough off without actors: they appear to be capable of any of three feats—of making the grossly vulgar appear acceptably mediocre; of making the acceptably mediocre appear what it is; and of making the distinguished appear acceptably mediocre. In any event, they cannot read poetry, for they try to make it appear to be something else, something, in brief, which they themselves can understand.

A poem calls for a formal reading, partly because the poem itself is of its own nature a formal statement, and partly because only such a reading will render the rhythm with precision. Furthermore, it is only with a formal tone as a basis that variations of tone within the poem can be rendered with precision: without such a formal tone to unify the poem, the poem becomes merely a loose assortment of details. The situation here is precisely analogous to that which I have described elsewhere[2] with regard to rhythm and meter: the firmer the metric structure, the more precise can be the rhythmic variations, and the greater the effect obtainable with a very slight variation; whereas if the structure is loose the variations lack significance.

A formal reading which avoids dramatic declamation will necessarily take on something of the nature of a chant. This kind of reading itself has dangers, however, for the reader may carry the procedure so far as to appear precious, and worse, he may deform syllables in the interests of what he considers musical intonation, much as a musical composer will draw syllables out or hurry over them in setting a poem to music. I never heard the late W. B. Yeats read aloud, but I have been told that he was guilty of both of these vices: if it is true that he was guilty of them, one has some reason to suspect that he never properly heard his own poems, a fact which may have been responsible for a number of curious rhythmical mishaps which are scattered through his works. A poem should, on the contrary, be conceived as having a movement of its own, an autonomous movement, which should be rendered as purely and as impersonally as possible. The reader has no more right to revise the rhythms in the interest of what he considers an effective presentation than he has a right to revise any other aspects of the language. The poem, once set in motion, should appear to move of its own momentum.

A more or less recent poet who went farther than any other has gone in deforming the inherent rhythmic elements in our language and so rendering the structure of his poems indecipherable is Gerard Manley Hopkins. Hopkins held a theory of dramatic or declamatory reading, and I suspect from a few passages in his prose that he combined this with a theory of musical intonation. Hopkins was an eccentric and extremely egoistic man, and he worked in isolation. He apparently failed to realize that his own dramatic and musical deformations of language were not based on universal principles but were purely private. As a result one can often be only dumfounded when he indicates his intentions by metrical signs, and one can often be only baffled when he fails to do so. In *Spelt from Sibyl's Leaves,* for example, Hopkins uses an extremely long line, which, if it is read with normal accentuation, produces the effect of a loosely irregular but still readable verse. He does not provide us with many accent marks until he is about halfway through the poem; from there on he provides marks in abundance, frequently with strange results. The last two lines will serve as illustration:

> But thése two; wáre of a wórld where bút these / twó tell, each off the óther; of a rack
> Where, selfwrung, selfstrung, sheathe- and shelterless, / thoughts against thoughts in groans grind.

We have here a kind of bad writing which is purely the result of bad reading; and even the best reading, if superimposed upon what the poet offers, can salvage the poem but very imperfectly.

In T. S. Eliot's reading of *The Waste Land,* as we have it on the recordings issued by The Library of Congress, we have another kind of dramatic reading, and conceivably a relationship between the way of reading and the way of writing. In those portions which exhibit a more or less definite rhythmic structure—for example, in *Death by Water*—Eliot reads more or less in the fashion which I am recommending, with a minimum of dramatic improvement on the text, and with a maximum of attention to movement. But in those portions of the poem—and they are the greater part of it—in which the rhythm does not cohere, in which the poem tends to fall apart in sandy fragments, Eliot reads dramatically; he does this with a good deal of skill, but most of what he puts into his voice is not in the poem—he descends to the practice of the actor who is salvaging a weak text. It would be interesting to know whether Eliot devised this mode of reading in order to rescue a weak poem, or whether the weak poem resulted in part from his having come gradually to employ such a mode of reading, so that he tended to see in his text as he was composing it something which he was not actually getting down on paper. This latter procedure in any event probably accounts for a good deal of the unrealized poetry of our time. For example, Randall Jarrell's reading of his poem *Lady Bates*, in The Library of Congress series, is very dramatic, very emotional, and very bad: I am unable to hear it without the conviction that Jarrell felt his emotions about his subject so readily and so uncritically that he did not trouble himself to write the poem. The poem itself is formless and dull.

The dependence upon superimposed rhythms or other effects which we get in a grotesque form in some of Hopkins and in a more skillful form in Eliot's reading of *The Waste Land* can lead to an astonishing degree of imperception on the part of critics (which is merely an impressive way of saying on the part of readers). In the volume entitled *Gerard Manley Hopkins,* by the Kenyon Critics, Mr. Harold Whitehall informs us that from about the year 1300 English poetry has become less and less amenable to being read aloud, because less and less rhythmical. And in another volume on Hopkins, edited by Norman Weyand, S.J., and written by a group of Jesuits, a volume entitled *Immortal Diamond,* Walter J. Ong arrives at similar conclusions. Both of these writers believe that there is no real rhythm without heavy stress; both believe that meter is based on declamatory rather than mechanical stress. Ong gives us no clue as to how we are to recognize our stressed syllables, and he fails to explain how Hopkins arrived at any of the stresses which he marked. Whitehall gives us his own system of stressing Hopkins, but it is quite as arbitrary as that of Hopkins, and when Whitehall's marked passages are finished we are left with no means of proceeding. Ong, convinced that there is no fine rhythm without heavy and obvious stress, is oblivious of the sensitivity of Sidney and the post-Sidneyan metrists, and equally of the structural principles of their verse; and his concept of reading aloud is indicated by the following passage: "If the poem calls for shouting, the shouting need not be kept imaginary for fear the beat of the rhythm will go. Shout, declaim, and you will only have thrust this rhythm home. So, too, if the shout should need to die to a whisper. . . ." This clerical type of rendition strikes me as about equally impractical, insensitive, and indecorous.

Nevertheless, rhetorical stress has a certain relationship to the structure of meter, but it is not the relationship sought by Hopkins. As I have already said, the language does not divide itself evenly into accented and unaccented syllables, but there is almost infinite variation in degrees of accent. For this reason, the basic rule of English scansion is this: that the accented syllable can be determined only in relationship to the other syllable or syllables within the same foot. The accented syllable of a given foot, as we shall eventually see, may be one of the lightest syllables in its line. But with this rule as a reservation, we may go on to say that poetic meter must be constructed out of the inherent (or mechanical) accentual materials of the language, so that the accented syllable of a foot will be naturally heavier than the unaccented; and if the poet desires to indicate a rhetorical stress he should do it by a metrical stress, or if he is using two syllables either of which might receive heavier stress than the other, then the rhetorical stress should fall where the reader as a result of the previously established pattern will expect the metrical stress.

Keats neglects these considerations in the first line of his last sonnet. The inexpert reader who endeavors to render this line conversationally or dramatically will read it as if he were a sociable lady addressing another sociable lady at a party:

> Bright star,   would *I* were steadfast   as *thou* art,

and the rhythm is destroyed along with the possibility of a proper rhyme. The fault, however, lies largely with Keats. It is natural to stress the two contrasting pronouns somewhat, although one need not carry the stress all the way to the ridiculous. Furthermore, on the first pronoun the metrical stress indicates the rhetorical, so that the two are not in conflict. If we consider the words *would I* in isolation, we shall see that so far as their mechanical properties are concerned, either can be stressed at the expense of the other; however, in this line the stressing of *would* would result in an inverted foot in the second position, and although inversion is possible in this position, it is difficult and generally unlikely, so that we naturally expect the stress to fall on *I,* which likewise is the natural recipient of the rhetorical stress. If we employ the four words *would I were steadfast* in isolation, the stress may fall variously according to our meaning. If we are implying a contrast between steadfastness and our lack of it, the heaviest stress falls on *would;* if we are implying a contrast between steadfastness and another particular quality, a light stress falls on *would* and a heavy on *stead-;* if we are implying a contrast between our own lack of steadfastness and the steadfastness of another, the heavy stress falls on *I,* as in the actual line, but if, as in this line, the comparison is completed, an equal stress should fall on the second pronoun; but since this pronoun also is coupled with a verb which is mechanically its equal and on the basis of its inherent nature could as well take the accent, and since the foot ends the line, and a rhymed line at that, the accent must fall on *art.* This blunder by Keats could scarcely have occurred as a result of his reading poetry in a dramatic fashion, for he understood the structure of English poetry very well, and had he read the line dramatically he would have noticed the error. It probably occurred as a result of his reading with a somewhat mechanical scansion, so that he failed to observe that the meaning was struggling with the meter. One can read it, of course, by means of a more or less evasive glide, but it constitutes an unhappy moment.

One can observe a related difficulty in the sixth line of Wordsworth's sonnet *Upon Westminster Bridge*:

> Ships, towers, domes, theatres, and temples lie.

The first four words of this line are coördinate in grammatical function and in importance, and in ordinary prose the first four syllables would be indistinguishable to the ear in the matter of accent. The average reader, if asked to mark the scansion of this poem, will indicate two spondees at the beginning of the line, but the first two feet are not spondaic—in spite of everything they are iambic. The truly spondaic foot is extremely rare in English; presently I shall have occasion to illustrate it, but for the present I shall merely describe it. It can occur as a variant in iambic verse, only if the accented syllables in the iambic feet are heavily accented and the unaccented are very light, and only if the cesural pause is heavily marked; and these conditions must prevail not merely in the line in question, but throughout much of the poem. The true spondee is a violent aberration—it is a form of what Hopkins calls sprung rhythm—and it is possible only where the rhythm is heavy and obvious. It can be found at least as early as Barnabe Googe and as late as the songbooks of John Dowland, and within these limits it may conceivably be found in as many as thirty poems, but I think it will be difficult to find it elsewhere except in the work of Gerard Hopkins, although something approaching it occurs occasionally in Henry Vaughn. In this sonnet by Wordsworth an extremely smooth iambic movement has been established in the first five lines (so effectively established that it dominates the sixth line) and almost any reader who is aware of rhythm at all will be forced to impose a very light iambic emphasis on the first two feet of the sixth line; to do otherwise will bring the poem apart in ruins. This can be done; but the difficulty indicates a defect in the poem, and a defect again which probably stems from faulty reading on the part of the poet. The difficulty is enhanced by the length of the syllables (a length increased by the commas) and by the all but insufferable series of dentals.

The relationship of rhetorical stress to metrical stress, and hence to reading, would appear, then, to be real, although the relationship can obviously be abused. Perhaps I should conclude the matter by offering these rules for poet and reader alike: (1) There should be no conflict between rhetorical stress and metrical stress, but insofar as it is possible the metrical stress should point the meaning; (2) where the mechanical potentialities of the language indicate the possibility of a stress in either of two directions, the grammatical structure should be so definite that a certain rhetorical stress will be unmistakable and will force the metrical interpretation in the right direction; and (3) the reader should deal with rhetorical stresses with the utmost restraint—he should indicate them as far as the occasion requires, but he should not become enthusiastic, undignified, or unmetrical about them. They are not to be superimposed upon the basic rhythm, nor can the basic rhythm be constructed from them.

I would like next to illustrate the importance of reading, by illustrating certain very marked differences in rhythm which may occur within the limits of the iambic pentameter line. English verse is predominantly iambic in structure, and although this fact has irritated certain poets and stirred them to curious experiments, the fact that so vast a number of eminent poets have found the iambic movement more useful than any other must have some kind of explanation. In the anapestic or dactylic foot the accented syllable must be definitely heavy or the identity of the foot and of the line will disappear, and this necessity makes for monotony and a jingling obviousness:

> I sprang to the stirrup, and Joris, and he;
> I galloped, Dirck galloped, we galloped all three. . . .

The unequivocally trochaic line tends to exhibit some of the same heaviness (as in *Hiawatha,* for example) although the reason for this is less clear. The seven-syllable tetrameter line may be described as trochaic, with a monosyllabic foot in the last position, or as iambic with a monosyllabic foot in the first position; since it is frequently used as a variant on iambic tetrameter, the second classification would seem the better. When this line is used throughout a poem, the poem will be short, or else will become monotonous: the accents again are usually heavy most of the time, and although the meter may be used in a short poem for the purpose of obtaining a didactic or semi-songlike effect, it appears to have few other uses. The iambic movement, however, appears to be natural to the language; it asserts itself easily, and the poet does not have to hammer his accents out to maintain it. This situation allows the poet to vary the degrees of his accents widely, to vary his cesuras, and to employ substitution with a certain freedom. Contrary to the views of Mr. Whitehall and of Father Ong, this type of meter lends itself very well to audible reading, but one must first know how to read. And when well written and well read it is far more flexible and perceptive than any other kind of English verse thus far devised.

My first example is by Barnabe Googe and was written early in the reign of Elizabeth, before the advent of Spenser and Sidney:

> Give money me, take friendship who so list,
> For friends are gone, come once adversity,
> When money yet remaineth safe in chest
> That quickly can thee bring from misery;
> Fair face show friends, when riches do abound,
> Come time of proof, farewell they must away;
> Believe me well, they are not to be found,
> If God but send thee once a lowering day.
> Gold never starts aside, but in distress,
> Finds ways enough to ease thine heaviness.

This poem has certain characteristics which one would expect to find in a period in which the pentameter line was new, when the misunderstandings of Wyatt had been only recently overcome: first of all there are no inverted feet and no trisyllabic feet; secondly the accented syllables are almost all heavy and of nearly the same weight—there are only two feet in the poem in which the accented syllables are noticeably light; thirdly the cesuras are all heavily marked, and in six of the ten lines they fall at the end of the second foot. The poem shows only one type of metrical variation; that is, the use of spondaic feet (or what I have elsewhere called syllabic sprung meter). The introduction of this variation into the newly acquired iambic pentameter line is Googe's principal contribution to the technique of English verse, and it is a contribution of no mean importance. There are two spondees at the beginning of line five; there is one at the beginning of six; there is one at the beginning of nine; and the first foot of the last line may be read with equal success as a spondee or as an iamb. All of these spondees can be forced into the iambic pattern, but they will have to be forced, and the poem will suffer. It is only in a poem such as this one, in which the rhythm is strongly and obviously marked by a great and regular distinction between accented and unaccented syllables that the true spondee can occur; in a smoother and subtler type of structure, such as my next example, two syllables of nearly the same degree of accent will be absorbed into the iambic pattern and will not stand out as approximately equal to each other; furthermore, any attempt to read them as spondees will destroy the movement of the poem.

My next example is from Shakespeare. Before this sonnet was written, Sidney and other early experimenters had rendered the line smoother, more varied, and more subtle:

> When to the sessions of sweet silent thought
> I summon up remembrance of things past,
> I sigh the lack of many a thing I sought,

And with old woes new wail my dear time's waste:
Then can I drown an eye unused to flow,
For precious friends, hid in death's dateless night,
And weep afresh love's long-since-cancelled woe,
And moan th'expense of many a vanish'd sight:
Then can I grieve at grievances foregone,
And heavily from woe to woe tell o'er
The sad account of fore-bemoaned moan
Which I new pay as if not paid before.
    But if the while I think on thee, dear friend,
    All losses are restored and sorrows end.

The position of the cesura in this sonnet is less varied than in the poem by Googe; it falls after the second foot in eleven out of fourteen lines; but the cesura is much less noticeable, partly because it is not emphasized by heavy grammatical breaks, and partly because of other qualities of the rhythm. Aside from this difference in cesural value, the most considerable rhythmic difference between this poem and the poem by Googe resides in the fact that there are great differences in the degrees of accent to be found *among the syllables which count metrically as accented.* It will be remembered that I remarked earlier that the accented syllable can be recognized as such only with reference to the other syllable or syllables within the same foot, for no two syllables bear exactly the same degree of accent: it is this fact which gives the rhythm of the best English verse its extreme sensitivity. But rhythm, in poetry as in music, is controlled variation from an arithmetical norm; and the rhythm ceases to be rhythm, and becomes merely movement, whenever the norm itself is no longer discernible.

I will illustrate what I have been saying by two lines from the sonnet. The scansion of the first line gives us a trochee followed by four iambs. The third foot, however, which is composed of the second syllable of *sessions* followed by the preposition *of* (the accented syllable), is very lightly accented. In the following foot, which is composed of *sweet,* followed by the first syllable of *silent, sweet,* the unaccented syllable, is more heavily stressed than the accented syllable of the preceding foot, so that we have in effect a series of four degrees of accent within two successive feet. Furthermore, if the reader should suffer from the delusion (a common one) that the second of these feet is really a spondee, let him read it the way he is forced to read the true spondees in the poem by Googe, and he will discover that spondaic rhythm is a very different matter from what he has here, and that the attempt to introduce it into this poem will be disastrous. The same thing occurs in the fourth and fifth feet of line nine:

> Then can I grieve at grievances foregone.

It occurs in the first two feet of Bryant's line:

> Where thy pale form was laid with many tears.

It occurs in the last two feet of Ben Jonson's line:

> Drink to me only with thine eyes.

It is, in fact, one of the commonest phenomena in English verse, yet I have seen a good many distinguished scholars and eminent poets interpret it wrongly.

I shall now quote a well-known song from John Dowland's *Second Book of Aires:*

> Fine knacks for ladies, cheap, choice, brave and new!
> > Good pennyworths! but money cannot move.
> I keep a fair but for the fair to view;
> > A beggar may be liberal of love.
> Though all my wares be trash, the heart is true.
>
> Great gifts are guiles and look for gifts again;
> > My trifles come as treasures from my mind.
> It is a precious jewel to be plain;
> > Sometimes in shell the Orient's pearls we find.
> Of others take a sheaf, of me a grain.
>
> Within this pack, pins, points, laces, and gloves,
> > And divers toys, fitting a country fair.
> But my heart lives where duty serves and loves,
> > Turtles and twins, court's brood, a heavenly pair.
> Happy the heart that thinks of no removes.

There are sprung, or spondaic, feet in the first, second, sixth, seventh, eleventh, thirteenth, and fourteenth lines of this poem. These feet represent the same kind of variant which we found in Googe, and for the most part we have the same strongly marked difference between accented and unaccented syllables and similarly strong cesural pauses, even in lines in which no spondees occur. Yet whereas the rhythm of Googe is hard, fast, and didactic, the rhythm of this poem is slower, more complicated, and very songlike. The result is partly due to more spondaic variants than we found in Googe, and to spondaic variants in other positions than the initial ones; it is partly due to the introduction at certain points of the type of line which we found in Shakespeare, such as the following:

It is a precious jewel to be plain,

a line in which the iambic fourth foot, composed of the second syllable of *jewel* and the preposition *to,* is extremely light and short and is followed by a final foot (*be plain*) in which the unaccented syllable is heavier than the accented syllable *to* before it; yet in this last foot the difference between *be* and *plain* is so marked that no one would be tempted to call the foot a spondee.

The author likewise does certain strange and ingenious things with his spondees. The first line, for example, goes as follows:

Fine knacks for ladies, cheap, choice, brave and new!

The first foot is spondaic, the second iambic; the third foot, consisting of the second syllable of *ladies* and of *cheap,* is likewise iambic, but the cesura, reinforced by the comma, in mid-foot, throws the accent onto *cheap* with unusual force, and *cheap* is then followed by the spondaic foot consisting of two syllables which are almost exactly equal to it, and which are likewise set off by commas, so that we have the illusion of a foot consisting of three accented syllables, or an English molossus. The author does something similar but almost more adventurous in the eleventh line, where the heavily iambic foot *this pack* is followed by the heavy spondee *pins, points,* which in turn is followed by the heavily inverted foot, *laces,* with the result that we get four strong accents in sequence, though only one spondee. Technically, this is one of the most brilliant poems in the language. Dowland (or his unknown poet) learned what he could from Googe and improved upon it; and he complicated the method (without destroying it—a difficult feat) by rhythms acquired from the refiners of the intervening period.

I shall now show the use of different types of iambic pentameter rhythm employed in a regular pattern. To do this, I shall employ a song by Campion. The song rhymes in couplets. The metric pattern begins with two lines of what one might call the primitive type, with heavy stresses and heavy cesuras, but with no spondees: in these two lines the first and third feet are inverted, the rest iambic, and the cesura falls after the second foot. The third and fifth lines are evenly iambic and are less heavily stressed, and the cesuras in these lines occur in different positions and are so light as to be all but imperceptible. The fourth and sixth lines are of the same type of iambic movement as the last lines mentioned, but contain seven feet instead of five.

There are two stanzas, and the pattern in the two is as nearly identical as the inescapable variations of language permit:

Follow your saint, follow with accents sweet!
Haste you, sad notes, fall at her flying feet!
There, wrapt in cloud of sorrow, pity move,
And tell the ravisher of my soul I perish for her love:
But if she scorns my never ceasing pain,
Then burst with sighing in her sight, and ne'er return again.

All that I sung still to her praise did tend;
Still she was first, still she my songs did end;
Yet she my love and music both doth fly,
The music that her echo is and beauty's sympathy:
Then let my notes pursue her scornful flight!
It shall suffice that they were breathed and died for her delight.

I shall now quote a sonnet by Gerard Hopkins, which is basically iambic pentameter, but which employs every conceivable variant. I have marked and described the scansion of this sonnet in my essay on Hopkins, and at this time I shall make only a few general remarks about the structure. The poem contains iambic feet, trochees, spondees, one molossus (a foot of three accented syllables), monosyllabic feet, trisyllabic feet of one accent each, and one or two feet which must be considered either as containing more than three syllables or else as containing syllables which are extrametrical or elided. The poem is successful as regards structure and rhythm, and it offers a rhythmic departure from the norm about as extreme as anyone is likely to achieve:

No worst, there is none. Pitched past pitch of grief,
More pangs will, schooled at forepangs, wilder wring.
Comforter, where, where is your comforting?
Mary, mother of us, where is your relief?
My cries heave, herds-long; huddle in a main, a chief
Woe, world sorrow; on an age-old anvil wince and sing—
Then lull, then leave off. Fury had shrieked 'No ling-
ering! Let me be fell: force I must be brief.'

O the mind, mind has mountains; cliffs of fall
Frightful, sheer, no-man-fathomed. Hold them cheap
May who ne'er hung there. Nor does long our small
Durance deal with that steep or deep. Here! creep,

> Wretch under a comfort serves in a whirlwind: all
> Life death does end and each day dies with sleep.

By the use of five short poems I have indicated a number of widely varying rhythms all of which are measured by iambic pentameter. So far as meter and rhythm are concerned all five are masterpieces; and in spite of any faults which may be found in them with regard to other matters, all five are brilliant poems and should be part of the literary experience of any man using the English language. Yet not one of these poems amounts to anything if its rhythm is not rendered with great precision; to read the poem so that its rhythm does not emerge in its totality and in every detail is to reduce the poem to lifeless fragments. You cannot buy expert readings of these poems on disks, as you can buy expert renderings of Bach and Mozart; nor can you go to a concert and hear them—every man is his own performer. It is important, therefore, that one read properly. But to read properly one must understand the principles both of English meter and of English rhythm, and not in a haphazard manner, but precisely; and one must understand the use of one's own voice; and after that one must practice.

I am at a disadvantage in dealing with a subject of this kind before an audience whom I cannot reach with my voice, for I cannot demonstrate, but am forced to try to describe. The nearest thing to a demonstration that I can offer is my reading of my own poems in the Library of Congress series. I do not consider myself a finished performer, nor, I think, are these readings the best of which I am capable. But they are all I can offer, and they will serve to indicate the method in a general way.

I have been told that this method of reading makes all poems sound alike, but this can be true only for those persons to whom all poems sound alike in any event, or for whom essential differences are meaningless. The virtue of the method, on the contrary, is that it gives each poem its precise identity, and no other method will do this. If this precise identity does not interest you, then you are not interested in poetry and you will in all likelihood never discover poetry. Some time ago, when I was defending this method of reading in public, a well-known scholar objected to my theories with a good deal of indignation, and he objected especially to my reading of the Dowland poem which I have quoted in these pages. He said that it was a street song, or peddler's song, and should be rendered as such. I do not know exactly how Elizabethan street songs were rendered, and I do not believe that he knew; but any attempt so to render it would be, I am sure, unfortunate, even if one had the necessary information. The poem is not a street song; it is a poem on love and on the art of poetry and on a relationship between the two, and it is one of the most deeply serious and deeply moving short poems in the Elizabethan period—the peddler is purely metaphorical, and his part in the poem is both indicated and formalized by the metrical structure and it should remain formal and no more than indicated in the reading. If the poet refers by way of metaphor to a cow, the reader is not, I trust, expected to moo. I refer the reader back to my quotations from Valéry, especially the last sentence. Of the "meaning" of the poem he says: "You will introduce it at the end as the supreme nuance that will transfigure the poem without altering it." By "the end," he means the end of the process of studying the poem and arriving at the proper rendering.

Bad reading and bad (or no) training in metrical theory are largely to blame, I believe, for the insensitive literary judgments by many critics who in other matters are very brilliant, and they are to blame also for a fair amount of bad academic work in literature. At Stanford University, at this writing, we have over one hundred graduate students in English, and about half of these are candidates for the doctorate. We are in a position to select our graduate students very carefully. We accept none who have not made excellent records here or elsewhere, and although some come to us from the smaller institutions (and incidentally some of our best), many come from places like Yale, Harvard, Chicago, Columbia, Princeton, and the better state universities. These people have made excellent records in the past, and most of them make excellent records here; yet almost none can read a line of poetry aloud so that one can discern the structure, and very few can mark the scansion from a line of Shakespeare's sonnets. These people are in these respects the products of their teaching, and the teaching should be improved. Most of our best critics and many of our best-known poets are not much better off. We have sunk into amateurism; and as a result we have in our time the meters of Eliot and of his imitators at the fifth remove, instead of meters comparable to those of the Elizabethans. And we have, worse still, a coherent (and fairly vocal) body of readers so ignorant that they prefer the incompetent to the expert.

If you answer that there are different kinds of poetry and hence we have different kinds of reading (this, of course, is the genteel answer which points to my lack of gentility), I am bound to reply that you are right: there are inferior kinds of poetry. By "inferior," I mean inferior in quality, not smaller in scope. The kind of reading which I defend is equally appropriate to a song by Campion or to an epic by Milton. Any poem which cannot endure the impersonal illumination of such a reading or which requires the assistance, whether expert or clumsy, of shouting, whispering, or other dramatic improvement, is to that extent bad poetry, though it may or may not be a good scenario for a vaudeville performance.

There will never be a first-rate poet or a first-rate critic who lacks a first-rate ear; and no one will ever acquire a first-rate ear without working for it and in the proper manner. Poetry, alas, like painting and music, is an art—it is not a form of happy self-indulgence; and to master an art or even understand it, one has to labor with all of one's mind and with at least a part of one's body.

NOTES

[1.]*Extracts from "A Discourse on the Declamation of Verse,"* by Paul Valéry, translated by Louise Varese. *Paul Valéry, Selected Writings,* New Directions, 1950.

[2.]"The Influence of Meter on Poetic Convention," in *Primitivism and Decadence,* the essay on John Crowe Ransom, Section IX, in *The Anatomy of Nonsense,* both reprinted in *In Defense of Reason,* Alan Swallow, 1947.

W. K. WIMSATT
AND MONROE C. BEARDSLEY

The Concept of Meter:
An Exercise in Abstraction

In this classic statement Professors Wimsatt and Beardsley argue for the traditional graphic scansion of English syllable-stress meter. They speak critically of what they call "deviations from good sense in metrics." Chief among the metrical deviationists are the structural linguists and the musical scanners. The fundamental error of the linguist is to neglect the abstract, two-valued metrical pattern in favor of emphasizing such less normative features as the stress-pitch-juncture patterns of English speech. The musical scanner (to put it briefly and over-simply) does not scan the meters but urges a preconceived musical notation on poetry; or worse yet, writes a score for a particular performance of the poem. Both Professors Wimsatt and Beardsley have somewhat softened their position vis-à-vis the linguists and musical scanners. Professor Wimsatt has, with qualifications, conceded that the linguistic theory of Halle and Keyser "asks the right kind of questions about the nature of a meter, and in my opinion gives some very good answers. . . ." Professor Beardsley, in his suggestive essay "Verse and Music," allows that musical notation can prove useful in scanning strong-stress meter, and that the arguments for the existence of isochronism in English verse (and prose) merit reexamination.

Wimsatt and Beardsley also accept the principle of relative stress. Meter is generated not by any scientifically measurable alternation of stress, but by the overall abstract pattern: this pattern need only be

This essay appeared originally in *PMLA*, LXXIV (1959). From *Hateful Contraries*, by W. K. Wimsatt. Copyright © 1965 by the University of Kentucky Press and used with their permission.

approximately maintained to be recognized. Wimsatt and Beardsley stress the paradigmatic nature of meter; as an element in poetic form, it is capable of precise abstraction. "You can write a grammar of the meter. And if you cannot, there is no meter."

I

Let us first of all confess that we do not have a novel view to proclaim. It is true that the view which we believe to be correct is often under attack today and is sometimes supposed to be outmoded by recent refinements. Its proponents too are often not sure enough of its actual character to defend it with accuracy. At the same time, a look into some of the most recent handbooks and critical essays reveals that there are some teachers and writers on our subject today who expound this view in a perfectly clear and accurate way. We have in mind, for instance, *A Glossary of Literary Terms* revised by Meyer Abrams for Rinehart in 1957 from the earlier work by Norton and Rushton, or the handbook by Laurence Perrine, *Sound and Sense: An Introduction to Poetry,* published in 1956 by Harcourt, Brace. In the lengthy *Kenyon Review* symposium on English verse, Summer 1956,[1] we admire the niceties of Mr. Arnold Stein's traditionally oriented discussion of Donne and Milton. There is also Mr. Stein's earlier *PMLA* article (LIX [1944], 393–97) on "Donne's Prosody." In the *Kenyon* symposium there is, furthermore, Mr. Ransom. It would be difficult to frame a more politely telling, persuasive, accurate retort than his to the more extravagant claims of the linguists.

We are, therefore, in a position to do no more than take sides in a debate which is already well defined. Still this may be worth doing. Our aim is to state as precisely as we can just what the traditional English syllable-accent meter is or depends upon, to rehearse a few more reasons in its support, perhaps to disembarrass it of some of the burdens that are nowadays needlessly contrived for it.

II

This essay is about the scanning of English verse. We want to consider two influential current schools of thought about scanning, and to examine critically a fundamental mistake which we believe is made by both of them, though in different ways. These two deviations from what we consider good sense in metrics may be conveniently designated as on the one hand the linguistic and on the other the musical or temporal. The linguistic view, as it happens, has been authoritatively illustrated in the contributions to the *Kenyon* symposium of 1956 by Harold Whitehall and Seymour Chatman. The musical view has been very well represented in the more recent volume *Sound and Poetry, English Institute Essays 1956,* and especially in its introductory essay "Lexis and Melos," by the editor, Northrop Frye—and no less in the same writer's larger book *Anatomy of Criticism,* published at Princeton in 1957.

Mr. Whitehall gives us an admirable summary of the linguistic system of George L. Trager and Henry Lee Smith, in part a reprint of his 1951 *Kenyon* review of their treatise, *An Outline of English Structure* (1951). But his essay is more than a summary; it is a celebration. Indeed it makes a very large claim for what this system can contribute to the modern study of metrics:

> as no science can go beyond mathematics, no criticism can go beyond its linguistics. And the kind of linguistics needed by recent criticism for the solution of its pressing problems of metrics and stylistics, in fact, for all problems of the linguistic surface of letters, is not semantics, either epistemological or communicative, but down-to-the-surface linguistics, microlinguistics not metalinguistics. (*Kenyon Review,* XVIII, 415)

To Mr. Chatman falls the pioneer task of showing how these extraordinary claims are to be substantiated. He presents us with a careful and interesting analysis of eight tape-recorded readings of a short poem by Robert Frost, one of the readers being Frost himself. Mr. Chatman's essay is full of passages of good sense. Still we have some objections to urge against him: the gist of these is that through his desire to exhibit the stress-pitch-juncture elements in spoken English, he shows an insufficient concern for the normative fact of the poem's meter. It is true that he does not deny that the poem has an "abstract metrical pattern," and he acknowledges the "two-valued metrics of alternating stresses" (p. 422). But in his actual readings these seem to be of little interest.

We are not quite sure we understand Mr. Chatman's idea of the relation between meter and Trager-Smith linguistics. One subheading of his essay, "Prosody and Meaning Resolution," probably ought to read "Intonation and Meaning Resolution." ("An 'intonation pattern'," let us note well, "is an amalgam of features of stress, pitch, and juncture which occurs as part of a spoken phrase."—p. 422) Mr. Chatman has learned from Frost's reading of his poem the correct intonation and meaning of the phrase "scared a bright green snake." Very well. Correct understanding *produces* correct intonation, and correct intonation *reveals* correct understanding. And one may choose or may not choose to indicate the intonation by Trager-Smith notation. And this intonation (whether indicated by Trager-Smith notation or not) may or may not affect the meter in the given instance. In this instance there is nothing to show that what Mr. Chatman learned about the intonation did change the meter. The same observations hold for Mr. Chatman's discovery of the meaning and intonation of the concluding phrase of the poem, "and left the hay to make." Through recorded readings of a poem Mr. Chatman learns something that another person might know through boyhood experience on a farm, or through a footnote. But again no need for Trager-Smith. And no change in meter. The point is brought out even more clearly in another recent article by Mr. Chatman, in the *Quarterly Journal of Speech*. He makes a shrewd observation about a passage in Spenser's *Faerie Queene* (I.ii.13. 4-5): "And like a Persian mitre on her head / She wore. . . ." "We must," he says, "resist the temptation to read *And líke a Pérsian mítre.*" The obvious meaning is rather: "Like a Persian, she wore. . . ."[2] Quite true. One stresses *Persian* a little more strongly, one pauses between *Persian* and *mitre*. But there is no change in meter, and no change in intonation that an old-fashioned comma will not provide for.

One of the good things about Mr. Chatman's *Kenyon* contribution is that, like Victor Erlich, whose *Russian Formalism* (1955) he aptly quotes (p. 438), Mr. Chatman prefers a "phonemic" analysis to the now somewhat old-fashioned total "acoustic" way of trying to study either language or metrics. (Phonemic differences, we can never remind ourselves too often, are those that make a real difference in the structure of a language, like the difference between *d* and *t* in English, rather than the difference between your pronunciation of *t* and mine.) Phonetic studies, observes Mr. Chatman, "before the discovery of the phonemic principle," were not really getting anywhere with the understanding of language. "It is unfortunately a truism that one cannot get more structure out of a machine than one puts in" (p. 422). We hold that for metrical study it is indeed necessary to remember the phonemic principle—in the broadest sense, the principle of linguistic significance in phonetic difference. But it is also necessary, while we work within that principle, to practice an even further degree of abstraction. Not just all or any phonemic features—not all or any intonational features—but a certain level of these is organized by the poet to make a metrical pattern.

Let us turn for a moment to our other authority and point of departure for the present argument, Northrop Frye. Mr. Frye's chief emphasis, both in his English Institute essay and in his *Anatomy,* is on the similarity or continuity between the pentameter line of Milton or Shakespeare and the older (and newer) English strong-stress meter, *Piers Plowman, Everyman, Christabel, The Cocktail Party.* "A four-stress line," he says, "seems to be inherent in the structure of the English language" (*Anatomy,* p. 251; cp. *Sound and Poetry,* pp. xvii, xx). It is true that Mr. Frye does not identify the four-stress pattern of the pentameter line with its meter; he clearly thinks of the "stress" pattern and the "meter" as two different things; for example, in a reading of Hamlet's soliloquy, "the old four-stress line stands out in clear relief against the metrical background" (*Anatomy,* p. 251). Nevertheless, it is also apparent from his neglect of any specific discussion of "meter" that he attaches little importance to it; he does not seem to believe that it has much to do with what he calls, in his special sense, the "music" of poetry. "To read poetry which is musical in our sense we need a principle of accentual scansion, a regular recurrence of beats with a variable number of syllables between the beats. This corresponds to the general rhythm of the music in the Western tradition, where there is a regular stress accent with a variable number of notes in each measure" (*Sound and Poetry,* p. xvii). Rather than object more emphatically to Mr. Frye's views at this point, we allow our difference from him to emerge, as we go along, in later parts of our essay.

Let us round out our preliminary account of strong-stress rhythm by a return to Mr. Whitehall. Mr. Whitehall is much impressed by Kenneth L. Pike's principle (e.g., *The Intonation of American English* [Ann Arbor, 1945], p. 34) that in English "the time-lapse between any two primary stresses tends to be the same irrespective of the number of syllables and the junctures between them" (*Kenyon Review,* XVIII, 418). Mr. Whitehall distinguishes a type of "rhythm" which he calls the *isochronic*: it "depends on equal time-lapses between primary stresses" (p. 420). And he finds in a line of Gray's *Elegy* three "primary stresses" and hence three isochronic sequences of syllables. It is not wholly clear whether the term "rhythm," as Mr. Whitehall uses it, embraces, excludes, or nullifies the concept of "meter," for Mr. Whitehall eschews the latter term. But when we consider his other technical terms, we can assemble a view very much like that of Mr. Frye. He speaks of *syllabic* "rhythms" (p. 420) and among these the *isoaccentual,* and he says that in Pope's *Essay on Man* there is "undoubtedly isoaccentual counterpointed with isochronic rhythm," while "in much of Milton" there is "isochronic counterpointed with isoaccentual rhythm." The nature of Mr. Whitehall's "prosodic" observations might be made clearer if we were to substitute for one of his terms an apparent synonym: for "isoaccentual rhythm" read "meter," i.e., syllable-stress meter of the English pentameter tradition, Chaucer to Tennyson. In Pope and Milton there is both syllable-stress *meter* and an occasional pattern of strong stresses which can, if one wishes, be taken as a moment of the older strong-stress *meter.*

Again: when Mr. Whitehall speaks of "isoaccentual" rhythms, and when he speaks of "isosyntactic" rhythms, he is talking about ascertainable linguistic features, and hence about ascertainable and definable metric patterns. But when he adds that "the other type [of nonsyllabic rhythm] is isochronic," he has slipped into another gear. This term is not on all fours with the others. Isochronism, observes Mr. Whitehall himself on an earlier page, is "not mentioned in the [Trager-Smith] *Outline*"; it is "not directly a significant part of the English linguistic structure" (p. 418). It is something which may or may not occur in correct English speech.

At the same time, let us observe that if isochronism *were* a general principle, or even an approximate principle, of all English speech, it would clearly be a different thing from meter. It would not serve to distinguish the metrical from the nonmetrical. Isochronism, according to the Pike theory, is not a special feat of language, managed by the poet, but a common feature of language. So long as a poet's lines had some strong stresses, and they always must have, the isochronism would take care of itself. In the actual English meters of the poets, even in the old strong-stress *Beowulf* and *Piers Plowman* meter, something quite determinate and special always *is* added: an approximately equal number of weaker syllables between the strong stresses, "configurational" heightening of the stresses, as by alliteration, and the syntactic entity of the lines and half-lines.

III

Some, though perhaps not all, of those who approach the sound of poetry from the two viewpoints we are here debating will want to reply to our argument by saying that we have lost sight of the primary poetic fact, which, they will say, is always this or that reading of a poem out loud—as by the bard with a harp, by the modern author for a tape-recording, or by actors on a stage. What our argument takes as the object of scansion will be referred to disrespectfully as a mere skeleton of the real poem. Mr. Chatman, for example, "attempts to describe the verse line as it is actually 'performed'." And he likes the Trager-Smith system because it "demands a comparison between actual oral performances of poetry and traditional meters." "It incorporates both formula and performance" (p. 423). Let it be so. Let the difference between our view and that of the linguistic recorders be something of that sort.

There is, of course, a sense in which the reading of the poem is primary: this is what the poem is *for*. But there is another and equally important sense in which the poem is not to be identified with any particular performance of it, or any set of such performances. Each performance of the poem is an actualization of it, and no doubt in the end everything we say about the poem ought to be translatable into a statement about an actual or possible performance of it. But not everything which is true of some particular performance will be necessarily true of the poem. There are many performances of the same poem—differing among themselves in many ways. A performance is an event, but the poem itself, if there *is* any poem, must be some kind of enduring object. (No doubt we encounter here a difficult ontological question; we are not inclined to argue it. It seems necessary only to expose the fundamental assumption which we take to be inevitable for any discussion of "meter.") When we ask what the meter of a poem is, we are not asking how Robert Frost or Professor X reads the poem, with all the features peculiar to that performance. We are asking about the poem as a public linguistic object, something that can be examined by various persons, studied, disputed—univocally.

The meter, like the rest of the language, is something that can be read and studied with the help of grammars and dictionaries and other linguistic guides. In this objective study, Trager-Smith principles, for instance, may be largely helpful. At the same time they may be in excess of any strictly metrical need. For the meter is something which for the most part inheres in language precisely at that level of linguistic organization which grammars and dictionaries and elementary rhetoric can successfully cope with. So far as Trager-Smith is a refinement on traditional ways of indicating intonation patterns (by punctuation, by diacritical marks, by spelling and word separation), Trager-Smith may well be a help to saying something about meter. On the other hand, it may well become only a needless fussiness of symbols by which somebody tries to be scientific about the ever-present, the ever-different disparities and tensions between formal meter and the linguistic totality. Our argument is not specifically against Trager-Smith, but against certain ways of combining Trager-Smith with multiple readings. It is interesting to study the tape-recording of various performances of Frost's "Mowing." But we must not let this mass of data blind us to the possibility that some of our readers have failed to get the meter right.

In the same way we argue against the temporal theorists, the timers. In the broadest sense, we define their theory as one which says that meter either consists wholly in, or has as an essential feature, some principle of recurrence in equal, or approximately equal, times—analogous to musical pulse. And we respond, in brief, that meter must be a character of the poem, but that timing is a character of performance: what is done or can be done by a reader, a chanter, or a singer. Mr. John Hollander, in a recent article ("The Music of Poetry," *Journal of Aesthetics and Art Criticism,* XV [1956], 232–44), has warned us against confusing a "descriptive" with a "performative" system of prosody. This is just what the timers have done since the beginning. Reciting poetry in equal times is a matter related to music, and there is no question that music can be imposed on verse—very readily on some verse—and that here and there in the history of poetic recitation music has been invoked to fill out what the meter did not do—where in effect the meter was insufficient. But the musician or the musicologist who comes in to perform these services or to point out their possibility ought to remember what he is doing.

Discussion of English meters seems to have been badly misled for a long time now by a prevalent supposition that the two main alternative, or complementary, principles of English meter are time and stress. Karl Shapiro's handy guide to modern English metrical theory (*A Bibliography of Modern Prosody*, 1948) reports that this is indeed the major split in the whole field of English metrical theory (of which the two great champions are Lanier for the timers and Saintsbury for the stressers), and Mr. Shapiro himself seems to welcome this alignment and to consider it more or less correct and inevitable. But the two main alternative principles of English meter, as we shall argue more in detail a little later, are actually two kinds of stress—strong stress (the Old English, the *Piers Plowman* tradition) and syllable stress (the Chaucer-Tennyson tradition). The difficulty of describing the difference between these kinds of stress meter and their occasional difficult relations with each other account in part for the experiments of the temporal theory.

The basic arguments against the temporal theories of English meter are now almost universally accepted so far as one main branch of these theories is concerned, namely, the "quantitative"—the theory of long and short *syllables,* on the classical analogy. The history of English prosody affords the futile instances of the Elizabethan "Areopagus" and in the eighteenth and nineteenth centuries the luxuriance of theories described in T. S. Omond's sympathetic *English Metrists* (1921). So far as the Greek and Latin patterns of long and short (dactylic hexameters, sapphics, hendecasyllabics, or the like) have been *successfully* reillustrated in English, this has been done on strictly accentual (plus syllable-counting) principles:

> This is the forest primeval. The murmuring pines and
>   the hemlocks . . .

> Needy Knife-grinder! whither are you going?
> Rough is the road, your wheel is out of order—
> Bleak blows the blast;—your hat has got a hole in't,
>   So have your breeches.

> O you chorus of indolent reviewers,
> Irresponsible, indolent reviewers. . . .

Syllables, number of syllables, and stresses, primary, secondary, and weak, are linguistic features which you can find in the English dictionary. But long and short syllables are not found in the English dictionary. Some syllables are, of course, often, perhaps nearly always, spoken more rapidly than others. But the length of the syllable is not a part of correctness or incorrectness in speaking English. Quantity, so far as it appears in any determinate way, more or less rides along with stress. We can drag or clip the syllables of English words, and we may sound odd, affected, or funny, but still we shall not be *mis*pronouncing our words, or changing their meaning. Quantity is a dimension where you cannot make mistakes in pronouncing English. And where you cannot make mistakes, you cannot be right, as opposed to wrong. It follows that in such a dimension a writer in English cannot create a public pattern. The English language will not permit a quantitative meter.

It would seem, however, that some kind of quantitative assumption must inevitably reappear (or be added to the linguistic facts) whenever the other main kind of temporal theory, the "isochronic," is applied in an actual scansion of lines of English verse. Syllables which in themselves may be recognized as having no correct quantity, either long or short, now have quantity conferred on them by crowding or jamming ("accelerating and crushing together"—Mr. Whitehall's terms) or by stretching, to meet the demands of the isochronic assumption. This kind of processing or adjustment of syllables is taken as a justification for, and is symbolized by, the use of musical notation, and such notation is sometimes called "scansion."

Let us ask the question whether it is *actually the case* that readers of poetry always, or even generally, do perform their readings isochronically.[3] (That this *can* be done, by a sufficiently skilful, or a sufficiently musical, reader no one of course denies.) It may be that we have here to acknowledge a distinction between two rather different kinds of verse. Perhaps it *is* true that nursery rhymes and ballads, at least some ballads, are usually, and normally, and even *best*, read with an approximation to isochronism. (This may have something to do with their origin in close connection with music.) The most convincing examples of musical notation produced by the equal-timing prosodists are in this area: "Mary, Mary,"—"O what is that sound that so thrills the ear?"—"It was 'Din! Din! Din!'" But then a Shakespeare sonnet or *Paradise Lost* or a lyric by A. E. Housman is a very different kind of thing.

When a poem is set to music, definite values have to be assigned to its notes and rests, and consequently to its measures and phrases. And however this is done, we are introducing an extralinguistic element, a precision of timing that does not belong to the linguistic elements, the words and syllables, as such. Consider, for example, the opening of Ralph Vaughan Williams' setting of a Housman poem:

Thus we make "on" twice as long as "Wen-," or "Edge" three times as long as "wood's." For another good example, compare a normal *reading* of Edith Sitwell's poems in *Façade* with the way she recites them to the accompaniment of William Walton's music.

Both printed words and printed musical score are prescriptions, or directions, for performance. Our point is that they are different prescriptions—perhaps complementary and cooperating, but still different and independent. One, the musical score, is not an explication or explanation (like diacritical marks) of the other, the words, but an addition to it.[4]

Music—or at least music with bar-lines, which is all we are concerned with here—is precisely a time-measuring notation; it divides the time into equal intervals and prescribes a felt underlying "pulse."[5] It calls for the metronome or the tapping foot. If we ourselves wish to add to the poet's notation our own rhythmic pattern, say

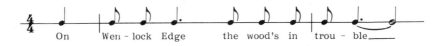

we are not scanning the verse, but either reporting on the way one reader performed it or else recommending that others perform it this way. Thus, Mr. Frye gives the following analysis of a line from Meredith's *Love in the Valley* (*Anatomy,* p. 254):

But another reader might, with equal plausibility, read it this way:

Meter involves measurement, no doubt, or it can hardly with much meaning be called "meter." But all measurement is not necessarily temporal measurement—even when the things measured occur in a temporal succession. If a person walks along the street hitting every third paling in a fence, he sets up a pattern, but he may or he may not do this in equal lengths of time. Better still, let every third paling be painted red, and we have a pattern which our person does not have to set up for himself but can observe objectively. He will observe or experience this pattern in time, but not necessarily in equal lengths of time. In either case, that of striking or that of simply seeing, we may further suppose the palings for some reason to be spaced along the fence at irregular intervals. Musical meter is a matching, or coordination, of two patterns, stress and time. But poetic meter is only one of these patterns. Why does one kind of measurement have to be matched with another kind? or translated into it? The measurement of verse is determined by some recurrent linguistic feature, peg, obstacle, jutting stress, or whatever. If we read this recurrence so as to give it equal times, this is something we do to it. Maybe we actually do, and maybe this is a part of our aesthetic satisfaction; still it is not a part of the linguistic fact which the poet has to recognize and on which he has to rely in order to write verses.

IV

The meter inheres in the language of the poem, but in what way and at what level? We hold that it inheres in aspects of the language that can be abstracted with considerable precision, isolated, and even preserved in the appearance of an essence—mummified or dummified. An appropriate example is to hand and does not have to be invented.   Back in the 1920's I. A. Richards was much concerned, and properly, to show that the movement or rhythm of poetry was closely inter-dependent with its other kinds of meaning. The movement, he argued, could hardly be said to occur at all except as an aspect of some linguistic meaning. Or at least it had no poetic value except as an aspect of some meaning. It is not quite clear which point Richards was making. But for the sake of his argument he exhibited, in his *Practical Criticism,* a contrivance which he called a "double or dummy"— "with nonsense syllables"—"a purified dummy." The dummy showed several things, perhaps a good deal more than Richards had in mind. For it certainly was not a *pure* dummy. How could it be? It was a linguistic dummy. And so this dummy did have a meter—perhaps even a kind of rhythm. If it did not have a meter, how could it be adduced as showing that movement, or meter, apart from sense did not have poetic value? You can't illustrate the poetic nullity of a certain quality taken pure by annihilating that quality. You do it by purging or purifying, isolating, the quality. And if you can do that, you prove that the quality can be isolated—at least from *certain* other qualities, in this case, the *main lines* of the linguistic meaning. In order to get even this dummy of a meter, Richards had to leave in a good many linguistic features.

> J. Drootan-Sussting Benn
> Mill-down Leduren N.
>   Telamba-taras oderwainto weiring
> Awersey zet bedreen
> Ownd istellester sween. . . .

"If any reader," says Richards, "has any difficulty in scanning these verses, reference to Milton, *On the Morning of Christ's Nativity, XV,* will prove of assistance."[6] There are, indeed, several uncertainties in Richards' composition which correspond to greater certainties in Milton's full linguistic archetype. Still the Milton is not necessary. Let us list some of the things we know about this dummy. The "nonsense syllables" are divided into groups (words). As English readers we find little difficulty pronouncing them. Some of the groups are English words ("Mill," "down,"); others are English syllables, even morphemes ("ing," "ey," "een," "er"). The capital initials, the monosyllables, the hyphens, the rhymes, give us very strong indications, absolutely sure indications, where some of the stresses fall. And there are some syllables, notably some final syllables, which are surely unstressed. If we don't inquire too closely how much any given stressed syllable is stressed more than another (and who is to say that we should make that inquiry?), we will indicate the scansion of Richards' dummy somewhat as follows:

> J. Dróotan-Sússting Bénn
> Míll-dówn Lédùren Ń.
>   Télàmba-táras óderwáinto wéiring
> Àwersey zét bidréen
> Ównd istéllèster swéen. . . .

The main uncertainties will be with the groups "Leduren," "Telamba," "Awersey," istellester," where there will be a choice or guess in placing the stress. But the choice in no one of the four cases is crucial to the meter. You can choose either way and not destroy the iambics. And Richards' readers who have read this dummy and admired the ingenuity of the argument have certainly all along been giving the dummy the benefit of some implicit scansion.

The dummy does two things for the present argument. It illustrates or strongly suggests the principle that meter may inhere at certain rudimentary levels of linguistic organization, and more specifically, that the kind of English meter of which we are speaking, so far as it depends on syllabic stress, depends not on any kind of absolute or very strong stress, but merely on a relative degree of stress—on a certain moreness of stress in certain positions. Of this latter we want to say something further before we finish. It is not a principle which is challenged by the linguists—though the exact sense in which they wish to apply it seems doubtful.

Let us now make some general prosodic observations. And first, that to have verses or lines, you have to have certain broader structural features, notably the endings. Milton's line is not only a visual or typographical fact on the page, but a fact of the language. If you try to cut up his pentameters into tetrameters, for example, you find yourself ending in the middle of words or on weak words like "on" or "the." Much English prose is iambic or nearly iambic, but it is only very irregular verse, because if you try to cut it regularly, you get the same awkward and weak result. Lines of verse are syntactic entities, though not necessarily similar or parallel entities. Depending on the degree of parallel, you get different kinds of tension between the fact of the lines and the fact of the overall syntax or movement.

Given the line then or the typographical semblance of a line (the possibility of a line) on the page, let us ask the question how we know we have a meter and know what meter it is. The line may indeed be only a syntactic entity and not metrical in any more precise way—as perhaps it is throughout Robert Bridges' *Testament of Beauty*[7] and in much so-called "free verse." With Mr. Whitehall we can call this a kind of "rhythm," *nonsyllabic, isosyntactic,* so long as the syntactic entities, the phrases or clauses, are "in strictly parallel sequence," as in Hebrew verse and in *some* "free verse." But this is in fact a very narrow restriction. It rules out all mere cutting of ordinary prose into its phrases or clauses (as in much free verse, and perhaps in Bridges or in parts of Bridges). For again, like Pike's isochronism, phrases and clauses are inevitable, and if they by themselves make a "rhythm" (or a meter), it is impossible not to write in this "rhythm" or meter. To get a meter, some other kind of equality has to be added to the succession of syntactic entities. (Even strictly parallel syntactic entities will be improved metrically by the addition of some more precise kind of equality.) The meter in the sense that it is internal to a given line or that it is something that runs through the series of lines is some kind of more minute recurrence—some exact or approximate number of syllables, with probably some reenforcement of certain syllables, some repeated weighting, what Mr. Whitehall calls a "configurational feature."

Here if we take a wide enough look at the world's languages and literatures (at Chinese and classical Greek, as well as the Western vernaculars of our immediate experience), we can talk about pitch and quantity, as well as accent or stress. But for our discussion of English meters, stress is the thing. (Rhyme, assonance, alliteration too are auxiliary "configurational" and metric features though Mr. Whitehall seems to count them out.)

The important principle of stress or accent in English verse is, however, a rather ambiguous thing, for there are in fact two main kinds of stress meter in English: the very old (and recently revived) meter of strong stress with indeterminate or relatively indeterminate number of syllables between the stresses, and the other meter, of the great English art tradition (Chaucer to Tennyson), which is a syllable-stress meter, that is, a meter of counted syllables and of both major and minor stresses.

There are certainly some lines of syllable-stress meter which taken alone could be read also as strong-stress meter (four beats instead of five). To use only one of Mr. Frye's examples:

> To be, or not to be, that is the question:
> Whether 'tis nobler in the mind to suffer
> The slings and arrows of outrageous fortune. . . .

But the precise number of syllables in syllable-stress meter is always somewhat against the strong-stress interpretation. One stress out of five in a pentameter line will inevitably be the weakest; still, because of the numbering of the syllables, and the alternation of the stresses, this fifth too calls out for some recognition.

> To be, or not to be, that is the question.
> With loss of Eden, till one greater man. . . .

And then we have the matter of the whole passage, the whole act and scene, the whole book, the whole long poem to consider. And Mr. Frye admits that the strong stresses vary in number from eight (the maximum apparently possible within the conditions of the pentameter—a virtuoso feat achieved by Milton) to the scarcely satisfactory three (eked out in musical terms, for a line of Keats by Mr. Frye's assumption of a preliminary "rest"). But the "pentameter" in a long poem by Shakespeare, Milton, Pope, Wordsworth, or Keats is not subject to such fluctuations. The pentameter is always there. It is *the* meter of the poem. The strong-stress lines of four, of three, of eight, and so on, come and go, playing along with the steady pentameter—and it is a good thing they do come and go, for if every line of *Hamlet* or *Paradise Lost* had the four strong beats which Mr. Frye finds in the opening four or five lines, Mr. Frye would begin to detect something marvelously monotonous; he wouldn't be so happy about his "inherent" and "common" four-stress rhythm. One principle of monotony is enough; it is *the* meter of the poem. In "pentameter" verse it is the iambic pentameter.

A few lines of Chaucer, Shakespeare, Spenser, Pope, Wordsworth, Tennyson, read consecutively, can hardly fail to establish the meter. What makes it possible for the lighter stresses to count in syllable-stress meter is the fact that it *is* a syllable meter. Following French and classical models, but in an English way, the poets count their syllables precisely or almost precisely, ten to a pentameter line, and this measuring out makes it possible to employ the minor accents along with the major ones in an alternating motion, up and down. The precise measurement tilts and juggles the little accents into place, establishes their occurrence as a regular part of all that is going on.

Likewise, the clutter of weaker syllables in a strong-stress meter is against an accurate syllable-stress reading, most often prevents it entirely. A few lines of *Piers Plowman* or of *Everyman* ought to suffice to show what is what.

> In a somer seson, whan soft was the sonne,
> I shope me in shroudes, as I a shepe were,
> In habits like an heremite, unholy of workes,
> Went wyde in this world, wondres to here.
>
> Lorde, I wyll in the worlde go renne over all,
> And cruelly out-serche bothe grete and small.
> Every man wyll I beset that lyveth beestly
> Out of Goddes lawes, and dredeth not foly.

This other kind of meter is older in English poetry and may be more natural to the English tongue, though again it may not be. Here only the major stresses of the major words count in the scanning. The gabble of weaker syllables, now more, now fewer, between the major stresses obscures all the minor stresses and relieves them of any structural duty. (Sometimes the major stresses are pointed up by alliteration; they are likely to fall into groups of two on each side of a caesura). Thus we have *Beowulf, Piers Plowman, Everyman,* Spenser's *February Eclogue,* Coleridge's *Christabel,* the poetry of G. M. Hopkins (who talks about "sprung rhythm" and "outrides"), the poetry of T. S. Eliot, and many another in our day.[8]

Let us now return and dwell more precisely for a moment on the principle of relative stress. This is a slight but very certain thing in English; it is the indispensable and quite adequate principle for recognizing and scanning verses composed precisely of a given number of English syllables—or more exactly, for seeing if they *will* scan (for not all sequences of equal numbers of syllables show a measured alternation of accents). This is the main point of our whole essay: simply to reassert the fact of English syllable-stress meter, to vindicate the principle of relative stress as the one principle of stress which in conjunction with syllable counting makes this kind of meter. Mr. Chatman has already quoted the landmark statement about relative stress made by Otto Jespersen in his "Notes on Metre," 1900 (*Linguistica* [Copenhagen, 1933], pp. 272-74), and we need not repeat this. In speaking of this principle let us explain firmly, however, that we do not find it necessary to follow either Jespersen or Trager-Smith in believing in any fixed or countable number of degrees of English stress. We wish in the main to avoid the cumbersome grammar of the new linguists. For all we know, there may be, not four, but five degrees of English stress, or eight.[9] How can one be sure? What one can nearly always be sure of is that a given syllable in a sequence is more or less stressed than the preceding or the following. Or, suppose that there are, as Jespersen and Trager-Smith seem to agree, just *four* degrees of English stress. The discriminations are not needed for discerning the meter—but only the degrees of more and less. How *much* more is always irrelevant.

The main thing to observe about the principles of relative stress and counted syllables is that by means of these you can explain the necessary things about English syllable-stress verse. For one thing, quite starkly, you can tell an iambic line from one that is not iambic.

> Preserved in Milton's or Shakespeare's name.

When a student misquotes this Popean line in a paper, it is not our perfect memory of the poem but our sense of the meter (and our belief in meter) which tells us he has left out a word. The four-beat theory of the pentameter could not make this discovery.

To take another kind of example: let us suppose that Pope had written:

> A little advice is a dangerous thing.

Persons who say that the line is one of Pope's four-beat lines will be hard put to explain why it isn't a good line; it still has its four strong beats. Yet nobody can actually say that the revised line is a good Popean line and goes well with the other lines of the *Essay on Criticism*. And all we have changed is the position of one relative accent, which makes it impossible that the syllable "is" should receive a stronger accent than the preceding syllable, and hence impossible that there should be five iambs in the line.

> /   /   /   /
> A little advice is a dangerous thing.

That one shift of accent throws us immediately into the anapestic gallop, and we have a line that belongs in Anstey's *Bath Guide.*

Another kind of example:

> Ah, Sunflower, weary of time.

Hardly the Goldsmith or Anstey anapestic gallop. Yet unmistakably an anapestic line. The strong syllables "Ah," and "flow-," coming where they do, create a heavy drag. Nevertheless, "sun" is even stronger, at least stronger than "flow-," a fact which is crucial. A reader can take the two opening syllables as he likes, as iamb, trochee, or spondee (if there is such a thing), and still not defeat the subsequent anapests. The very weak syllables "er" and "y" in two key iambic stress positions make it unthinkable that the line should be read as iambic.

Again: the beginning of the line is a characteristic place, in both iambic and anapestic lines, for the full inversion.

> Ruin hath taught me thus to ruminate.

> Whether 'tis nobler in the mind to suffer . . .

> Softly, in the dusk, a woman is singing to me;
> Taking me back down the vista of years, till I see. . .

But:

> Hail to thee, blithe spirit!

This is something different. The unquestionably iambic movement following the very strong first syllable[10] might, if we were desperate, be accounted for by saying that the word "Hail" breaks into two syllables, "Hay-ul," with a resultant needed extra weak syllable and the familiar opening pattern of iambic inversion. But a much more energetic and irrefutable assertion of the iamb appears in the progressive rise or stress increase of the three syllables "thee, blithe spirit." (Note well: the slack of a given foot can be stronger than the stress of the preceding foot.) For a trochaic reading of this line, you would have to have "thee, blithe," a rhetorical impossibility, making a nonsensically hopping line.

The notion of an accentual spondee (or "level" foot) in English would seem to be illusory, for the reason that it is impossible to pronounce any two successive syllables in English without some rise or fall of stress—and *some* rise or fall of stress is all that is needed for a metrical ictus. This fact produces in English iambic meter two kinds of ambiguous situations or metrical choices, that of two weak syllables coming together, and that of two strong syllables coming together. In each of these situations, the iambic principle is saved merely by the fact that certain unhappy choices are impossible.

> Rocks, caves, lakes, fens, bogs, dens, and shades of death.

Certainly it is impossible to pronounce the first two, the first three, the first six syllables of this line with a perfectly even stress. On the other hand, no determinate pattern of stresses seems dictated. No doubt several are possible and are actually employed or experienced by various readers of this Miltonic passage. To us the most plausible seems as follows:

> Rocks, caves, lakes, fens, bogs, dens. . .

The more regularly iambic reading,

> Rocks, caves, lakes, fens . . .

seems forced. The only reading which will clearly defeat the iambic movement is absurd:

> Rocks, caves, lakes, fens. . .

Two weak syllables together present perhaps the more difficult problem. But all cases will not be equally difficult.

> In profuse strains of unpremeditated art.

Here certainly the crucial fact is that "strains" is *more* stressed than "-fuse." Only observe that much—come out on the fourth syllable with an ictus, and the first two syllables can be stressed any way anybody wants. There are only two possible ways: "In pro-" or "In pro-". The second way, invoking a kind of Miltonic indult for the disyllable beginning with "pro-," makes the line more regularly iambic, but it is not necessary.

> Upon the supreme theme of Art and Song. . . .

This is the same thing, only pushed ahead to the second and third feet of the line. The situation of the four syllables here, two weak and two strong, has been described as a kind of compensation, a "hovering" of the accent, or as a "double or ionic foot" (Ransom, *Kenyon Review,* XVIII, 471). And doubtless some such notion does something to help our rationalizations. But we may observe also that only the coming together of the two strong accents makes possible the coming together of the two weak. "The " and "su-" are so weak only because "-preme" is so strong; and because "-preme" is so strong, "theme" has to be yet stronger. (Imagine a group of persons arguing about themes. One says theme X is good. Another says theme Y is good. Another says, "Yes, but the supreme theme is Zeta." Just the reverse of the stress required in the Yeats line.) In a system where the only absolute value, the ictus, consists only in a relationship, we needlessly pursue a too close inquiry into the precise strength of the stronger point in the relationship. A somewhat more difficult, double, example of the two-weak, two-strong pattern is provided by Marvell.

> To a green thought in a green shade.

One may begin by observing that whatever we do with the two pairs of weak syllables, it remains absolutely certain that "thought" is stronger than "green," and that "shade" is stronger than "green." (The relative strength of the two "greens" produces of course the peculiarity of the logico-rhythmic character of the line—the interaction of its sense with its meter. But here we speak precisely of the meter.) "To a," because of its introductory position, presents no difficulty. "In a," is more curious just because of its medial position. Probably a rather marked caesura, in spite of the continuing syntax and the shortness of the line, is created by the head to back juxtaposition of the two ictuses "thought" and "in." This again is part of the peculiar gravity of the line. The most plausible reading seems to us:

> To a green thought in a green shade.

If anybody wants to read:

> To a green thought in a green shade,

arguing for two anapests compensated for by two single-syllable strong feet, there is probably no triumphant way to refute the reading. Still the lack of pause between "green" and the nouns which follow it is against the single-syllable foot. The single-syllable foot occurs in lines that sound like this: "Weave, weave, the sunlight in your hair."

Some of the most perplexing problems confronting the theorist of English meter—no matter to what school he belongs—are those arising in connection with the "dipody" or double-jump single foot (x x́ x x̂). This foot was much used by narrative poets of the late Victorian and Edwardian eras and also, because of its accentual difficulties and ambiguities, has been a favorite ground for exercise in several kinds of temporal scansion. Regular or nearly regular instances of the dipody are perhaps easy enough.

I would I were in Shoreham at the setting of the sun.

A recent handbook remarks very sanely: "Although the meter is duple insofar as there is an alternation between unaccented and accented syllables, there is also an alternation in the degree of stress on the accented syllables . . . the result is that the two-syllable feet tend to group themselves into larger units" (Laurence Perrine, *Sound and Sense* [New York, 1956], p. 160). "You will probably find yourself reading it as a four-beat line." It is a kind of strong-accent meter, with number of syllables and minor stresses tightened up into a secondary pattern. An easy enough substitute for the dipody will be of course the anapest (x x x́). The iamb also (x x́) is available, and also the single strong-stress syllable, either at the start of the line, or just after a medial pause.

Brooding o'er the gloom, spins the brown eve-jar.

Thus dipodic meters can occur where no single line has more than two dipodies, and many lines have only one, and in these latter the reader may well have a choice just where to place the dipody. Meters of this sort are very slippery, elusive. One's first feeling on reading them may be that a strong lilt or swing is present, though it is hard to say just how it ought to be defined. A recurrent feature may be that the line seems to start on a strong stress, with falling meter, but then, with the aid of the agile dipody, swings up midway into a rising meter to the finish. The number of syllables in the line will vary greatly, and the principle of relative stress operates with a vengeance—the weaker syllable of the dipody showing all sorts of relations to the stresses of the other feet. It is a tricky, virtuoso meter, very apt in nursery rhymes and in the rakish, barrack-room, mad-hatter, pirate-galleon narratives of the era to which we have alluded above. Meredith's pleasant little monstrosity "Love in the Valley" is a striking instance of the difficulties. It seems safe to say that no *great* English poems have been accomplished in any variant of this meter. The theory of meter which we are defending is, we believe, better fitted to explain—and reveal the ambiguities of—the dipodic meter than any other theory. But the illustration and arguing of the point are perhaps beyond present requirements.

V.

It is one of the hazards of an argument such as this that it is often on the verge of slipping from questions about something that seems to be merely and safely a matter of "fact" to questions about value. It is quite possible that some prosodists of the linguistic and musical schools would grant that meter, as we have described it, is a fact, but in the same breath would put it aside as of little consequence, at least when compared to the strong-stress pattern or some principle of equal timing. This was, for instance, the spirit of D. W. Prall's attack on the traditional metric in his *Aesthetic Analysis* (New York, 1936, esp. pp. 117, 130). Such a metric was trivial, "artificial," misleading. Our own difference from some recent writers may partly be reduced to a difference in emphasis, which reflects a different estimate of significance. We maintain not only that meter, in our sense, does occur, but that it is an important feature of verse.

To make out a broad-scale case for this claim might require much space and effort. Fortunately, we can do perhaps all that is necessary at the moment if we work upon an assumption that is now quite widely entertained, or indeed is a commonplace with students of poetry today: that there are tensions between various poetic elements, among them meter and various aspects of sense, and that these tensions are valuable.

One of the good features of Mr. Chatman's *Kenyon* essay is his constant appeal to an idea of "tension" between the full spoken poem and some kind of metrical pattern. "I believe that the beauty of verse often inheres in the tensions developed between the absolute, abstract metrical pattern and the oral actualization of sequences of English sounds" (p. 436). A student in a seminar presided over by one of the present writers was stumped, however, in scanning a line at the blackboard and refused to put the next stress mark anywhere at all. "I don't see how to show the interaction between the meter and the sense." As if by scanning he *could* show the interaction. As if anybody expected him to. As if the meter itself could be the interaction between itself and something else. This interest in tension, or interaction, is excellent. But how can there be a tension without two things to be in tension?

Wóndring upón this wórd, quáking for dréde.
(Clerk's Tale, 1, 358)

Here is a very special relation of phrase to meter. The double inversion, at the start of the line and again after the caesura, gives the two participial verbs a special quiver. But this depends on the fact that there *is* a meter; the inversions otherwise would not be inversions.

You can write a grammar of the meter. And if you cannot, there is no meter. But you cannot write a grammar of the meter's interaction with the sense, any more than you can write a grammar of the arrangement of metaphors. The interactions and the metaphors are the free and individual and unpredictable (though not irrational) parts of the poetry. You can perceive them, and study them, and talk about them, but not write rules for them. The meter, like the grammar and the vocabulary, is subject to rules. It is just as important to observe what meter a poem is written in (especially if it is written in one of the precise meters of the syllable-stress tradition) as it is to observe what language the poem is written in. Before you recognize the meter, you have only a vague apprehension of the much-prized tensions.

Perhaps it needs to be said that there is a difference between deviations from a meter (or "exceptions," as Mr. Ransom calls them) and the constant strain or tension of a meter (as an abstract norm or expectancy) against the concrete or full reality of the poetic utterance. The deviations are a part of the tension, but only an occasional part. The deviations occur only here and there—though some of them, the inverted first foot, the dropping of the first slack syllable, the extra slack syllable internal to the line (elided, or not elided in the anapest)—occur so often as to assume the character of an accepted complication of the norm. But the tension in the wider sense is always there. Here one might discourse on the "promotion" and "suppression" of syllables to which both the linguists and Arnold Stein refer. These are useful terms. There is no line so regular (so *evenly* alternating weak and strong) that it does not show some tension. It is practically impossible to write an English line that will not in some way buck against the meter. Insofar as the line does approximate the condition of complete submission, it is most likely a tame line, a weak line.

And thus: "scanning" a line is not a dramatic, or poetic, reading of a line. Scanning a line is reading it in a special, more or less forced, way, to bring out the meter *and* any definite deviations or substitutions. Scanning will not bring out the other parts of the tension; it will tend to iron them out. On the other hand, a good dramatic, or poetic, reading will tend to bring out the tensions—but note well that in order to do this it must be careful not to override completely and kill the meter. When that is done, the tensions vanish. (Another reason why the meter must be observed is, of course, that if a line is truly metrical, a reading which actually destroys the meter can only be an incorrect reading—by dictionary and rhetorical standards.) A good dramatic reading is a much more delicate, difficult, and rewarding performance than a mere scanning. Yet the scanning has its justification, its use. We would argue that a good dramatic reading is possible only by a person who *can* also perform a scansion.

"The trouble with conventional metrics," complains Mr. Chatman, "is that because it cannot distinguish between levels of stress and intonation, it often cannot distinguish meaningful from trivial performances" (p. 436). The answer is that metric is not required to do this, though it is needed for it. Mr. Chatman or another reader will have to make his own reading as meaningful as possible, but he will be in a better position to do this if he recognizes the meter. We are speaking all along, if not about a sufficient, yet about a necessary, rule for poetic reading.

If we may insert a brief pedagogic excursus: Schoolteachers nowadays, beginning in grade school and going right up into graduate school, probably try much too hard to prevent their students from a "mechanical" or thumped-out scansion, telling them rather to observe the variations, the tensions—telling them in effect to promote all tensions as much as possible. But the fact is that the tensions and the variations will pretty much take care of themselves if the student lives long enough and provided he is equipped with just one principle (of no precise application) that the variations and tensions are there and ought somehow to be recognized. The variations and tensions tend to assert themselves. The meter, because it is artificial, precisely measured, frail if meticulous, tends to be overridden and, if not actually destroyed (as it cannot be in any correct reading), at least obscured. This you can see if you ask college freshmen to scan a passage of Milton or to write fifteen lines in imitation. The probability is that the student of average gifts, if he has never at any stage of his schoolroom education been required or allowed to whang out the meter, is not aware that it is there and hence has very little notion of what the teacher means by the tensions.

For the word "tension," let us substitute at this point, in a concluding suggestion, the word "interplay"—meaning the interplay of syllable-stress meter with various other features of linguistic organization, but especially with those which are likely to set up other quasi-metric or rhythmic patterns. One of the disadvantages of the old strong-stress meter is doubtless its limited capacity for interplay. The stress pattern of the meter is so nearly the same as the stress pattern of the syntax and logic that there is nothing much for the meter to interplay with. The same must be true for all meters depending on patterns of repeated or parallel syntax—such as the meter of the Hebrew Psalms and the free verse of Walt Whitman. Where such meters gain in freedom and direct speech-feeling, they lose in opportunity for precise interplay. Conversely, where syllable-stress meters lose in freedom and naturalness of speech-feeling, they gain in the possibility of precise interplay. Perhaps this suggests a reason why the greatest English poetry (Chaucer, Shakespeare, Milton, Pope, Wordsworth) has after all been written in the more artful syllable-stress meter—not in the older, simpler, more directly natural strong-stress meter.

It is no doubt possible to think of many kinds of interplay, with many resulting kinds of total poetic feel. Maybe some of the languor and soft drag of Tennyson's verse, for instance, comes sometimes from the interplay between the rising iambic motion of the line and the falling trochaic character of a series of important words.

> It little profits that an idle king . . .
> To follow knowledge, like a sinking star. . .

Again, and very frequently in English verse of the tradition, the special rhythmic effects arise from the fact that the stress pattern of the iambics either more or less coincides with or more or less fails to coincide with the pattern of the stronger logical stresses, thus producing a movement either slow or fast, heavy or light.

> That, like a wounded snake, drags its slow, length along . . .
> Flies o'er th'unbending corn, and skims along the main.

The same kind of thing combines further with the number and length of the words involved in a line to produce contours of tension so special as perhaps better not translated into any other kind of meaning but simply regarded as shapes of energy. The 10,565 lines of Milton's *Paradise Lost,* all but two or three of them iambic pentameter lines, abound in illustrations of Milton's virtuosity. To show two extremes in one respect, recall a line we have already quoted and set beside it another.

> Rocks, caves, lakes, fens, bogs, dens, and shades of death . . .
> Immutable, immortal, infinite. . . .

Eight strong stresses in one line; three in the other. But five *metric* stresses in either. And if that were not so, there would be nothing at all remarkable about the difference between eight and three.

It is, finally, possible, as we have already observed, that a given line in a given poet may invite scanning in either the older strong-stress way or in the Chaucer-Tennyson syllable-stress way—four beats by the old, five beats by the new. If a poem written on the whole in syllable-counting pentameters happens to show here and there lines which have one somewhat lighter stress and hence four stronger stresses, this is not very remarkable. For in the nature of things, as we have already observed, five stresses will always include one weakest. We have already sufficiently illustrated this phenomenon. But if a poem written on the whole in a meter of four strong stresses, with indeterminate number of syllables, at some point tightens up, counts syllables, and tilts minor accents into an iambic pentameter, this is something else. A wise and shifty modern poet, always in search of rhythmical invention, writes a stanza containing in the middle such a line as:

Her hair over her arms and her arms full of flowers,

and at the end:

Sometimes these cogitations still amaze
The troubled midnight and the noon's repose.

This is playing in and out of the metrical inheritance. Part V of *The Waste Land* begins:

After the torchlight red on sweaty faces
After the frosty silence in the gardens
After the agony in stony places . . .

Coming after four parts of a poem written largely in strong-stress meter, these lines, with their marked swinging parallel of construction, will most likely be read at a fast walk as strong-stress meter, four stresses to the first, three each to the second and the third. But each is also a perfectly accurate pentameter line, each complicated in the same two traditional ways, the inverted beginning and the hypermetric ending ("Whether 'tis nobler in the mind to suffer . . .").

It is probably not until about the time of Mr. Eliot and his friends that the free and subtle moving in and out and coalescing of strong-stress and syllable-stress meters in the same poem, the same stanza, begins to appear with any frequency. This is something remarkable in the history of metrics. But the understanding of it depends precisely upon the recognition of the few homely and sound, traditional and objective, principles of prosody upon which we have been insisting throughout this essay. Without recognition of the two distinct principles of strong-stress and of syllable-stress meter, it seems doubtful if anything at all precise or technical can be said about Mr. Eliot's peculiar rhythms and tensions.

NOTES

[1.] Harold Whitehall, Seymour Chatman, Arnold Stein, John Crowe Ransom, "English Verse and What It Sounds Like," *Kenyon Review,* XVIII, 411–77.

[2.] "Linguistics, Poetics, and Interpretation: The Phonemic Dimension," *Quarterly Journal of Speech,* XLIII (October 1957), 254.

[3.] The question is, of course, a psychological one, but the psychologists have not dealt much with it. A search of *Psychological Abstracts* for the last twenty years turns up (XXI [September 1947], 387) one article (abstract 3211): Marguerite Durand, "Perception de durée dans les phrases rhythmées," *Journal de Psychologie Normale et Pathologique,* XXXIX (1946), 305–21. But Mlle. Durand apparently took isochronism for granted and had her passages (French and Czech) spoken to the beats of a metronome. Albert R. Chandler, *Beauty and Human Nature* (New York, 1934), pp. 244–56, gives a good account of some earlier investigations. Ada L. F. Snell, "An Objective Study of Syllabic Quantity in English Verse," *PMLA,* XXXIII (1918), 396–408; XXXIV (1919), 416–35, presents experimental evidence against the assumption that readers of English verse observe any kind of "equal time intervals."

[4.] A kind of middle or double service is performed by traditional marks of prosodic scansion—which in part, in large part, call attention to objective features of linguistic structure, but to some extent also are used for "promoting" or "suppressing" (or indicating the promotion or suppression of) such features in favor of a certain pattern. This double character of scansion marks has perhaps caused much of the difficulty in metrical theory.

[5.] We take this term from Leonard B. Meyer's excellent discussion of musical rhythm in *Emotion and Meaning in Music* (Chicago, 1956), pp. 102–103. Pulse is the division of time into "regularly recurring, equally accented beats." What Meyer calls "meter" in music depends on pulse; but in this respect it is different from meter in verse. What he calls "rhythm"—e.g., the difference between an iambic and an anapestic or trochaic pattern—can occur without pulse and meter, he holds, as in plain chant or *recitativo secco.*

[6.] *Practical Criticism* (New York, 1935), p. 232.

[7.] Elizabeth Wright, *Metaphor, Sound and Meaning in Bridges' "The Testament of Beauty"* (Philadelphia, 1951), p. 26, says that Bridges' lines are to be timed equally, with the help of pauses at the ends of the lines.

[8.] Yvor Winters, *The Function of Criticism* (Denver, 1957), pp. 79–100, 109–23, expresses a view of English meter in general and of Hopkins which we take to be substantially in accord with our own.

[9.] Alexander J. Ellis, "Remarks on Professor Mayor's Two Papers on Rhythm," *Transactions of the Philological Society 1875–1876* (Strasburg, 1877), p. 442, distinguished "nine degrees" of "force" or stress in English and likewise nine degrees of "length," "pitch," "weight," and "silence."

[10.] The problem of "rising" and "falling" meters is one which we are content to touch lightly. Temporal theorists, working on the analogy of the musical downbeat, tend of course to make all meters falling. George R. Stewart, Jr., a moderate timer, makes the following revelatory statement: "If a person comes upon a road and walks a few rods before arriving at the first milestone, he will have to pass five milestones, counting the first, before he has walked four measured miles; in other words, since the start and the finish must be shown, five markers are necessary to establish four units. In verse the stresses are the markers, and the feet are the units. Five stresses can mark off only four intervals, so that what we ordinarily call a five-foot line might be more properly described as a four-foot line with a little left over at beginning and end" (*The Technique of English Verse* [New York, 1930], p. 42). (For Mr. Stewart "rising" and "falling" are qualities of phrasing, not of meter, p. 37.) Suppose, however, that we are counting not "measured miles" but precisely milestones—not equal times but precisely stresses. And suppose that a man walks not a "few rods" but a full mile before reaching the first milestone. The first slack syllable of the iambic line is as much a mile as any other slack syllable. The line begins at the beginning of that syllable. The iambic line which starts with a strong and then *one* weak syllable is a more difficult matter. But many such lines, like the one from Shelley's *Skylark* which we discuss above, can be shown in one way or another to be in fact iambic. The shape of the phrases is likely to have much to do with it. Other lines of this sort, such as some in Tennyson's *The Lady of Shalott,* may in fact be ambiguous—that is, they may be susceptible of being satisfactorily read either as iambic or as trochaic.

MORRIS HALLE AND
SAMUEL J. KEYSER

The Iambic Pentameter

Professors Halle and Keyser are concerned to determine the nature of "metricality" in English verse. Why is the first of these lines a "lawful embodiment" of the iambic pentameter, but the second not?

(1) The curfew tolls the knell of parting day.
(2) How many bards gild the lapses of time.

An experienced reader of English verse knows that "something" is wrong with (2), a "tacit rather than explicit" awareness of rules being violated. The so-called standard theory (as expounded by Robert Bridges and other traditional metrists) explains that a trochee (*lapses*) in the "sensitive" fourth foot, preceded by another trochee (*gild the*) in the third foot, unsettles the rhythmic stability of the line. Or in the terminology of Gerard Manley Hopkins, the line is "counterpointed" or syncopated by the anomalous feet.

Professors Halle and Keyser discard the concept of the foot and consider the entire line the metrical unit. They use "symbol strings" to indicate the positions of the syllables in the line and formulate "correspondence rules" to construct a theory of metricality "more powerful, and hence to be preferred over the standard theory. . . ." The rules function to actualize or "generate" metrical effect; the Halle-Keyser theory established the methodology for what has come to be known as generative metrics.

Reprinted from *Versification: Major Language Types*, ed. W. K. Wimsatt. Copyright © 1972 by New York University. Used by permission of the New York University Press.

Generative metrics has a number of advantages over the traditional foot-based prosody. Its rules more adequately account for departures from the metrical norm; it is the violence of *stress maxima* thrust into normally W (weak) positions that generates the prosodic energy of these lines:

(3) Let me not to the marriage of true minds.
(4) Captain Carpenter rose up in his prime.

But the intrusions of stress maxima need not destroy metricality nor necessarily generate violent effects. The second of these lines (6) shows stress maxima in two W positions:

(5) Can shee excuse my wrongs with vertues cloake:
(6) Shall I call her good when she proves unkind?
    Dowland, *First Booke of Songes* (1597), V

The rhythm is pleasing and any sense of "unmetricality" faint; the line follows the hemiola rhythm of its musical setting, a characteristic pattern of the Elizabethan galliard.

Generative theory has been widely accepted and applied; it also has been, in the dozen years since it was first formulated, considerably modified. Other linguists have tried to account for numerous exceptions and apparent operative illegalities. Their scansions have become increasingly complex, their terminologies increasingly hermetic. The poetry tends to disappear into the methodology; we cannot hear the meters and rhythms because so much intervenes between ear and eye. Perhaps a more inclusive theory of greater conceptual elegance—and greater simplicity—may eventually emerge.

What, then, exactly is Prosody? Our English word is not carried over from the Greek word with its uncertain and various meanings, but it must have come with the French word through the scholastic Latin; and like the French term it primarily denotes the rules for the treatment of syllables in verse, whether they are to be considered as long or short, accented or unaccented, elideable or not, etc., etc. The syllables, which are the units of rhythmic speech, are by nature of so indefinite a quality and capable of such different vocal expression, that apart from the desire which every artist must feel to have his work consistent in itself, his appeal to an audience would convince him that there is no chance of his elaborate rhythms being rightly interpreted unless his treatment of syllables is understood. Rules must, therefore, arise and be agreed upon for the treatment of syllables, and this is the first indispensable office of Prosody.

Robert Bridges, "A Letter to a Musician on English Prosody"

When a poet composes metrical verse, he imposes certain constraints upon his choice of words and phrases that ordinary language does not normally obey.[1] The poet and his readers may not be able to formulate explicitly the nature of the constraints that are operative in a given poem; there is little doubt, however, that neither the poet nor the experienced reader would find great difficulty in telling apart wildly unmetrical lines from lines that are straightforwardly metrical. Thus few people familiar with the canon of metrical English verse from Chaucer to Yeats would disagree with the proposition that (1*b*) and 1*c*) are lawful embodiments of the iambic pentameter, whereas (1*a*) is not, even though (1*a*) has the same number of syllables as (1*b*), but (1*c*) does not.

(1) (*a*) Ode to the West Wind by Percy Bysshe Shelley.
    (*b*) O Wild West Wind, thou breath of Autumn's being.
    (*c*) The curfew tolls the knell of parting day.

In addition, readers of verse possess the ability to categorize metrical lines as more or less complex. Thus, most readers would no doubt judge (1*b*) as a more complex iambic pentameter line than (1*c*).

We shall look upon these readily observable abilities of experienced poetry readers as crucial facts that must be accounted for by an adequate theory of prosody. A good theory, however, would be expected to do more than that; it would also help us to understand the nature of metrical verse and illuminate the relationship between a speaker's everyday linguistic competence and his ability to judge verses as metrical or unmetrical, as complex or simple. We restrict this study to the favorite meter of English poets, the iambic pentameter. The approach used here can readily be extended to other meters; see, for example, Halle "On Meter and Prosody" and Halle and Keyser, *English Stress*.

We propose that the ability of readers and poets to judge verse lines as metrical or unmetrical, and as more or less complex, is due to their knowledge of certain principles of verse construction. This knowledge—much like the average speaker's knowledge of his language—is tacit rather than explicit. People when questioned may be unable to give a coherent account of the principles that they employ in making the above judgments of verse lines. It is, therefore, the task of the metrist to provide a coherent and explicit account of this knowledge, just as it is the task of the grammarian to make explicit what it is that the fluent speaker of a language knows about it.

We shall assume that this knowledge consists of two distinct parts: one concerns the abstract pattern underlying the meter; the other, the rules that relate the abstract pattern to concrete lines of verse. We regard this assumption as a working hypothesis to be justified by showing that insightful and important results can be obtained with its help.

The sequences of abstract entities that underlie the meter are symbol strings such as those in (2):

(2)   (*a*) XXXXXXXXXXXX
      (*b*) WSWSWSWSWSWS(W(W)) where parenthesized entities are optional.

These abstract patterns are related to concrete lines of verse by correspondence rules such as those illustrated in (3):

(3)   (*a*) Each abstract entity (X, W, S) corresponds to a single syllable.[2]
      (*b*) Stressed syllables occur in S positions only and in all S positions.[3]

We scan particular lines by establishing a correspondence between the syllables of the line and the abstract entities in the abstract pattern such as those in (2). Lines are judged metrical if such a correspondence can be established exhaustively without violating the applicable correspondence rules. In (4) we illustrate the scanning of a line from Robert Bridges' "Testament of Beauty," a poem written in the pure syllable-counting meter defined by the abstract pattern (2*a*) and the correspondence rule (3*a*):

(4)   Long had the homing bees plundered the thymy flanks.

In (5) we illustrate the scanning of an iambic pentameter line which is defined by the pattern (2*b*) and the correspondence rules (3*a*) and (3*b*). It should be noted that (3*a*) and (3*b*) together imply that an unstressed syllable must occur in each W position. We shall see below that the somewhat indirect formulation adopted here is actually required in order to characterize the full variety of stress patterns that may lawfully actualize the iambic pentameter pattern.

(5)   The cúrfew tólls the knéll of párting dáy.

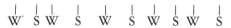

The characterization of the iambic pentameter that has been given here with the help of the pattern (2*b*) and the correspondence rules (3*a*) and (3*b*) is essentially a more formal statement of the description to be found in many of the standard treatises. Thus in Robert Bridges' important *Milton's Prosody* we are told that the normal iambic pentameter line can be defined as

(6)   a decasyllabic line on a disyllabic basis and in rising rhythm (i.e.
with accents or stresses on the alternate even syllables); and the
disyllabic units may be called *feet*. (p. I)

We discuss the question of feet below. At this point we wish only to note
that the normal iambic line defined by (6)—or equivalently by (2*b*), (3*a*),
and (3*b*)—does not characterize (1*b*) or any of a huge number of lines that
appear commonly in iambic pentameter verses, e.g.,

(7)   As ook, firre, birch, aspe, alder, holm, popler,
Wylugh, elm, plane, assh, box, chasteyn, lynde, laurer,
Mapul, thorn, bech, hasel, ew, whippeltree—
                                        Chaucer, *Knight's Tale*, 11., 2921–23.

(8)   Batter my heart, three-person'd God, for you
As yet but knock, breathe, shine, and seek to mend;
That I may rise, and stand, o'erthrow me, and bend
Your force to break, blow, burn, and make me new.
                                        Donne, "Holy Sonnet 14"

(9)   O Wild West Wind, thou breath of Autumn's being
Thou from whose unseen presence the leaves dead
Are driven like ghosts from an enchanter fleeing, . . .
                                        Shelley, "Ode to the West Wind"

(10) Speech after long silence; it is right,
All other lovers being estranged or dead, . . .
                                        Yeats, "After Long Silence"

The existence of such lines has not escaped the attention of Bridges or of any
other serious student of prosody. In fact, immediately below the definition
(6) Bridges notes that in Milton one may find three types of exception to the
norm:

  I Exceptions to the number of syllables being ten.
 II Exceptions to the number of stresses being five.
III Exceptions in the position of the stresses.

In other words, each of the three properties of the line that are specifically
regulated in the definition (6) is violated on some occasion in the iambic
pentameter of Milton's *Paradise Lost*.

To account for these exceptions Bridges and many other metrists sup-
plement the definition of the norm with a list of allowable deviations, which
commonly includes the items below:

(11)   1. unstressed foot (pyrrhic)
       2. heavy foot (spondee)

3. initial foot inverted (trochee)
4. verse-medial foot inverted (trochee)
5. extra slack syllable inserted verse-medially
6. dropping of verse-initial slack syllable (headless)

We shall refer to the account based on the norm (6) and the allowable deviations (11) as the standard theory of the iambic pentameter. We examine next the lines in (7)–(10) in order to illustrate the functioning of the standard theory.

The lines from Chaucer (7) are metrical by a liberal invocation of allowable deviation (11.2), for heavy feet abound in (7). Moreover, there is an initial trochee (11.3) in the last two lines, and an extra slack syllable (11.5) in the second line.

The first line of Donne's sonnet (8) has an initial trochee (11.3) as well as a verse-medial heavy foot (11.2) in the phrase *three-person'd God.* The second line contains a spondee (11.2), as does the fourth line; whereas the third line has an initial pyrrhic foot (11.1) and an extra slack syllable (11.5) *me and.*

The first line of Shelley's poem (9) exhibits two spondees (11.2). The second line contains an initial trochee (11.3) and the pyrrhic foot (11.1) *-ence the,* and a verse-final spondee (11.2). The third line has an extra slack syllable *en* in *driven* (11.5) and a pyrrhic (11.1).

In the Yeats verses (10) the first line is headless (11.6) and contains one verse-medial spondee (11.2) and a pyrrhic foot (11.1). The second line begins with a spondee (11.2) and includes an extra slack syllable in *being* (11.5).[4]

Although the standard theory consisting of the abstract pattern (2*b*), the correspondence rules (3), and the list of allowable deviations (11) correctly establishes the lines in (7)–(10) as metrical, it has a number of inadequacies that suggest rather fundamental revisions. Consider first the line (1*a*) which we have been using as our prime example of an unmetrical line:

$$\acute{\text{O}}\text{de to the West W\'ind by P\'ercy B\'ysshe Sh\'elley.}$$

The line contains an inverted first foot (11.3), a heavy foot (11.2), and two verse-medial trochaic substitutions (11.4). Since all these are admissible deviations, the line must be judged metrical by the standard theory. But this surely is an unacceptable consequence.

The difficulty arises from the fact that the standard theory expresses allowable deviations in terms of feet. (In fact, it is only in this domain that the entity *foot* plays a significant role.) Implicit in this view is the notion that deviations in one foot are independent of deviations in adjoining feet. Deviations in one foot, however, are not independent of deviations in adjoining feet. Thus the line just scanned was unmetrical because it had two consecutive trochaic feet, and such lines are ruled out in iambic meters. It is, of course, possible to modify (11.4) so as to take account of this possibility. But if adjoining feet are not independent, there is a serious question as to the sense of setting up feet as entities intermediate between the line and the weak and strong positions that constitute the line. We shall propose below an account that does not make use of the concept *foot,* and we shall attempt to show that such an account is superior to the standard theory even where the latter is patched up to handle cases like the one just discussed.

We have already noted that an important shortcoming of the standard theory is that it deals with allowable deviations by means of a list, thus implying that there is nothing in common among the allowable deviations, for in the standard theory there are no qualifications for membership in this list. By characterizing the allowable deviations with the help of a list, the standard theory renders itself incapable of explaining certain facts about English verse which an adequate theory would be expected to explain. It was noted many years ago by Jespersen (p. 262) that whereas an iambic line could tolerate a trochee in the first two syllables,[5] a trochaic line could not tolerate an analogous iambic substitution in the first two syllables. He cites the following lines from Longfellow:

(12)   Tell me not in mournful numbers
        Life is but an empty dream

and observes that the second line may not be replaced by:

(13)   A life's but an empty dream.

There is no explanation for this phenomenon in the standard theory.

There is a further systematic correlation which is suggested by Jespersen's observation. If iambic verse permits the dropping of an initial slack syllable (see the first line of (10)), trochaic verse admits of an extrametrical slack syllable at the beginning of a line. The following trochaic couplet is illustrative:

(14)   All the buds and bells of May
        From dewy sward or thorny spray.
                                        Keats, "Fancy"

Indeed, if one did not know that "Fancy" was written in trochaic meter the above couplet would be metrically ambiguous since it can easily have occurred in an iambic tetrameter poem. This second correlation between iambic and trochaic verse also remains unexplained in the standard theory.

Thirdly, Jespersen (p. 255) notes that major syntactic breaks—what he refers to as pauses—appear to play an important role in the metrical behavior of a line. This break is commonly indicated orthographically by a comma, semi-colon, colon, or period. It is noteworthy that two of the categories on the allowable deviation list are commonly associated with major syntactic breaks. These two are internal trochaic substitution, which often occurs after a major syntactic break (see 28*c–d*), and the heavy foot, which is composed of two positions separated by a major syntactic break (see (7)). Once again a deeper generalization is hinted at here which the standard theory does not capture.

To meet the objections just sketched we propose to replace the standard theory by the account below:

(15)   (*a*) *Abstract metrical pattern* (cf. (2*b*))
    *(W) S W S W S W S W S (x) (x)
    where each x position may only be occupied by an unstressed syllable and where elements enclosed in parentheses may be omitted.

   (*b*) *Correspondence rules* (cf. (3))
       (i) A position (S or W) corresponds to either a single syllable,
         or
         a sonorant sequence incorporating at most two vowels (immediately adjoining to one another, or separated by a sonorant consonant).

         Definition: When a stressed syllable is located between two unstressed syllables in the same syntactic constituent within a line of verse, this syllable is called a *stress maximum*.

       (ii) Stressed syllables occur in S positions and in all S positions;
         or
         stressed syllables occur only in S positions, but not necessarily in all S positions;
         or
         stress maxima occur only in S positions, but not necessarily in all S positions.[6]

The order of alternatives of the correspondence rules is significant. Each earlier alternative is subsumed by each later alternative and the later alternatives can be viewed as enlarging the class of lines which are deemed metrical. For example, in (15*b*i) the first alternative allows only ten- to twelve-syllable lines to realize the abstract metric pattern whereas the second alternative increases to twenty the number of syllables in lines which realize the abstract metrical pattern. At first sight the correspondence rules given here with their several alternatives may appear to differ but little from the list of allowable deviations incorporated in the standard theory. This, however, disregards the very important fact that while in the standard theory there is no limitation as to what is to be included in the lists, the alternative statements of the revised theory are subject to the limitation that later statements must subsume—and hence be generalizations of—earlier statements. In addition, we propose that the order of statements in the correspondence rules reflects the complexity of a line. The order is, therefore, our formal device for capturing the important concept of tension. The intuitive basis for this is reasonably straightforward. If the means whereby a given abstract pattern is actualized are narrowly restricted, the pattern is readily perceived as being present in the data. On the other hand, when the means whereby a pattern is actualized are allowed to be of a great variety, it becomes correspondingly difficult to discern that the pattern is encoded in a given sequence of words. Thus no one can miss the iambic pentameter pattern in

The cúrfew tólls the knéll of párting dáy

whereas it takes considerable sophistication to see that the same pattern is present in Donne's line

Yet deárly I lóve you and would be lóvèd fáin.

This increased difficulty in perception of the pattern which results from utilizing more complex correspondence rules explains also why there are no lines in which all or only the most complex correspondence rules are utilized. Such lines exceed the threshold of the reader's ability to perceive the pattern. We return to questions of this type in the last part of the paper.

To begin our discussion of the revised theory let us simply see how the theory permits a line to be scanned. The procedure is as follows: in each line we first establish position occupancy by numbering the different syllables in the line from left to right.[7] If the number is ten, a one-to-one occupancy of positions by syllables is assumed, in accordance with the first alternative of (15*b*i). If the number is one less than ten, a check is made to determine if a one-to-one syllable-to-position assignment can be made by assuming a head-less line. If the number of syllables is more than ten, a check is made to determine whether the line contains any extra-metrical syllables, or whether two adjacent syllables may be assigned to a single position in accordance with the second alternative of (15*b*i). (See also below.)

Having established the syllable-to-position assignments, we next locate stressed and unstressed syllables in the line. We then check to see if the location of stressed and unstressed syllables satisfies one of the three alternatives of (15*b*ii). We begin by checking the first alternative and underlining all positions in which this alternative is not satisfied; i.e., we underline each position where an S is occupied by an unstressed syllable or a W by a stressed syllable. Next we examine the line by means of the second alternative of (15*b*ii) and underline all positions where it is violated; i.e., a W occupied by a stressed syllable now receives a double underline. Finally, we check out the third alternative; if any position violates this alternative—i.e., if any W is occupied by a stress maximum—the line is judged unmetrical. Below we illustrate the procedure just outlined:

(16)   The cúrfew tólls the knéll of párting dáy.

$$
\begin{array}{ccccccccc}
| & | & | & | & | & | & | & | & | \\
W & S & W & S & W & S & W & S & W & S
\end{array}
$$

This line satisfies in its entirety the first alternative of both (15*b*i) and (15*b*ii).

(17)   And léaves the wórld to dárkness <u>and</u> to mé.

$$
\begin{array}{cccccccccc}
| & | & | & | & | & | & | & | & | & | \\
W & S & W & S & W & S & W & S & W & S
\end{array}
$$

In line (17) the fourth S violates the first but not the second alternative of (15*b*ii).

(18)   <u>Bátter</u> my héart, <u>threé</u>-pérson'd Gód, for yóu.

$$
\begin{array}{cccccccccc}
| & | & | & | & | & | & | & | & | & | \\
W & S & W & S & W & S & W & S & W & S
\end{array}
$$

In (18) the first S violates the first alternative of (15*b*ii) but not the second, and the first and third W violate the second alternative, but are allowed by the third alternative. An example of cases where all three alternatives are violated is provided by the triply underlined and barred position in the unmetrical line (19*a*).

(19*a*) Óde to the Wést Wínd by Pércy Býsshe Shelley.[8]

    W   S W   S   W   S W S W   S W

The revised theory provides a great deal of freedom within the iambic pattern while at the same time providing sufficient constraints to make the art form an interesting one for the poet to work in. It is for this reason that when one finds a poet moving outside of the constraints of the meter, one is tempted to search for some aesthetic reason for his doing so. Consider, in this regard, the following opening line from a sonnet by Keats:

(19*b*) How many bárds gíld the lápses of tíme.

    W   S W S   W   S W S W S

This line is unmetrical since it contains a stress maximum in the fourth W position in violation of the last alternative of (15*b*ii). However, it seems quite clear that the poet is purposely moving outside of the meter in order to caricature metrically the sense of the line. The line is literally what it speaks of figuratively, a "lapse of time." This metrical joke requires that the line be treated as unmetrical.

Returning to metrical lines, we note Donne's line (20) as an instance where later alternatives of both (15*b*i) and (15*b*ii) apply:

(20) Yet dearly I lóve you and would be lóvèd fáin.

    W   S W S   W   S   W SW   S

The second and third W in (20) violate the first alternative of (15*b*i) but not the second, while the third S violates the first but not the second alternative of (15*b*ii). Note that the assignment of two syllables to a single position has to be done in the way shown. If different syllables were to be assigned to a single position the line would be unmetrical because stress maxima would occupy W positions.

The assignment of syllables to positions is, of course, a strictly metrical assignment. It does not imply that the syllables assigned to a single position should be slurred or elided when the verse is recited. The correspondence rules are not instructions for poetry recitations. They are rather abstract principles of verse construction whose effect on the sound of the recital verse is much more indirect.

It is obvious that the second alternative of (15*b*i) subsumes the first alternative as a special case. Poets appear to differ a great deal as to the precise extension of the second alternative. For example, Chaucer not only makes use of elision, but allows for monosyllabic words to be assigned to a single position along with an adjacent syllable under certain special conditions.[9] Other poets seem to modify elision as defined in (15*b*i) by allowing it to operate on two vowels separated by an optional fricative consonant (s, f, v, etc.) as well as across an optional sonorant.[10] Still other poets allow for an extra-metrical syllable internally before a major syntactic break. Examples of the latter are:

> (21)   And as I past I worshipt: if those you seek
> > Milton, *Comus*, l. 302
>
> From mine own knowledge. As nearly as I may
> > Shakespeare, *Ant.* II, ii, 91

and Shelley as well (see (25) below).

Whatever the usages may be from one poet to another, they can readily be accounted for by suitable extensions of the correspondence rules, and, as they appear to have only limited general theoretical interest, we shall not attempt to deal further with these rules here.

We recall that in rejecting the standard theory we stressed the fact that the list of allowable deviations (11) was not otherwise restricted, and that there was no mechanism for excluding from this list such obviously absurd items as (22):

> (22)   1. Insertion of a parenthetic phrase in a line.
> > 2. Trochaic foot followed by a dactyl.
> > 3. Elision of exactly three syllables verse-finally.

We must now show that the allowed deviations of the standard theory (11) are in fact subsumed by the various alternatives of the revised theory advanced here, and that it excludes the absurdities collected in (22).

That the revised theory excludes (22) is really unnecessary to demonstrate in detail since there is no way in which even the last (i.e., most general) alternatives of (15*b*i) and (15*b*ii) can be stretched so as to include (22). It is equally self-evident that (11.5), which allows an extra slack syllable in the line, and (11.6), which admits headless lines, are included by the revised theory. The latter is specifically allowed by (15*a*), where the first W is marked as optional and parenthesized. It ought to be noted here that the omission of the line-initial W contributes to the complexity of the line, whereas the omission of the line-final, extra-metrical syllable leaves the complexity of the line unaffected. We have reflected this difference between the two parenthesized sub-sequences by supplying an asterisk to the first parentheses in (15*a*). We have, however, at this point no explanation for this difference. Examples of headless lines in iambic pentameter are given in (23):

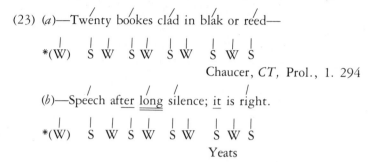

(23) (*a*)—Twénty boókes clád in blák or reéd—

Chaucer, *CT,* Prol., 1. 294

(*b*)—Speéch after lóng sílence; it is ríght.

Yeats

Extra slack syllables in the line (11.5) are allowed by the later alternatives of (15*b*i), as we have already seen in our discussion of (20) above. The third line of (8), repeated here as (24), is an additional example:

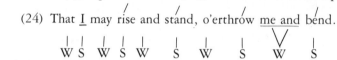

(24) That I may ríse and stánd, o'erthrów me and bénd.

Turning now to the remaining allowable deviations, we recall that the unstressed foot (11.1), has already been illustrated in (17) above. The third line of (9), repeated here as (25), offers an additional example:

(25) Are dríven, like ghósts from an enchánter fleéing.

Here the third S contains an unstressed syllable, a realization allowed by the second alternative of (15*b*ii). (For the assignment of *driven* to a single position, see above.)

The next allowable deviation (11.2), the heavy foot (spondee), requires invocation of the last alternative of (15*b*ii). We have already invoked it in our discussion of (18) above. Notice, however, that it is required to accommodate all of the lines of (7), the second of which is repeated here by way of illustration:

(26) Wýlugh, élm, pláne, ássh, bóx, chásteyn, lýnde, laurér.

In (26) the first W violates the first alternative of (15*b*i) and both the first and second alternatives of (15*b*ii). The second and third W's violate the first two alternatives of (15*b*ii) but are allowed by the last alternative.

The two final allowable deviations of the standard theory concern inverted feet; by (11.3) these are allowed verse-initially, by (11.4) they are allowed verse-medially. We have shown in (18) above how examples of the former type would be scanned by the revised theory. An additional example of a line beginning with an inverted foot is scanned in (27).

(27) Sĺlent upon a péak in Dárien.

$$\begin{array}{ccccccccc} | & | & | & | & | & | & | & | & || \\ W & S & W & S & W & S & W & & S & WS \end{array}$$

Keats

Verse-medially inverted feet may appear in two distinct positions, after stressed syllables (cf. (28 *a*–*b*)) and after a major syntactic boundary (cf. (28 *c*–*d*)).

(28) (*a*) The Mĺllere was a stóut cárl for the nónes.

A. Prol. 1. 545

(*b*) The cóurse of true lóve never díd rún smóoth.

MND, I, i, 134

(*c*) Appéare in pérson hére in Cóurt. Sĺlence.

$$\begin{array}{ccccccccc} | & | & | & || & | & | & | & || \\ W & S & W & SW & S & W & [S & WS \end{array}$$

WT, III, i, 10

(*d*) Frĺends, Rómăns, countrýmĕn, lénd mĕ yoŭr éars.

$$\begin{array}{ccccccccc} | & | & | & | & | & | & | & | & | \\ W & & S & W & S & W & S & W & S & W] & S \end{array}$$

JC, III, ii, 78

The occurrence of two stressed syllables back to back as in *stout carl* and *true love* may correspond to any verse internal W S or S W sequence by virtue of the last alternative of (15*b*). To illustrate this we scan (28*a*) and (28*b*) below:

(28) (*a*) The Mĺllere was a stóut cárl for the nónes.

$$\begin{array}{ccccccccccc} | & || & | & || & | & | & | & || \\ W & SW & SW & S & W & S & WS W \end{array}$$

(*b*) The cóurse of trúe lóve never did rún smóoth.

$$\begin{array}{ccccccccc} | & | & | & | & | & || & | & | \\ W & S & W & S & W & SW & SW & S \end{array}$$

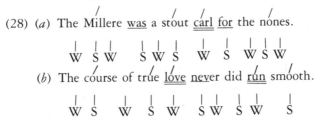

Instances of two stressed syllables corresponding to a W S sequence were scanned in (18), (23*b*), and (26) above.

It is an interesting fact that inverted feet appear only under the following three conditions in an iambic pentameter line; verse-initially, after a stressed syllable (see (18)), and after a major syntactic boundary (see above), across which the stress subordination rules of English do not operate. In the standard theory this is just another fact, to be noted down, of course, but not to be endowed with any special significance. In the revised theory, on the other hand, these three environments are the environments where a stressed syllable will not constitute a stress maximum and hence where a stressed syllable may occupy a W position. Note, in particular, that line (28*d*) would be unmetrical, were there no major syntactic boundary before *lend*. Thus, in the light of the revised theory, the restriction of inverted feet to the above three environments is anything but a curious coincidence; it rather reflects a significant property of the meter. It is one of the reasons for our assertion that the revised theory is more powerful than, and hence to be preferred over, the standard theory.

There is yet another odd fact noted by metrists that finds a ready explanation in the light of the revised theory, but is just a curiosity from the point of view of the standard theory. This is an asymmetry cited above between trochaic and iambic lines with regard to the admissibility of inverted feet in verse-initial position (see above). The abstract metrical pattern for a trochaic line must be of the form

(29)   SWSWSWS(W)

and its correspondence rules, those of (15*b*). If one allows an inverted foot (i.e., an iamb) at the beginning of a trochaic line, one places a stress maximum in a W position, thereby violating the last alternative of (15*b*ii). We illustrate this with the help of the line concocted by Jespersen on the model of Longfellow's "Psalm of Life":

(30)   A life's but an émpty dréam.

                        S   W   S W S   W   S

Here the second syllable violates all three of the alternatives of (15*b*ii), and hence renders the line unmetrical. As we have seen above the same does not happen when a trochee is substituted for the first iamb in an iambic line. Such lines (see (28*a*)) are allowed by the third alternative of (15*b*ii) and are therefore perfectly metrical lines.

Notice also that the introduction of an initial extra-metrical syllable will have no effect on a trochaic line, but its inclusion in an iambic line will be limited to lines without inverted first feet since, otherwise, a stress maximum will be realized in a W position in violation of the last alternative of (15*b*ii).[11]

Once again the revised theory shows certain facts to be lawful consequences which are deducible from certain other facts, and thus provides a more adequate explanation for the phenomena than the standard theory.

The final argument in favor of the revised theory is that, as noted above, it is relatively easy to reconstruct the notion of metrical complexity or tension within the revised theory. In the standard theory it is possible to attribute increasing complexity to each succeeding item in the list of allowable deviations. This procedure, however, is quite *ad hoc*. There is no independent justification for ordering the allowable deviations as in (11); hence nothing can be deduced from that order. This does not hold for the order of the alternatives in the correspondence rules (15*b*): here the alternatives are ordered in increasing generality, beginning with the least general and ending with the most general. As already remarked above, the degree of difficulty that a reader will experience in discerning the abstract metrical pattern in a line can be plausibly assumed to be directly related to the richness and variety of the means that can be employed in actualizing the pattern. It should follow, therefore, that when a greater variety of correspondences is employed, the pattern is more difficult to perceive. The number of underlines in the different lines scanned in accordance with our procedure can then be taken as a measure of the complexity of the line. As demonstrated above this measure works properly in extreme cases. Whether it works properly in all cases cannot be determined at this stage in the progress of our science. Questions can naturally be raised about our decision to assign equal complexity to later alternatives regardless of source. It is perfectly conceivable that the increase in complexity due to the need to invoke the third rather than the second alternative of the correspondence rule (15*b*ii) should be a fraction of that resulting from the invocation of the second alternative of (15*b*i). Such questions, however, can be answered only when a massive body of verse has been subjected to the type of analysis proposed. The best that can be done at this point is to list in order of increasing complexity all the lines that have been analyzed above so as to show that the judgments made by our scheme are not totally implausible.[12]

Complexity of

(31)   1. The curfew tolls the knell of parting
             day (16)   0

2. Twenty bookes clad in blak or reed (23*a*)   1
3. And leaves the world to darkness and to
   me (17)   2
4. Are driven like ghosts from an enchanter
   fleeing (25)   2
5. Yet dearly I love you and would be lovèd
   fain (20)   3
6. Appeare in person here in Court.
   Silence (28*c*)   3
7. The Millere was a stout carl for the
   nones (28*a*)   4
8. Speech after long silence; it is right (23*b*)   5
9. Silent upon a peak in Darien (27)   5
10. Batter my heart, three-person'd God,
    for you (18)   5
11. Friends, Romans, countrymen, lend me
    your ears (28*d*)   6
12. Wylugh, elm, plane, assh, box, chasteyn,
    lynde, laurer (26)   7

It will be observed that the lines in (31) vary in complexity from zero to seven. Lines with considerably greater complexity can be readily invented (cf. (32) with the complexity of (17)), but such lines do not appear to be attested in the poets. The theory, thus, allows for a greater variety of line than anyone ever found use for. When faced with such a fact, one may attempt to revise the theory so as to restrict the number of unattested cases that are allowed by the theory. Alternatively one may attempt to explain the unattested cases in some plausible fashion leaving the theory intact. Since we are unable at this point to come up with a significant improvement over the revised theory, we must look for an explanation for the observed facts within the theory. If it is granted that the complexity of a line is directly related to the difficulty that the line in question poses for the reader, and if one further supposes that poets normally do not wish to turn their poems into difficult crossword puzzles the artistry of which cannot be appreciated without laborious pencil and paper calculations, then it is not unreasonable to assume further that there is an upper bound on the complexity that a given poet would ever wish to impose on his lines. A supposition of this sort is perfectly natural in the case of syntax: while clearly there is no upper bound on the number of nouns that can be conjoined in a noun phrase, it would surprise no one to learn that a perusal of the collected works of all American novelists from Hawthorne to

Henry James did not reveal a single conjoined noun phrase composed of more than twenty-seven (or, for that matter, none of more than sixty-nine) nouns.[13]

The case of the iambic pentameter does not appear to us so dissimilar as to rule out an analogous explanation for the absence of lines such as (32) in verses written in iambic pentameter.[14]

(32) Billows, billows, serene mirror of the marine boroughs, remote willows.

NOTES

[1.] This essay is a shortened version of a part of a larger study dealing with English metrics. The full study constitutes the third chapter of Halle and Keyer, *English Stress* (Harper and Row). (Permission to reproduce material from this book granted by publisher.) This work was supported in part by National Institute of Mental Health Grant No. MH-13390-02 and in part by National Science Foundation Grant No. GS-2005 at Brandeis University. We wish to acknowledge the extremely helpful comments of Edward Weismiller and W. K. Wimsatt. We are indebted to them for many improvements in the exposition which follows; responsibility for its imperfections is, of course, our own. For full reference for all works cited in these notes, see the selected bibliography at the end.

[2.] We use the term "syllable" here as the equivalent of "sequence of speech sounds consisting of one syllabic sound ('vowel') preceded and followed by any number of consecutive nonsyllabic sounds ('consonants')." In particular, we do not take a position on the vexing question of whether or not utterances can be unambiguously segmented into syllables.

[3.] By stressed syllable we mean here the syllable that has the main stress in the word; all other syllables in the word are subsumed under the term "unstressed." Thus in the word *instrumentality*, the antepenult syllable will be viewed as "stressed" and all other syllables lumped together as "unstressed." We regret this imprecise language, but we see no ready way out of this terminological embarrassment.

[4.] An example of a verse-medial inverted foot (11.4) can be found in (28).

[5.] See W. K. Wimsatt (in Thomas A. Sebeok, *Style in Language*): " . . . it is not at all clear to me why the trochaic substitution in the first foot is so acceptable in the iambic line. I'm never able to make up my mind whether it is because it just happened, as Mr. Ransom, I think, suggests, sort of got established, or whether there is some peculiar reason" (p. 206).

[6.] In previous studies (see, e.g., Halle and Keyser, "Chaucer and the Study of Prosody," we proposed that a stress maximum is constituted by a stressed syllable located between two syllables with lesser stress. The definition of stress maximum given here limits more severely the syllables that can be stress maxima. Since in metrical lines, stress maxima may *not* correspond to W positions, an immediate consequence of the more restrictive definition of the stress maximum is to admit as metrical certain lines that previously had been judged as unmetrical; e.g., from Chaucer:

1. "With this quyksilver, shortly for to sayn" (C.Y., 1, 1111); cf. "for quyksilver, that we it hadde anon" (C.Y., 1. 1103);
2. "He was short-sholdered, brood, a thikke knarre" (A. Prol., 1. 549);
3. "Ther nas quyk-silver, lytarge, ne brymstoon" (A. Prol., 1. 629);
   from Spenser:
4. "Ne let house-fyres, nor lightnings helplesse harmes" (Epithalamion xix. 7);
   from John Donne:

5. "Askt not of rootes, nor of cock-sparrows, leave" ("Progress of the Soule," 1.217);
6. "Th'hydroptique drunkard, and night-scouting thiefe" ("Holy Sonnet III," 1.9).

Though lines of this kind are clearly unusual, they do occur and thereby provide justification for "weakening" the theory in the manner outlined here. The need for a revision of the definition of the stress maximum given in Halle and Keyser, "Chaucer and the Study of Prosody," was noted independently by J. Meadors, "On Defining the Stress Maximum." Note, finally, that "unstressed" in (15*a*) means literally "without stress." This may not be invariant from one poet to another but seems correct for Chaucer and the major poets of the Renaissance.

[7.] It is important to keep in mind that extra-metrical syllables, both in verse-initial and verse-final position, are not included in the numbering.

[8.] Edward R. Weismiller (in a personal letter) has pointed out that lines which exhibit a violation of our rules do, in fact, occur in the work of many Renaissance poets; for example, in the metrically experimental poet Sidney's *Astrophel and Stella:*

$$\text{With sw\'ord of w\'it, g\'iving w\underline{}nds of dispr\'aise.} \quad (10.10)$$
$$\text{W} \quad \text{S} \quad \text{W} \quad \text{S} \quad \text{W} \quad \text{S} \quad \text{W} \quad \text{S} \quad \text{W} \quad \text{S}$$

It is Weismiller's belief that such lines are in imitation of an Italian model, the so-called double trochee. Since we have no relevant statistical studies for the major poets of the Renaissance, we are not in a position to judge how common lines like the above are. A reading of the first thousand lines of the metrically conservative poet Spenser's *Faerie Queene* yielded three clear examples: I.i.12.9, I.ii.36.4, I.iii.7.9, which suggests that the so-called double trochee was far from common. They are, in any case, unmetrical in terms of (15) and, if Weismiller's contention is correct, we should expect few lines of this type to occur in poets and in periods known not to be influenced by the Italian model. For a fuller discussion of the term metricality see Halle and Keyser, "Illustration and Defense of a Theory of the Iambic Pentameter."

[9.] For a discussion of Chaucer's rule in some detail see Halle and Keyser, "Chaucer and the Study of Prosody," and for a criticism of the rule as given there see Hascall, "Some Contributions to the Halle-Keyser Theory of Prosody." Hascall's modification is based upon the observation that in the overwhelming number of instances in which a monosyllabic word is assigned with another syllable to a single position, the monosyllabic word is not a member of a major lexical category (i.e., not an adjective, noun, adverb, verb). This seems to us a correct observation and requires modification of the rule along the lines specified by Hascall.

[10.] Extensions of the class of consonants which participate in elision are suggested in Hascall and in Freeman, "On the Primes of Metrical Style." It is one of the contributions of Bridges, *Milton's Prosody,* that the content of this rule actually changes in Milton between *Paradise Lost* and *Samson Agonistes.*

[11.] Notice that the occurrence of an extra-metrical syllable in verse-initial position in a trochaic line will have the same effect as a verse-final extra-metrical syllable in an iambic line; namely, both may turn a main stress into a stress maximum. This suggests that stress maxima in these positions are not crucial to the meter, which would then be a purely internal matter. If this is so, the last position of an iambic line and the first position of a trochaic line would have to be given a rather different theoretical status. Bridges was aware of this: "Tyrwhitt is quoted as saying that one of the indispensable conditions of English blank verse was that the last syllable should be strongly accented. The truth seems to be that its metrical position in a manner exonerates it from requiring any accent.—Whether the 'last foot' may be inverted is another question.—A weak syllable can very well hold its own in this tenth place, and the last essential accent of the verse may be that of the 'fourth foot'" (p. 39).

[12.] Recent studies (see Beaver, "A Grammar of Prosody" and Freeman, "On the Primes of Metrical Style") have dealt with the question of metrical style in terms other than line complexity. They have taken into account such things as the number and position of stress maxima, the number and position of unactualized S positions, and so forth. For example, in a discussion of the following lines from Pope's "An Essay on Criticism":

1. When Ajax strives some rock's vast weight to throw

2. The line too labours, and the words move slow.

Freeman notes that the heavy stresses back to back contribute to the overall impression of slowness: "Stress neutralization is at work even more clearly in another of Pope's deliberately and exaggeratedly 'slow' lines:

$$(/)$$
And ten low words oft creep in one dull line
W S W S W S WS W S

The line is perfectly metrical, but the monosyllabic Adjective-Noun and Adverb-Verb combinations create so much stress neutralization that no stress maxima, or at most one, are actualized in the line" (p. 78).

It is perhaps worth noting that while the large number of heavy stresses back to back in this line is in part responsible for the impression of slowness, it is not in itself a sufficient condition. Thus, we can paraphrase this line by a simple permutation, and while the complexity level remains the same, the line seems impressionistically quite different:

And ten low words in one dull line oft creep.

Conversely, note that (18) above can be made to seem much slower by performing a similar inversion which leaves the complexity level unchanged:

Batter my heart, for you, three-person'd God.

The precise relationship to a theory of metrical style of such factors as line complexity and the arrangement of syntactic structures within the line remains to be explored. The most that can be said at this juncture is that the revised theory, we hope, provides an adequate tool for such explorations.

[13.]We have tried to demonstrate the existence of an inverse relation between metrical complexity of a verse type and the frequency of this type by studying the statistics of different verse types in *Beowulf*; see Halle and Keyser, *English Stress,* pp. 153–55.

[14.]In May 1970 (see Bibliography), two articles appeared: Wimsatt: "The Rule of the Norm," and Magnuson and Ryder, "The Study of English Prosody," which take issue with the theory of prosody in Halle and Keyser, "Chaucer and the Study of Prosody," and Keyser, "The Linguistic Basis of English Prosody." The theory presented above anticipates in certain instances the objections raised. A more detailed reaction to these critics, which touches also upon a number of points not treated above, appears in Halle and Keyser, "Illustration and Defense."

SELECTED BIBLIOGRAPHY

BEAVER, JOSEPH C. "A Grammar of Prosody," *College English,* 29 (January 1968), 310–21.

BRIDGES, ROBERT. *Milton's Prosody.* Oxford: Clarendon, 1921.

_____"A Letter to a Musician on English Prosody." Rpt. Gross (see below), pp. 86–101.

FREEMAN, DONALD C. "On the Primes of Metrical Style." *Language and Style,* 1 (Spring 1968), 63–101.

GROSS, HARVEY, ed. *The Structure of Verse: Modern Essays on Prosody.* Greenwich, Conn.: Fawcett, 1966.

HALLE, MORRIS. "On Meter and Prosody," In *Progress in Linguistics.* Eds. Manfred Bierwisch and Karl Erich Heidolph. The Hague: Mouton, 1970. Pp. 64–80.

_____and S. JAY KEYSER. "Chaucer and the Study of Prosody." *College English,* 28 (December 1966), 187–219.

_____ and S. JAY KEYSER. *English Stress: Its Form, Its Growth, and Its Role in Verse.* New York: Harper, 1971.

HASCALL, DUDLEY. "Some Contributions to the Halle-Keyser Theory of Prosody." *College English,* 30 (February 1969), 357–65.

JESPERSEN, OTTO. "Notes on Meter." *Linguistica.* Copenhagen: Levin & Munksgaard, 1933.

KEYSER, S. JAY. "The Linguistic Basis of English Prosody." In *Modern Studies in English: Readings in Transformational Grammar.* Eds. David Reibel and Sanford A. Schane. Englewood Cliffs, N.J.: Prentice-Hall, 1969.

————— and MORRIS HALLE. "Illustration and Defense of a Theory of the Iambic Pentameter." *College English,* 33 (November 1971), 154–76.

MAGNUSON, KARL, and FRANK G. RYDER. "The Study of English Prosody: An Alternative Proposal." *College English,* 31 (May 1970), 789–820.

MEADORS, JAMES. "On Defining the Stress Maximum." M.I.T., 1969. Unpub.

SEBEOK, THOMAS A., ed. *Style in Language.* Cambridge: M.I.T. Press, 1960.

WEISMILLER, EDWARD. "The 'Dry' and 'Rugged' Verse." In *The Lyric and Dramatic Milton.* Ed. Joseph H. Summers. New York: Columbia University Press, 1965. Pp. 115–52.

WIMSATT, W. K. "The Rule and the Norm: Halle and Keyser on Chaucer's Meter." *College English,* 31 (May 1970), 774–88.

CHARLES L. STEVENSON

The Rhythm
of English Verse

This closely argued essay makes a strong case for the temporalist or "musical" scansion of English verse. Professor Stevenson follows in the tradition of previous musical scanners, notably George Stewart, Sidney Lanier, and Joshua Steele. It is important to emphasize that Professor Stevenson not only offers a theory of metrical effect, but also deals with rhythm, the movement of the poem "broadly conceived." Thus he analyzes the function of metrical stress, of pauses and silences, of syllabic quantity, and of verbal phrasing.

Like Jespersen and Halle and Keyser he rejects the concept of the foot but maintains that metricality is a matter of stress arrangement; there is "the right place for a stress" in the line of verse and a supporting metrical paradigm that generates a pattern of expectation. Unlike the linguists Professor Stevenson argues that the stresses in metrical verse occur at approximately equal intervals: "The metrical stresses of verse correspond to the *beats* of music." However, the correspondence is not exact because verse shows what Professor Stevenson felicitously names *limited variability.* While the musician can introduce "few or many notes between his on-beat notes," the poet is restricted to the number of syllables that can intervene between metrical stresses.

Musical scansion, as it is skillfully and cautiously employed by Professor Stevenson, allows us insight into elements of verse structure that

This essay appeared originally in *The Journal of Aesthetics and Art Criticism,* XXVIII/3, Spring 1970. Copyright © 1970 by *The Journal of Aesthetics and Art Criticism.* Reprinted by permission of the author and publisher. Professor Stevenson has made some additions and corrections for this collection.

neither traditional prosody nor generative metrics account for: namely, the *silences* that occur within or at the end of the verse line, and the phenomenon of syncopation. Syncopation is an especially fascinating deviation from the metrical norm, charged with the significance of "felt experience":

> I no longer strive to strive towards such things.
> T. S. Eliot, *Ash Wednesday*

Because stress maxima occur in the second and third W positions, the generative metrists would label the line "unmetrical"; however, musical annotation shows emphatic and psychologically arresting syncopation:

Professor Stevenson notes, "A musical annotation of verse rhythms is always a little misleading: by correlating metrical stresses with beats it exaggerates the extent to which the metrical stresses become recognized by their timing." He is fully aware of the divergences between verse and music, and makes none of the extravagant claims that previous musical scanners have made. Indeed, this essay is a singularly eclectic performance that treats fully a whole range of rhythmic effects in English verse.

I

The concept of a foot, as used in scanning English verse, was borrowed many years ago from the prosodists of Greece and Rome; and as Omond (1907) has remarked, it was borrowed "without enquiry into the actualities of English speech-sounds." These actualities have subsequently demanded attention: they have led to progressive revisions of the concept, with the result that it is now more suited to English than it used to be. But the concept continues to be perplexing. It still shows signs of not being at home in our language.

Those who seek a more instructive prosody, accordingly, can proceed in one of two ways. They can revise the concept of a foot more thoroughly; or they can reject it, replacing it by one or more concepts of another sort.

In the present paper I shall deal with the second of these alternatives. I shall outline an analysis of verse-rhythms that rejects the foot, together with the more specific concepts (of iambs, trochees, etc.) that are used in classifying feet. In that way, and with the help of neighboring concepts, I shall attempt to show that English prosody can be at once simplified and strengthened.

My views will often be mine only by adoption. I am much indebted to the work of G. R. Stewart (1930) and C. E. Andrews (1918), and to the work of the musically-minded prosodists whose progenitor was Joshua Steele (1775).

II

More than half of my paper will be concerned with *stresses*. I must separate them from their connection with feet, and comment on their nature and function.

In a familiar sense a syllable is said to be stressed when it is louder or (on occasion) higher in pitch than the syllables that are near to it. English makes much of stresses, as will be evident to anyone who realizes that *"in*valid" and "in*val*id" are different words. In prosody, however, it is convenient to use *stress* in a broader sense than this example suggests—a sense in which stresses sometimes depend on their loudness or pitch and sometimes on their position within a context. In general, stresses may be metrical or non-metrical, and the former may be accentual or non-accentual—as can best be explained by the following examples.

In the line quoted below all the stresses are both metrical and accentual:

(1)   But whén the sún his béacon réd

That is not true, however, of the next line in the same poem:

(2)   Had kindled on Benvóirlich's héad

Here the dot-marked stress on "on" is not accentual, but is nevertheless metrical. Any experienced reader, that is to say, is not likely to push this innocent word beyond its normal loudness or pitch; but it "passes" as a stress even so, because it occurs at the right place for a stress. And in the next line,

(3)   The deép-moûthed bloôdhoûnd's heávy baý

the syllables marked "s" are accentual only, their place in their context preventing them from being metrical.

These distinctions seem to me to be in keeping with our "sense" of rhythm; for we are inclined to feel that "on," in (2), has a different status from that of the other weak syllables in the line, such as the first and third syllables of "Benvoirlich's"; and we are inclined to feel that "mouthed" and "hound's," in (3), have a different status from that of "deep" and "blood," etc.

We have, then, (a) stresses that are both metrical and accentual, which I mark by acute accents, (b) stresses that are metrical but not accentual, which I mark by dots, and (c) stresses that are accentual but not metrical, which I mark by s's.

Stresses may be accentual in varying degrees; so for particularly strong non-metrical stresses I could use S's rather than s's, and for somewhat lightly accented metrical stresses I could use grave accents rather than acute accents. For the present, however, I shall not do so.

Let me be emphatic in saying that marks for stresses, like all other marks used in prosody, presuppose or recommend a certain style of reading. That is of little importance for the examples given above, where the rules of English pronunciation virtually insist upon the stresses that I have indicated. But many lines freely lend themselves to divergent readings, and the stress-marks must then be placed one way or another, depending on the reading that is in question. Consider, for example, the alternative markings given below:

(4)   When to the Séssions of sweet silent thought
(5)   When to the Séssions of sweet silent thought

I prefer (4) to (5), feeling that it suggests a reading in which the word "sweet" more spontaneously acquires its importance; but for the purpose of analyzing rhythms I do not want to insist on my own taste. So I am content to mark the one written line in accordance with two possible readings.

In the examples that are to follow there will be further possibilities of divergent readings, and possibilities that I shall often leave unmentioned. I shall presuppose just one style of reading, selecting a style that I take to be rather usual. That will be permissible, I trust, so long as my examples illustrate a notation in which other styles of reading could also be indicated.

III

Metrical stresses have a particularly important function in verse, as we shall see presently; so let us now consider how they become recognized as such. Why do they give us a stress-like impression even when they are not accentual? And how are they distinguished from the accentual but non-metrical stresses that sometimes neighbor them? I have suggested that metrical stresses must occur at the right places; but the nature of these right places has still to be explained.

A part of the explanation is concerned with timing: metrical stresses are recognized as such because they tend to recur, in any standard reading, at intervals that *sound* approximately equal. What happens is this. In the full context of a poem there are usually regular lines like (1), where all stresses are accentual and where the temporal intervals between them are much alike. The stresses in these lines—subject to an important qualification to be made just below—are spontaneously heard as metrical; and the intervals between them tend to be *expected* in other lines. Two further things may then happen. In the first place, a weak syllable rather than a strong one may occur after the expected interval; and the fact that it "ought" to be strong makes it impress us, in spite of its weakness, as doing the work of a strong one. Its stress is accordingly metrical but not accentual. In the second place, a strong syllable rather than a weak one may occur *within* an expected interval; and the fact that it "ought" to be weak makes it impress us, in spite of its strength, as replacing a weak one. Its stress is accordingly accentual but not metrical.

Such is a part of the explanation, but it is not the whole of it. Timing is only one of the vectors that establish metrical stresses. There is a further vector that is equally important—one that normally reinforces timing, but which can also make up for its occasional irregularity, or offset its normal effect. This further vector is concerned with the number of syllables that *lie between* those that are stressed. If the stresses are to impress us as being metrical, this number must be small, and it must also be somewhat uniform. Let me explain further.

In examples (1), (2), and (3) there is just one syllable between those that are metrically stressed; and when we turn to further examples we find that the number, though not always just one, is never large.

(6)   The Assýrian came dówn like the wólf on the fóld,
      And his cohórts were gléaming in púrple and góld

(7)   And whát is so ráre as a dáy in Júne?
      Then, if éver, come pérfect days.

(8)   Únder yonder béech-tree síngle on the gréen-sward,
      Cóuch'd with her árms behínd her gólden héad.

In (6), it will be noted, there are two syllables between those that are metrically stressed; in (7) there are either two or one (though none between "June" and "Then"); and in (8) there are either three or two or one. (Light metrical stresses, of the sort marked by a dot or a grave accent, could be recognized as lying between those marked in (8); but for the moment we can neglect them.) When we consider (7) and (8) we cannot, of course, say that the number of syllables between the metrically stressed ones is usually constant throughout a given poem. We can, however, say that the number varies only within narrow limits. Examples in which the number is as high as four are extremely rare. And in examples where only *one* such syllable *typically* occurs (as is the case for by far the greater part of English verse), the number is seldom changed to more than two.

Now I am suggesting that this *limited variability,* as I shall call it, is no less important than timing in making certain stresses become recognized as metrical. It usually reinforces the timing; but it also has the important effect of permitting the timing to be *decidedly* approximate. It opens the possibility of a style of reading in which the timing is subject to many accelerandos, ritards, and holds, and in which the metrical stresses, in spite of these "flexibilities in tempo," continue to be unambiguously evident.

Consider the following example, where limited variability is particularly important:

(9)   Daúghters of tíme, the hýpocritic daýs.

Here any effort to time the stresses equally will yield a reading that sounds artificial. There virtually must be an accelerando on the words "hypocritic days." The accelerando is so abrupt that one might be inclined, if he judged only by timing, to take the second stress on "hypocritic" to be non-metrical, and thus to take the line as having four metrical stresses rather than five. But since the line occurs among others that obviously have five metrical stresses, most of us, to preserve symmetry, would be inclined to hear this one too as having five. And we can hear it in that way mainly because the metrical stresses are made evident by limited variability. This vector, then, makes up for the sudden irregularity of the temporal vector.

Let us now consider a further example, in which limited variability is not preserved:

(10)   Ac*cor*ding to an edi*tor*ial in the *Gazette,*
       the *gov*ernor is *hope*lessly inef*fic*ient.

It is possible, and without artificiality, to time these stressed syllables (italicized) in an equal manner. But such a timing does not transform the prose into verse. The stresses refuse to sound verse-like; they are heard neither as metrical stresses nor as contrasting (like those that would be s-marked) with metrical stresses. The number of syllables between them is too large for verse, and too greatly varied.

We can, of course, get a better imitation of verse by means of additional stresses:

(11)   Accórding tȯ an editórial in thė Gázette,
       the góvernȯr is hópelessly inefficient.

The accentual metrical stresses are so few, however, that they give us meager help in hearing where the non-accentual stresses occur. To compensate for this we are likely to read the dot-marked syllables as if they were marked by grave accents, and to time them mechanically—with the result that the "verse" becomes stilted.

In sum: metrical stresses come to be recognized as such because of approximately equal timing and because of limited variability. These vectors can compensate for the absence of an accent on some of the metrically stressed syllables (though as (11) reminds us, the accents cannot be repeatedly absent), and they can help us to distinguish metrical stresses from non-metrical stresses.

I shall do no more than mention some of the other vectors that bear on metrical stresses. These include a systematic use of alliteration—an old device which subsequently enabled Hopkins, in particular, to avoid some of the restrictions of limited variability. They include the effects of a fixed stanza form, in which obvious metrical stresses in one line help us to recognize not so obvious metrical stresses in a corresponding line. And they also include certain inflections of the voice—as in the line,

(12)   But being too happy in thy happiness

where the stress on "too" can best be made to sound non-metrical by a sudden rise in pitch. Various other contextual vectors here enter, however, as is evident from the fact that "thy," with its obviously metrical stress, can also be high in pitch.

IV

Why do metrical stresses need to be recognized as such? What is their special interest and function?

I can best answer with the help of a spatial analogy, as provided by the pattern below:

(13)   ——— — — ——— ——— ——— — — ——— ———

We are not likely, even after examining this pattern rather closely, to be aware of any orderly way in which the dashes are arranged. But if we now add ascending lines to some of the dashes, like this,

(14)   ——— — — ——— ——— ——— — — ——— ———

we find that an orderly arrangement, with symmetries and asymmetries, becomes much more apparent. We are likely to see the right half of the pattern as repeating the left half; or we are likely, throughout, to see a long-short-short combination as alternating with a long-long combination.

It will be evident that the ascending lines have partitioning effect: they help us to see the pattern as composed of sub-patterns. So perhaps we may say, though still tentatively, that the ascending lines provide consecutive "frames" that divide the total "picture" into smaller "pictures." The frames, moreover, are similar frames. So they invite us to compare the pictures within them, noticing when they are alike and when they are different. It is for that reason, presumably, that (14) gives us an immediate sense of being organized, whereas (13) does not. The frames help us to make the visual comparisons on which our sense of organization depends.

Let us now consider a slightly more complicated design:

(15) — — / — — / — — / — — — — /

Here the conspicuous sub-patterns are those separated by the spaces, with the ascending lines lying within them. But the *uniformity* of the ascending lines has still a strong effect: it makes them frame additional (though less conspicuous) sub-patterns, of a sort that are overlapped or included by those due to the spaces. And the more we notice the additional sub-patterns, the more we are likely to make comparisons (eye-comparisons, so to speak) throughout the whole design.

Thus in (15) we are still likely, as in (14), to compare the *line-generated* sub-patterns with one another. We then see the ascending lines "primarily" as frames, with the spaces as gaps within the framed pictures; and we easily notice that the first two pictures have these gaps, whereas the third does not. And we are likely, as well, to compare the *space-generated* sub-patterns with one another. We then see the ascending lines only "secondarily" as frames; for the separating effect of the spaces (as said above) makes the ascending lines look like elements *within* pictures. The ascending lines, however, help us to compare even the latter pictures, of which the first two are noticeably similar and the third looks like the first two tied together by an extra short dash.

When the ascending lines are seen only secondarily as frames, they are nevertheless seen as enough like frames to reveal the uniform intervals between them. Otherwise they would be less conspicuous, and less useful in helping us to compare the space-generated pictures in which they provide centers of interest.

It will be convenient to say that the ascending lines of both (14) and (15) act as "reference points" (in spite of the fact that *points* is not quite the right term). In general, reference points are conspicuous, recurrent elements in a pattern, yielding next-next-next serial effects that invite comparisons. They invite comparisons both in the sub-patterns that they themselves generate and in other sub-patterns generated in a different and often contrasting way.

Let me now show that my designs of dashes and ascending lines are analogous to the rhythmic patterns of verse. A perfect analogy cannot, of course, be hoped for. But roughly speaking, the dashes correspond to the syllables of verse, and the ascending lines correspond to metrical stresses. The spaces in (15) correspond to divisions between words or between short phrases (though the analogy is there particularly slender). And just as the ascending lines provide a spatial pattern with reference points, so the metrical stresses of verse provide a temporal pattern with reference points.

In explaining this I shall again speak of frames for pictures, though with the reminder that these terms, as applied to verse, will be stretched even further from their literal senses. Let us consider, bearing that in mind, the example that follows:

> (16)   Who knows whither the clouds have fled?
> In the unscarred heaven they leave no wake.

In any usual reading of these lines we are likely to notice the similar rhythm of "Who knows whither" and "unscarred heaven." We seldom notice it as "dissectively" as we do when analyzing it; but we are likely to notice it quite enough to get an aesthetically interesting half-impression of it. And that can be explained, partially at least, in this way. The pictures presented by "Who knows" and by "unscarred" are both similarly framed by stresses; and their similar frames help us to notice that both pictures contain two syllables, each rather strong, and each of much the same length. (I assume that "unscarred," in this context, bears its main stress on the first syllable.) Moreover, "Who knows" is not an altogether complete picture; it needs to be completed by "whither," which is only a part of the next picture. And in the same way, "unscarred" is not an altogether complete picture; it needs to be completed by "heaven," which is again only a part of the next picture. The manner in which the pictures lie within their frames, or need to be completed beyond their frames, greatly helps us to become aware of their similarity; and the framing stresses thus provide the rhythmic pictures with reference points.

The similarity in question is somewhat offset by the divergent beginnings of the lines. No preliminary words occur before "Who knows whither," whereas preliminary words do occur before "unscarred heaven."

But the stresses, as reference points, are of interest in revealing this very divergence. They show that the picture presented by "unscarred," as distinct from that presented by "who knows," needs to be completed in *both* directions beyond its frame.

When the pictures need to be completed beyond their frames, it will be evident that the latter are felt only secondarily as such. But like the ascending lines of (15), they are felt as enough like frames to reveal the uniform intervals between them, and they continue to facilitate comparisons for that reason.

Metrical stresses are as if ornamental frames, of aesthetic interest in their own right; so I do not want to suggest that their *only* function is to facilitate comparisons. I do want to suggest, however, that that is their main function.

V

In referring to the interval between framing stresses (no matter whether the frames are felt primarily as such or only secondarily as such) I shall hereafter use the term *stress-interval*. So each metrical stress in a poem, save for the first and last, will at once end a stress interval and begin a new one. Similarly, the mark on a yardstick opposite the figure 1, for instance, at once ends the first inch and begins the second inch.

It does not follow, however, that a stressed syllable, as distinct from the stress that it bears, can at once end a stress-interval and begin a new one. For a stressed syllable is felt as having a main body, so to speak, that occurs *after* its stress. Although its stress is felt at the beginning of its vowel sound, any preceding consonants tend to be pronounced so quickly that the stress gives the impression of occurring at the beginning of the syllable itself. A (metrically) stressed syllable, accordingly, always lies *within* the stress-interval that begins with its stress; it does not lie within the stress-interval that ends with its stress. Thus the first stress-interval of (16) contains only "Who knows." It does not contain the first syllable of "whither," even though it is ended by the stress on that syllable.

Since I am developing a foot-free prosody, I must now pause to show that a stress-interval need not coincide with a foot. To call a stress-interval by the name *foot*, as is sometimes done by the musically-minded prosodists, impresses me as being entirely misleading.

In the example that follows, for instance, the perpendicular lines mark traditional divisions into feet, and the colons mark divisions into stress-intervals:

(17)   Milton, | thou : shoulds't | be : liv- | ing : at | this : hour.

And none of the feet (in this case) coincides with a stress-interval. "Milton, thou" falls partly in one foot and partly in another; and so on.

In general, a stress-interval cannot coincide with an iamb, an amphibrach, or an anapest; for these feet do not begin with a stressed syllable. A stress-interval *need* not, moreover, coincide with a trochee or a dactyl. The initial trochee in (17) is shorter than the first stress-interval. And although the first stress-interval in (17) is like a dactyl in containing a stressed syllable followed by two unstressed syllables, it is there *not* (in any usual scansion) taken to be a dactylic foot.

VI

Many of the preceding remarks could be repeated, *mutatis mutandis,* in discussing music. Let me explain this briefly.

The metrical stresses of verse correspond to the *beats* of music. Thus when we march or dance to music we keep in step with its beats; and if we were to march or dance to verse—as we often could though we normally do not—we would in a similar way keep in step with its metrical stresses.

The stress-intervals of verse correspond to intervals between beats; and in the special case of music that has only *one* beat to a measure, they correspond to measures.[1]

Like metrical stresses, the beats of music sometimes bear no accent, and become recognized by their "place" in a larger context. That is true, for instance, of the fifth beat in "God Save the King." A note is sustained *through* this beat; so (if we may disregard those who sing "God save our grahacious king") it is a beat that has no semblance of an accent.

Non-metrical stresses (s-marked) are roughly similar to musical accents that are off-beat.

There can be little doubt, moreover, that the conception of reference points, as discussed above in connection with metrical stresses, has a bearing on musical beats as well. By "following" the recurrent beats we can more easily make comparisons. The comparisons are often concerned with length: we hear first a quarter note and then two eighth notes, for instance, because the beat helps us to get ear measurements of these (approximate) ratios. But the comparisons are often of other sorts. There is an immediately noticeable difference, for instance, between two neighboring on-beat notes separated by a weak note and two neighboring on-beat notes separated by a strong (accented) note. That is partly because the weak and the strong notes are heard as parts of divergent pictures—the divergence being emphasized by the similar frames that the beats provide for them.

And yet the metrical stresses of verse and the beats of music are not *quite* alike. That is true because of a difference in the vectors that cause them to be recognized as such. In verse, as we have seen, the principal vectors are timing and limited variability. In music only the first of these vectors is important, the second having virtually no importance. In other words, although a poet, in achieving a verse-like effect, must be careful not to have a large and varied number of syllables between his metrically stressed syllables, a musician, in achieving a musical effect, can introduce few or many notes between his on-beat notes, entirely as he pleases.

There are several reasons for this difference between verse and music, but the main one is presumably this: The stresses of our language are particularly important for distinguishing one word from another; so in our everyday discourse we get into the habit of noticing only that (phonemic) aspect of them. We tend to hear stresses only enough to make the words recognizable and thus understandable. If we are to hear them as reference points, then, they must be made more than usually conspicuous: they must be so conspicuous that they lead us to break through our everyday habits. And an approximately regular timing is insufficient to make them that conspicuous. A limited variability is needed as well. Without the latter we are not likely to "follow" the stresses, and thus not likely to get the next-next-next impression that invites comparisons. In music, on the other hand, we can listen to the sounds without having to break through everyday habits; so we can follow the beats without the help of limited variability—that being particularly the case because musical timing is on the whole more regular than that of verse.

VII

My discussion of stresses in verse has been mainly concerned with those that are metrical. I have pointed out that the latter are sometimes non-accentual; but I have so far been assuming that they occur *on a syllable.* Let me now ask a question that promises to challenge that assumption:

Does English verse ever embody *silent* metrical stresses—in other words, metrical stresses that occur on *pauses* that lie *between* syllables?

If so, the silent stresses will be reminiscent of musical beats that occur on rests; and of course such beats are of unquestioned importance in music. But the parallels between verse and music may or may not be close in this respect, so the question deserves a careful answer.

I can best handle the question by analyzing some examples, marking silent stresses in them experimentally. Whether the stresses are appropriate can then be subject to further discussion. My marks for silent stresses will again be dots, but placed over spaces rather than over syllables.

> (18)   There be none of beauty's daughters ˙
>   With a magic like thee; ˙
>   And like music on the waters ˙
>   Is thy sweet voice to me: ˙
>   When, as if the sound were causing
>   The charmed ocean's pausing, ˙
>   The waves lie still and gleaming, ˙
>   And the lull'd winds seem dreaming. ˙

Let me first discuss the ends of the lines. As in most verse, pauses of *some* sort are there often appropriate; but in most verse the pauses are merely time-out pauses, comparable not to musical on-beat rests but rather to musical holds. So my marks treat this example in an unusual way: they indicate not time-out pauses but rather pauses that conform to the meter— pauses whose metrical stresses arise from the psychological momentum, so to speak, of the metrical stresses that precede them. Can that be justified? I am inclined to think that it can, for such reasons as these:

By feeling a silent stress after "daughters," in the first line, I find that I can more easily go on to the next line. Consider the words,

> "daughters With a magic."

Without a silent stress there will be three syllables between the metrically stressed ones; and that number, which is not found *within* any of the lines, puts a certain strain (though only a slight one, to be sure) on limited variability. But with a silent stress, separating "daughters" from "With a," there will be fewer syllables between the metrical stresses, and the transition *between* the lines will continue the rhythmic flow that is found *within* them. The same can be said, *mutatis mutandis,* of the transition between the last two of the quoted lines.

In the second and fourth lines the silent stresses at the end seem to me justified for a different reason. They make these relatively short lines (without feminine rhymes) more closely match the other lines. The silent stresses do not prevent the lines from sounding relatively short, so far as the spoken syllables are concerned; rather, they provide a measure of their shortness.

In the fifth line,

$$\overset{/}{\text{When}},\ \overset{/}{\text{as if the}}\ \overset{/}{\text{sound}}\ \text{were}\ \overset{/}{\text{causing}},"$$

I mark *no* silent stress. The usual four metrical stresses are obtained with the help of an initial stress on "When," and the line then flows over, with enjambment, to the next line. If the line were forced into having only three metrical stresses—corresponding to the three that a more traditional scansion might indicate throughout the poem—then "When" would have to be deprived of its stress, and the words

$$\text{"When as}\ \overset{/}{\text{if}}"$$

would invite a hurried and jerky reading, overriding the poet's comma. But so long as four metrical stresses (including the silent ones) are recognized throughout, the reading of

$$\text{"}\overset{/}{\text{When}},\ \text{as}\ \overset{/}{\text{if}},"$$

with enjambment at the end of the line, impresses me as enhancing the rhythm of the verse, and as more clearly revealing its sense.

In "With a magic like thee" I have indicated a silent stress *within* the line, after "magic." I can think of no other way of making the line rhythmically convincing. The words "magic" and "thee" must be much stronger than the other words; and only the within-the-line silent stress, which makes it unnecessary to feel metrical stresses on the other words, can achieve this effect. The same is true of a later line in the poem (not previously quoted), namely, "Like an infant's, asleep," which becomes rhythmically convincing only with a silent stress after "infant's."

So in this example I find the silent stresses appropriate, and easily "felt." That is not to say, however, that silent stresses are ubiquitous in English verse. In most examples the pauses impress me as time-out pauses, giving no hint of an extra stress. And even in the present example I have reservations about some of the pauses at the ends of the lines, which are a trifle ambivalent. Let me explain this further, turning to an example in which the ambivalence is much more obvious.

Ambivalent pauses are midway between time-out silences and stressed silences, suggesting both but insisting on neither. Thus in my own reading of the lines,

$$(19)\quad \text{I}\ \overset{/}{\text{arise}}\ \text{from}\ \overset{/}{\text{dreams}}\ \text{of}\ \overset{/}{\text{thee}},\ \overset{/?}{}$$
$$\text{In the}\ \overset{/}{\text{first}}\ \text{sweet}\ \overset{/}{\text{sleep}}\ \text{of}\ \overset{/?}{\text{night}}$$

I feel that each has only three metrical stresses; but I also feel that the terminal pauses *almost* introduce a fourth one (whence the question marks). This ambivalence sometimes permits the lines to continue,without any conspicuous change in meter, into lines that definitely have only three metrical stresses; and it sometimes permits them to continue, again without any conspicuous change in meter, into lines that definitely have four metrical stresses. Thus in the first of the lines that follow (quoted from the same poem) I feel only three metrical stresses, with virtually no terminal pause:

(20)   And a spirit in my feet
       Hath led me—who knows how?—?

And in the first of these still later lines I feel (inevitably) that there are four metrical stresses:

(21)   My cheek is cold and white, alas!
       My heart beats loud and fast ?

I do not, moreover, find the ambivalent pauses in the poem rhythmically disturbing; on the contrary, I find them agreeable.

Ambivalences of this sort are peculiar to verse. In music they have no close parallel. On first hearing a musical composition, to be sure, even a skilled listener may *confuse* an on-beat rest with a held (i.e., a time-out) off-beat rest; but as he grows more familiar with the composition he will be likely to avoid his confusion. Silences that are midway between on-beat rests and held off-beat rests have no permanent place in music. But in verse, as I have been suggesting, corresponding silences do have a permanent place: they are not confusions but are simply special effects.

Why does this difference arise? Partly, I suspect, because the metrical stresses of verse become recognizable (to repeat) not only because of timing but also because of limited variability; and for silent stresses limited variability is not always decisive in its effect—being weaker in examples (19)–(21) than in (18). The unsupported vector of timing, accordingly, with its dependence on the "psychological momentum" of the preceding stresses, may poorly emphasize a silent stress, and may leave it ambivalent for that reason. But in music, where the beats depend much more on their timing, and where the timing is more exact, the "psychological momentum" of the preceding beats can add a silent beat in a manner that is free from ambivalence.

A musical rest often lasts through several beats, whereas in verse (in my opinion, which is contrary to that of Steele but in accord with some of the other musically-minded prosodists) it is unusual for a pause to last through more than one stress. Cases that one might suppose to be of the latter sort are often (as I feel them) cases in which a silent stress is also "held"—i.e., lengthened by a time-out pause. My remarks about timing, limited variability, and psychological momentum will serve, perhaps, to give a partial explanation of this further divergence between verse and music.

VIII

The possibility of silent stresses in verse suggests a further possibility—that of a metrical stress that occurs "well within" a syllable. Normally a stress on a syllable is felt at the beginning of its vowel sound, and nearly at the beginning of the syllable itself (see above); so a stress well within a syllable is one that is felt *after* the beginning of its vowel sound, during a period when the syllable is in the course of being sustained.

Such stresses raise the question as to whether the syllables of verse, like the notes of music, can be syncopated. For in music a note that is syncopated has a *beat* that can also be described as well within it. More specifically, a note is said to be syncopated when it is attacked off-beat (often with an accent), and when it is sustained long enough to receive at least one beat before it ends.

There can be no doubt that syncopated effects are much less frequent in verse than in music. When they are possible, moreover, a reader may wish to avoid them; he may wish to "place" his stresses on syllables in a way that yields a more usual effect. In the following example, however, I am myself decidedly partial to a style of reading in which syncopations are retained:

(22)   Wanting the sticky, salty sweetness
       Of the strong wind and shattered spray;
      Wanting the loud sound and the soft sound
       Of the big surf that breaks all day.

The marks indicate syncopations only for the word "sound," in both of its occurrences in the third line. The s-marked, non-metrical stress corresponds to a firm "attack" on this word, and the dot—placed over the last letter rather than over the vowel, and rather than over the following space—marks a metrical stress that is well within the word. In an effective reading of the third line the words "Wanting the" must be read quite differently than they are in the first line: they must suggest no stress, and must be hurried a little. The two words in "loud sound," like those in "soft sound," must be pronounced with equal emphasis and in both cases the word "sound" must be prolonged a little, so that its metrical stress can be plainly felt as well within it. In such a reading the syncopated effect, appropriate to a description of surf, becomes arresting, and in no way foreign to English diction. A musical annotation of verse-rhythms is always a little misleading: by correlating metrical stresses with beats it exaggerates the extent to which the metrical stresses become recognized by their timing. But even so, I venture to annotate my intended reading of a part of example (22) in this manner:

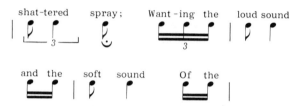

Much depends, let me repeat, on the style in which the example is read. An additional syncopation could be introduced in the second line, as indicated by these changed marks on the word "wind":

$$\text{/} \quad \text{s} \quad \cdot \quad \text{/} \qquad \text{/}$$
(23)   Of the strong wind and shattered spray.

Similarly, an additional syncopation could be introduced in the fourth line, as indicated by these changed marks on the word "surf":

$$\text{/} \quad \text{s} \quad \cdot \quad \text{/} \qquad \text{/}$$
(24)   Of the big surf that breaks all day.

On the other hand, even the syncopations of the third line could be avoided, as in the reading specified below:

$$\text{/} \quad \text{/} \qquad \text{/} \quad \text{/}$$
(25)   Wanting the loud sound and the soft sound.

(The words "loud" and "soft," rather than "sound," must then be prolonged.)

But syncopated effects are in any case quite possible in verse. A prosodist may or may not wish to *praise* a reading that emphasizes them, but he should at least use a notation that permits them to be specified and discussed.

Qualifications are needed, as usual, to provide for certain differences between verse and music. Consider, for instance, a reading of (24) above in which the word "surf" is followed by a brief silence (even a *very* brief silence). It then becomes hard to hear just where the second metrical stress in the line is occurring. Is it occurring well within "surf," or is it occurring on the silence that follows the word? The stress is placed indefinitely; whereas in music, for any parallel case, a beat is likely to be placed more definitely.

Given such a reading of (24), perhaps a better way of marking it would be

$$
\text{(26)} \quad \text{Of the b\'ig } \overset{s}{\text{surf}} \overset{\tiny\sim}{} \quad \text{that br\'eaks all d\'ay}
$$

where the wavy line under the dot shows the indefiniteness just mentioned.

An explanation of the indefiniteness takes us back (once again) to the two vectors of Section III. Timing is helped by limited variability in showing the neighborhood where the metrical stress must lie, but is not helped by limited variability in placing it just here or there within that neighborhood. And a further factor enters: we have no phonemic need, in everyday discourse, of noticing just where a word ends and a following silence begins.

IX

The first part of my paper is now completed. It has been concerned with stresses, and in particular with the various sorts of stresses that are metrical. As suggested in Section IV, metrical stresses are important mainly because of their function. They constitute the relatively fixed, recurrent elements in the rhythm of verse, acting as reference points that facilitate comparisons. It will be evident that the comparisons, in their turn, reveal the more varied elements in the rhythm of verse—elements that are essential to any rhythm that avoids monotony and acquires a positive aesthetic value.

I shall now discuss the latter, more varied elements in verse, though with continued attention to the manner in which metrical stresses help us to make comparisons between them.

Only *some* of these varied elements can be discussed, so I shall somewhat arbitrarily restrict myself to three topics: the relative lengths of syllables, phrase-units, and the rising or falling beginnings of lines. These will be discussed in order in the next three sections.

X

The topic of length (or "quantity") has had a curious history in prosody. The older writers had much to say about what they *called* length; but they systematically confused length with stress, and thus said nothing trustworthy about length in any ordinary, temporal sense of the term. More recent writers, happily, have corrected the length-stress confusion. But they have been so impressed by the importance of stress that they have emphasized it very nearly to the exclusion of length. In consequence, a careful study of syllabic length has not yet been developed.

The musically minded prosodists, however, made an important contribution to the topic. See in particular Lanier (1880) and Thomson (1904). They pointed out that the length of English syllables, unlike the length of Greek and Latin syllables, has only a little to do with vowels and consonants. It has mainly to do with the *context* in which the syllables arise.

Consider, for instance, the syllable *new*. If asked whether it is long or short, we can only answer that it all depends. In the context "new dress" it is relatively long; but in the context "newer dress" it becomes shorter; and in the context "newer address" it becomes still shorter. And this example, which is from Thomson, is only one of innumerable others that could be suggested. Thus it takes no longer to say "sixty dollars" than it does to say "six dollars." The syllable *six* simply shrinks in the former context.

Such examples illustrate a tendency that is quite strong in our spoken English: we tend to fit the length of our syllables to the length of our somewhat uniform stress-intervals. (I speak of verse, but much the same thing could be said of many "segments" of prose as well.) So when we have only one syllable within a stress-interval we tend to make the syllable relatively long, and when we have several syllables within a stress-interval, we tend to make them relatively short.

In fitting our syllables to our stress-intervals we are not as relentless, of course, as Procrustes was in fitting his guests to his bed. Our syllables, unlike Procrustes' guests, can usually be lengthened or shortened without suffering injury. And when they are in danger of injury the danger is avoidable; for our stress-intervals, unlike Procrustes' bed, can themselves be lengthened or shortened. It remains the case, however, that we lengthen or shorten our stress-intervals reluctantly; so we sometimes have more in common with Procrustes than we might at first suppose.

The vowels and consonants of a syllable have a somewhat modest importance in this connection. They determine the degree to which syllables resist being lengthened or shortened—the resistance being of the sort that we *tend* to take into account. So when several syllables occur in the same stress-interval we give them various shares of it. Thus in "He lounged on the sofa" we are likely to give "lounged," with its complex sounds, rather more length than we give to "on" or "the." Our rhythm is likely to be reminiscent of an eighth note followed by two sixteenth notes. Whereas in "He sat on the sofa" we are likely to give "sat," with its simpler sounds, very much the *same* length that we give to "on" or "the." Our rhythm is likely to be reminiscent of an ordinary triplet.

But the effect of vowels and consonants must not be overestimated. In "sat on the," for instance, we do not *always* equalize the syllables. To obtain a contrastive emphasis (as in "He sat on the sofa; he didn't lounge there") we are particularly likely to give "sat" a *large* share of its stress-interval. And quite apart from contrastive emphasis, we may lengthen the word simply because it is a verb, which we feel to "deserve" more length than a "mere" preposition or article. There are times, moreover, when we lengthen the word to suggest a slight punctuating effect, as in "He sat, I believe, on the sofa." (In this latter context, it is not necessary to introduce silences for the commas.)

Similarly, in "lounged on the" we do not *always* permit "lounged" to be long. That is particularly true in rapid diction, when the syllables of "lounged on the" tend (in triplet fashion) to share the stress-interval equally. The shorter stress-intervals in such a diction become crowded; so to prevent the "little" words from becoming unrecognizable we cut down the "big" one.

The length of English syllables, then, is governed mainly by our tendency to fit them in between stresses. It is also governed by other contextual factors, such as those arising from contrastive emphasis. So the vowels and consonants of syllables, though they remain factors that deserve theoretical attention, have a length-governing effect that is far from being decisive.

Let me now turn more specifically to our manner of making comparisons between syllabic lengths—or, rather, to our manner of "hearing" comparisons between them. In listening to verse we "hear" these comparisons by noticing how they *divide up* the stress-intervals in which they occur. So the stresses have their characteristic function of providing us with reference points. To return to a familiar metaphor, the stresses are inch marks on a built-in temporal yardstick by which the syllables are measured. The yardstick is noticeably elastic, and has no clear marks for half inches, quarter inches, etc. But in the lack of any other built-in yardstick we use this one; and we compensate for the lack of clear marks for half inches, quarter inches, etc., by making estimates of where they ought to be. We measure the lengths, then, but "in a certain sense": the measurements give us a heightened sense of *apparent* lengths.

Such measurements have no close correlation with the physical measurements that are made with the help of recordings. For the purposes of aesthetics, however, which are often the purposes of prosody as well, we need do little more than take note of that fact. For in aesthetics apparent lengths take precedence over physical lengths: they lay claim to our attention in their own right. So we must not suppose that our appearance measurements (if I may call them that) are intended to provide forecasts of physical measurements, and are somehow faulty when they do not. They are of interest for quite another reason. And the physical measurements of the experimental psychologists, let me add, would be of greater aesthetic interest than they are IF they could help us (as parts of a broader theory) to make forecasts of appearance measurements.

It is difficult to devise a good notation for syllabic lengths. I shall here simply revive the old dash-cup notation, with the reminder that I am divorcing it from any necessary connection with stresses. (The stresses will be marked also, in my usual way.) Whatever its faults may be, the dash-cup notation has the virtues of vagueness and indeterminacy—and for appearance measurements these *are* virtues. But to prevent an excess of the virtue of indeterminacy I shall use dashes of varying length, the very shortest dash being reserved for syllables that are not-quite-long. Using this notation let me now analyze several examples.

The lines that follow illustrate *metrically stressed* syllables that greatly *differ* in length:

(27)   And there the surly village churls,
       And the red cloaks of market girls
       Pass onward from Shalott.

It will be noted (given a style of reading that I take to be not unusual) that in "surly," "village," and "onward" the metrically stressed syllables are short whereas in "red cloaks of market" they are respectively very long, long, and not-quite-long. Such variations in the length of the metrically stressed syllables (together with corresponding variations in the unstressed syllables) impress me as typical of English verse: they protect it from monotony. Prosody has regrettably said little about them, its notation having been for so many years hampered by the length-stress confusion.

The same poem contains the line,

(28)   Willows whiten, aspens quiver

where a special effect is created by the *unvaried* shortness of the metrically stressed syllables. The line contrasts greatly with a neighboring one,

(29)   Four gray walls, and four gray towers

where the shortness of the stressed syllable in "towers" is rather less conspicuous, and where the words "four" and "gray," both being adjectives, and both being emphatic, virtually insist on our hearing them as having the *same* length.

The line that follows illustrates the possibility of assigning appearance-measured lengths to *silences*:

(30) Now, as at all times,
I can see in the mind's eye.

And it illustrates, further, the importance of syllabic lengths in emphasizing rhythmic similarities. If we read the line as marked, we readily hear a similarity between the first five words and the last five. But if we read it in an alternative manner, reducing the length of "see" to that of "in" or "the," and making no other change, we hear a less perfect and less arresting similarity.

Let me add an example that bears on the so-called paeonic verse—an example in which I mark only the full metrical stresses, and not the hinted ones that lie between them:

(31) Who shall put a bridle in a mourner's lips to chasten them.

In a rapid reading the stress-intervals of such a line become crowded; so in the interest of clear articulation we tend to let no words become "big," and to give *all* of the syllables an equal length (see above). The result, save in humorous verse, is intolerably monotonous; and in most cases the poet breaks the monotony for us by frequently reducing the number of syllables (as in example (8)). In the present example we can remedy matters by slowing down our tempo, or by interrupting it by holds and ritards. But the temptation to equalize the syllabic lengths is not easily resisted. In standard English verse, including virtually all of blank verse, the number of syllables in the stress-intervals is two, occasionally varied to three. That reflects the need of uncrowded stress-intervals, with syllabic lengths that are easily varied— lengths that yield to, rather than resist, the diversity of pressures to which they are subject.

Most of us are not in the habit of paying close attention to syllabic lengths. We notice them rather less than we notice stresses; for when a reader mishandles lengths we often know only that something-or-another is wrong, whereas when he mishandles stresses we often know just what is wrong. But it does not follow that we are insensitive to lengths. We hear them as entering into our "net impression" of a rhythm, even though we only half recognize them. Our prosodists would do well to analyze lengths more carefully; for that would both enrich our net impressions and help to explain them.

XI

I now turn to comparisons between what I shall call "phrase-units." A phrase-unit is a minimally small group of consecutive syllables that "want" to stay together, or else a single metrically stressed syllable that "wants" to stay somewhat by itself. For example:

(32)   The hungry, judges, soon, the sentence, sign,

And wretches, hang, that jurymen, may dine.

The degree to which the syllables want to stay together, in most of the phrase-units indicated, is very slight; but the wants are nevertheless discernible. Thus in "The hungry" the article wants to stay with the noun, and the second syllable of the noun wants to stay with its first syllable. And in "judges" the second syllable, once again, wants to stay with the first syllable. So these become the first and second phrase-units of the example. To a lesser extent, of course, all five of the syllables in "The hungry judges" want to stay together; but these syllables do not constitute a group that is minimally small, so for the purpose of obtaining phrase-units they must be subdivided after "hungry," where the want in question is least urgent. In "that jurymen" the wants are all so urgent that no corresponding subdivision is appropriate; so there the phrase-unit extends over two metrical stresses. In most cases, however, both in this example and in others, the phrase-units have just one metrical stress.

It is possible to use longer brackets that connect some of the phrase-units together, as below:

(33)   The hungry, judges,

soon, the sentence, sign,

And wretches, hang,

that jurymen, may dine.

And two still longer brackets could here be used, each of them corresponding to a full line. The brackets then become reminiscent of the phrase-marks in music, with the shorter brackets indicating phrases that are *subordinate* to those indicated by the longer ones. See Cooper and Meyer (1960) for an analysis of the many factors on which the good gestalten of musical phrases depend. (The gestalten may be "good," of course, in varying degrees.)

Phrase-units are quite distinct from what I have been calling stress-intervals and they are also quite distinct from what traditional prosodists call feet.

The stress-intervals of (32) often *cross* the phrase-units, as in "soon the" and "hang that." And they are often *crossed by* the phrase units, as in "hungry," "sentence," etc. The only stress-interval that coincides with a phrase-unit is the one containing "judges."

And the feet of (32), according to traditional prosody, are all iambs, save for a possible pyrrhic substitution in the last two syllables of "jurymen"; so the only foot that coincides with a phrase-unit is the one containing "may dine."

In general, phrase-units are less uniform than stress-intervals, and less uniform than (alleged) traditional feet. They tend to have several "shapes" within a single line—shapes that depend mainly on the place of their metrical stresses. A phrase-unit may be introduced by a stressed syllable, or terminated by it, or lie around it; it may also *be* a stressed syllable; and on occasion it may extend over more than one metrical stress.

Because of their lack of uniformity, phrase-units deserve special attention. They yield aesthetically interesting comparisons. The more we learn to "hear" these comparisons, the more we realize that phrase-units can lend a great variety to the rhythm of verse, and without disturbing its recurrent metrical stresses. Repetitions of phrase-units, though they occur, tend to be infrequent, and to stand out as special effects rather than as effects that are monotonously standardized.

Here is a further example, in which the phrase-units have "shapes" that change with great frequency:

(34) Sómewhere, súrely, afár,

In the sóunding lábour-house vást

Of béing, is práctised that stréngth,

Zéalous, benéficent, fírm.

To a limited extent, phrase-units have been granted theoretical attention. The prosodists of Greece and Rome used the term *diaeresis* to name a coincidence of word endings with the endings of feet; and they considered a persistent *diaeresis* to be a fault in verse—a fault that can be roughly correlated, of course, with phrase-units that lack variety. The same term, with the same implication of a fault, was subsequently carried over into English prosody, and reappears, for instance, in a recent work by Shapiro and Beum (1965). But *diaeresis,* by definition, is connected with poetic feet. For the purposes of the present paper, in which the concept of a foot is being avoided, it is important to realize that phrase-units can be handled in another way: they can be dissociated from feet and connected with syllables that are variously grouped around metrical stresses. In thus handling them I follow, in principle, the work of George Stewart (1930).

As noted in Section IV, when phrase-units and stress-intervals cross one another, we can hear them *as* crossing. The stresses are then heard only secondarily as frames, and for the rest are centers of pictorial interest; but the intervals between them are still sufficiently heard to cause them to retain their next-next-next effect—an effect that makes them correspond to one another in a way that invites comparisons.

XII

I now turn to comparisons between the beginnings of lines in verse. In a familiar terminology, lines are said to have "rising" beginnings when their first metrically stressed syllable is preceded by at least one other syllable, as in "The Assyrian" of example (6), and as in

(35)   Stand clóse around, ye Stygian set,
       With Dírce in one boat conveyed.

And they are said to have "falling" beginnings when a metrical stress occurs on their very first syllable, as in "Zealous, beneficent" of example (34), and as in

(36)   Sóldier, rest, thy warfare o'er,
       Sléep the sleep that knows no breaking.

Although line beginnings and traditional feet are related (as will be discussed in the next section), they must of course be distinguished from one another, if only because feet are taken to continue *throughout* a line. Line beginnings must also be distinguished from the shape of initial phrase-units: the former may remain the same even though the latter change. Thus in (35), with its rising line beginnings, the phrase-unit "Stand close" differs in shape from the phrase-unit "With Dirce"; and in (36), with its falling line beginnings, the phrase-unit "Soldier" differs in shape from the phrase-unit "Sleep."

There can be no doubt, I trust, that the rising line beginnings of (35) stand in sharp contrast to the falling line beginnings of (36). The divergent rhythmic effects are arresting. And there can be no doubt that the similar line beginnings of (35) make its two lines go easily together, just as the similar line beginnings of (36) make *its* two lines go easily together. Line beginnings, then, fully deserve theoretical attention.

In many poems the line beginnings are either rising throughout or falling throughout. But we must remember that our poets make no invariable rule of that practice, as is evident from example (34) and others.

Rising and falling beginnings are not peculiar to verse: they occur also in music. The principal and middle-sized phrases of music may begin during an up-beat, and in that case they resemble the rising beginnings of verse; or they may begin on a down-beat, and in that case they resemble the falling beginnings of verse. Consider, for instance, the tune (not the words, though the words are not unsuited to the tune) of "It Came upon a Midnight Clear." This conspicuously begins during an up-beat, and all of its subsequent middle-sized phrases (e.g., the one correlated with "That glorious song of old") begin in the same way. In that respect the tune differs from that of "Good King Wenceslas," in which the first middle-sized phrase and all the subsequent ones begin on a down-beat. Musical analysts have called attention to these disparate sorts of phrase beginnings. Mason (1930) repeatedly points them out in the themes of Brahms's chamber music, for example, and Cooper and Meyer (1960) have made a special study of them.

XIII

Throughout the preceding pages I have avoided making use of the concept of a poetic foot. I want now, in concluding, to suggest that there has been no loss in avoiding the concept—that the neighboring concepts that I have been emphasizing are sufficient to render it superfluous.

If we judge the meaning of the term *foot* by examples of its use—and in the absence of a clear definition that is the only way in which we *can* judge its meaning—we find that it has an extremely close connection with line beginnings. For rough purposes, in fact, we can take traditional feet as being groups of syllables that provide the best possible *echoes* of line beginnings—though always with the proviso that the line beginnings are *characteristic* of the poem in which they occur.

Let me explain this with the help of the following example, where the foot divisions, I trust, are those that a traditional prosody would accept:

(37) Can stor- | ied urn | or an- | imat- | ed bust
      Back to | its man- | sion call | the fleet- | ing breath?

Here the rising beginning of the first line—"Can stor-," with its ti-TUM effect—is characteristic of the whole poem from which the line is quoted. It is characteristic because most other lines in the poem begin in the same way. So all of the syllables in this particular line (by the implicit rules of traditional prosody) must be divided into groups that best echo the ti-TUM effect: they must be divided into iambs. And even in the second line the echoing must continue, as in the last four feet. The beginning of this line itself, however, has a stress-pattern that prevents it from being characteristic; so by a method of residues, so to speak, its first foot becomes a trochee. The trochee echoes a characteristic line beginning in an inverted fashion, changing the position of the metrical stress; it is an imperfect echo. But it remains a suitable substitution for an iamb because it does not disturb the echoes of ti-TUM that occur elsewhere in the line.

As the example reminds us, the "best echoes" do not have to take account of phrase-units (which here variously cross the feet). They do, however, have to take account of the pattern of stresses in a line, which may require the recognition of substitutions.

In certain cases there are divergent echoes, of which the best is not easily determined. Consider, for instance, the alternative scansions (both compatible with the same style of reading) that are given below:

$$(38) \quad \text{Are drív-} \mid \text{en like ghósts} \mid$$
$$\qquad\quad \text{iamb} \qquad\qquad \text{anapest}$$
$$\qquad \text{from àn} \mid \text{enchánt-} \mid \text{er fléeing}$$
$$\qquad \text{pyrrhic} \qquad \text{iamb} \qquad \text{amphibrach}$$

$$(39) \quad \text{Are dríven} \mid \text{like ghósts} \mid$$
$$\qquad\quad \text{amphibrach} \qquad \text{iamb}$$
$$\qquad \text{from àn} \mid \text{enchánt-} \mid \text{er fléeing.}$$
$$\qquad \text{pyrrhic} \qquad \text{iamb} \qquad \text{amphibrach}$$

Since the line occurs in a poem where the characteristic beginning is again ti-TUM, these scansions both yield as good echoes as the stress-pattern of the line permits. Perhaps (38) would be preferred by most prosodists, on the ground that the recognition of a subsitution should be delayed as long as possible, or on the ground that the anapest is a slightly better echo of a ti-TUM than is the amphibrach (the former preserving the wholly rising quality of an iamb).

So much for the "best echo" principle, which impresses me as central to foot divisions. If the principle were further developed, with attention to the many rhythms and meters that English poetry exemplifies, it would of course have to be variously amended. It would have to specify just how much of a line is to be considered its beginning, and to include rules (amid much controversy) for determining just when one echo is better than another. It

would have to make provision, moreover, for verse in which the line beginnings are characteristically of alternative sorts (such as ti-TUM *or* ti-ti-
TUM). And for verse with much enjambment, it would presumably have to
take account of not only line-beginnings but also the beginnings of long
phrases. But I suspect that such amendments could be introduced, yielding a
concept of a foot that was still recognizably traditional.

In the very course of examining the concept, however, one can scarcely
avoid having doubts about its utility. Although it properly emphasizes line
beginnings it makes altogether too much of echoes. It can fairly be suspected
of dealing with on-paper units that correspond only to theoretical echoes—
echoes that become audible, save under artificial conditions of attention, only
when they can borrow their audibility from other aspects of the rhythm of
verse.

The foot is not adequately defended when provided with "favorable"
illustrations like the one that follows:

(40)   Sweet dáy, | so cálm, | so cóol, | so bright.

For the feet of these favorable illustrations are also phrase-units; they have
what I have just called a borrowed audibility. And this borrowed audibility,
when sustained through several lines (as in the present poem it is not),
becomes the *diaeresis* that is commonly considered to be the mark of *poor*
verse.

In other examples the audibility of the foot divisions requires a decidedly strained sort of attention. That is evident from example (37) above,
or from such an example as this:

(41)   And nát- | ure, heart- | less, wít- | less náture
       Can néi- | ther cáre | nor knów.

A man would have to be courageous in his conservatism, surely, to maintain
that he hears, rather than sees, the foot divisions of this example. Even the
line beginnings, which for the purpose of these (entirely usual) foot divisions
must be taken as ti-TUMS, do not "want" to stop with the feet, but instead
want to go on to complete the initial phrase-units (here "And nature" and
"Can neither"). And the alleged echoes of the line beginnings, save for
"nor know," are also at variance with the phrase-units. Mere echoes, if heard
at all amid the rivaling units of the example, are far from being heard
spontaneously.

A man would be almost equally courageous in his conservatism, let me
add, to maintain that he *expects* units that correspond to the feet of the
example and hears the phrase-units as pleasantly crossing over them. That

roughly, is what Lascelles Abercrombie (1932) maintains; but expectations are not likely to be sustained when they have so little to confirm them.

My remarks do not, of course, question the audibility of the metrical stresses of the example, or of the limited variability of the syllables that lie between them. Nor do they question the audibility of the rising beginnings of the lines (which remain somewhat conspicuous even when they suggest ti-TUM-ti rather than ti-TUM). They question only the audibility of the *echoes* of the line beginnings.

I have always the suspicion, in reading the traditional prosodists, that they feel "forced" to retain the foot—forced because they need to recognize a uniformity in verse from which its variety becomes a departure. Now of course there *is* such a uniformity and one that helps to make the variety become noticeable. But it is best accounted for not with reference to feet but simply with reference to metrical stresses. When these are (a) distinguished from non-metrical stresses, and (b) conceived as being sometimes non-accentual, and (c) taken to imply a limited variability, then they are quite sufficient, along with the stress-intervals that they generate, to provide such uniformity in verse as we are able to hear.

It cannot properly be claimed that stress-intervals, like feet, have an artificiality that makes them too become inaudible. Some of my previous remarks have helped to show that. Metrical stresses, which bound these intervals, are particularly conspicuous, whereas the boundaries of alleged echoes of line beginnings are not. We hear stress-intervals only secondarily, as I have put it, when they are crossed by phrase-units; but we still hear them, just as we hear musical beat-intervals (corresponding to our steps in marching or dancing) when the latter are crossed by musical phrases.

The prestige of the concept of a foot has been partly due, perhaps, to the conviction that our poets "thought" in terms of feet, and that we, as readers, should follow their example. But that is a conviction that cannot stand up under examination. Our poets have led, rather than followed, our prosodists. And their thoughts, like their intentions, are best judged from their work itself. If the concept of a foot poorly illuminates their work, that is a reason for suspecting that they did *not* think in terms of it.

Although reluctant to discuss the poets' "thoughts," I want to show the implications of a *supposition* about them. Suppose that our poets thought first of the metrical stresses of their verse, together with the limited variability that is essential in making them recognizable. And suppose that they thought secondly of a uniformity (subject to exceptions) in their line beginnings. Their verse, so constructed, would then of necessity lend itself to scansions in which alleged echoes of the line beginnings could be "found."

For limited variability would insure a certain similarity between the line beginnings and the syllables that followed them. The similarity would sometimes be imperfect; but the imperfections would simply correspond to cases in which a usual foot is said to undergo substitution. As on-paper units, then, as distinct from audible units, the alleged echoes would seem faithful to the work of the poets, even though the poets were in no way concerned with them. And our prosodists, in deference to a long tradition, might be inclined to accept these on-paper units as counterparts of the feet of the Greeks and Romans—to accept them in spite of their inaudibility.

XIV

In making these suggestions about a foot-free prosody I cannot claim to have reached final conclusions. The "actualities of English speech-sounds," on which English prosody should be founded, are extremely complicated—as are the actualities of our psychological reactions to them. It is to be hoped that our linguists and psychologists, in continuing to investigate them, will eventually give prosody a secure place within a larger body of theory. But these more elaborate investigations must be guided by preliminary conceptions and hypotheses that provide them with a point of departure. I have dealt only with these preliminaries to a full study, feeling that traditional prosody, with its alien conception of a foot, has done little to reveal them and much to obscure them.

Poems quoted:

(1) (2) (3) Scott, *The Lady of the Lake.*
(4) (5) Shakespeare, *Sonnet XXX.*
(6) Byron, *The Destruction of Sennacherib.*
(7) Lowell, *The Vision of Sir Launfal.*
(8) Meredith, *Love in the Valley.*
(9) Emerson, *Days.*
(12) Keats, *Ode to a Nightingale.*
(16) Lowell, *The Vision of Sir Launfal.*
(17) Wordsworth, *England, 1802, ii.*
(18) Byron, *For Music.*
(19) (20) (21) Shelley, *Indian Serenade.*
(22)–(26) Millay, *Exiled.*
(27) (28) (29) Tennyson, *The Lady of Shalott.*
(30) Yeats, *The Magi.*
(31) Swinburne, *Erechtheus.*
(32) (33) Pope, *The Rape of the Lock.*
(34) Arnold, *Rugby Chapel.*
(35) Landor, *Dirce.*
(36) Scott, *The Lady of the Lake.*

(37) Gray, *Elegy*.
(38) (39) Shelley, *Ode to the West Wind*.
(40) Herbert, *Virtue*.
(41) Housman, *Last Poems*, XL.

Theorists quoted or mentioned:

Abercrombie, Lascelles. *Poetry, Its Music and Meaning*, London, 1932.
Andrews, C. E. *On Reading and Writing Verse*, New York, 1918.
Cooper, G. and L. Meyer. *The Rhythmic Structure of Music*, Chicago, 1960.
Lanier, Sidney. *The Science of English Verse*, New York, 1880.
Mason, D. G. *The Chamber Music of Brahms*, New York, 1930.
Omond, T. S. *English Metrists*, Oxford, 1907.
Shapiro, K. and R. Beum. *A Prosody Handbook*, New York, 1965.
Steele, Joshua. *Prosodia Rationalis*, Dublin, 1775 & 1779.
Stewart, George. *The Technique of English Verse*, New York, 1930.
Thomson, William. *The Basis of English Rhythm*, Glasgow, 1904, and *The Rhythm of Speech*, Glasgow, 1923.

NOTES

[1] I refer to beats that are plainly felt as such. Consider, for instance, a musical composition with a 6/8 time signature, performed at a rapid tempo. It is appropriate, to be sure, to say that each of its measures has six beats; but since only the first and fourth of those beats will normally receive enough psychological reinforcement to be plainly felt, it is also appropriate to say that each of its measures has only two beats. My remarks, throughout the paper, assume that beats will be counted in the latter manner.

Most of the musically-minded prosodists let their count of beats include those that are so rapid that they become plainly felt only if special attention is paid to them; and they tend to correlate each stress-interval of verse with a short musical measure that has either two or three of those beats. They tend, for example, to correlate the two stress-intervals of "cohorts were gleaming in" (see example (6)) with two full measures, each measure having three beats. So for their count of beats, and for their short measures, there is no correspondence between metrical stresses and *subordinate* beats, but only a correspondence between metrical stresses and *principal* beats. But by my slower, alternative count of beats their short measures are one-beat measures. Given my manner of speaking, then, I trust that I am correct in recognizing a correspondence between metrical stresses and beats in general, together with a correspondence between stress-intervals and beat-intervals, and (permissibly) between stress-intervals and one-beat measures.

PART THREE

Poets on Prosody

T. S. ELIOT

Reflections on Vers Libre

Like many of Eliot's early essays, "Reflections on *Vers Libre*" shows a terse brilliance and dogmatic assurance that make it memorable. It contains those kinds of detachable formulations, like the "objective correlative" and the "auditory imagination," which excite theoretical possibilities and tempt the critic into overambitious extrapolation. Whole theories are implicit in "between fixity and flux, this unperceived evasion of monotony"; whole modes of evaluation in "for there is only good verse, bad verse, and chaos."

Eliot's essay must be read in its historical context: as a polemic against shifting trends in the teens, and against the lack of craftsmanship in the verse of his contemporaries. Art, Eliot reminds us, is never easy; the supposed freedoms of *vers libre* are only "negatives: (1) absence of pattern, (2) absence of rhyme, (3) absence of metre." We also note that Eliot's theory of "interesting verse"—the evasion and approximation of "some very simple form, like the iambic pentameter"—was informing the structure of his own poetry. *Prufrock and Other Observations* was published a few months after "Reflections on *Vers Libre*" in June 1917. *Ara Vos Prec* appeared in 1920, containing the masterly "Gerontion." Lines like these reveal, in the analogy Eliot takes from *Hamlet*, "the ghost of some simple metre . . . lurk[ing] behind the arras . . . advanc[ing] menacingly as we doze, and withdraw[ing] as we rouse."

I that was near your heart was removed therefrom
To lose beauty in terror, terror in inquisition.
I have lost my passion: why should I need to keep it
Since what is kept must be adulterated?

Ceux qui possèdent leur *vers libre* y *tiennent: on n'abandonne que* le *vers libre.*
                                              DUHAMEL ET VILDRAC

A lady, renowned in her small circle for the accuracy of her stop-press
information of literature, complains to me of a growing pococurantism.
'Since the Russians came in I can read nothing else. I have finished Dostoevski, and I do not know what to do.' I suggested that the great Russian
was an admirer of Dickens, and that she also might find that author readable.
'But Dickens is a sentimentalist; Dostoevski is a realist.' I reflected on the
amours of Sonia and Raskolnikov, but forbore to press the point, and I
proposed *It Is Never too Late to Mend.* 'But one cannot read the Victorians at
all!' While I was extracting the virtues of the proposition that Dostoevski is a
Christian, while Charles Reade is merely pious, she added that she could no
longer read any verse but *vers libre*.

It is assumed that *vers libre* exists. It is assumed that *vers libre* is a school;
that it consists of certain theories; that its group or groups of theorists will
either revolutionize or demoralize poetry if their attack upon the iambic
pentameter meets with any success. *Vers libre* does not exist, and it is time
that this preposterous fiction followed the *élan vital* and the eighty thousand
Russians into oblivion.

When a theory of art passes it is usually found that a groat's worth of art
has been bought with a million of advertisement. The theory which sold the
wares may be quite false, or it may be confused and incapable of elucidation,
or it may never have existed. A mythical revolution will have taken place and
produced a few works of art which perhaps would be even better if still less of
the revolutionary theories clung to them. In modern society such revolutions
are almost inevitable. An artist happens upon a method, perhaps quite
unreflectingly which is new in the sense that it is essentially different from
that of the second-rate people about him, and different in everything but
essentials from that of any of his great predecessors. The novelty meets with
neglect; neglect provokes attack; and attack demands a theory. In an ideal
state of society one might imagine the good New growing naturally out of
the good Old, without the need for polemic and theory; this would be a
society with a living tradition. In a sluggish society, as actual societies are,
tradition is ever lapsing into superstition, and the violent stimulus of novelty

is required. This is bad for the artist and his school, who may become circumscribed by their theory and narrowed by their polemic; but the artist can always console himself for his errors in his old age by considering that if he had not fought nothing would have been accomplished.

Vers libre has not even the excuse of a polemic; it is a battle-cry of freedom, and there is no freedom in art. And as the so-called *vers libre* which is good is anything but 'free', it can better be defended under some other label. Particular types of *vers libre* may be supported on the choice of content, or on the method of handling the content. I am aware that many writers of *vers libre* have introduced such innovations, and that the novelty of their choice and manipulation of material is confused—if not in their own minds, in the minds of many of their readers—with the novelty of the form. But I am not here concerned with imagism, which is a theory about the use of material; I am only concerned with the theory of the verse-form in which imagism is cast. If *vers libre* is a genuine verse-form it will have positive definition. And I can define it only in negatives: (1) absence of pattern, (2) absence of rhyme, (3) absence of metre.

The third of these quantities is easily disposed of. What sort of a line that would be which would not scan at all I cannot say. Even in the popular American magazines, whose verse columns are now largely given over to *vers libre,* the lines are usually explicable in terms of prosody. Any line can be divided into feet and accents. The simpler metres are a repetition of one combination, perhaps a long and a short, or a short and a long syllable, five times repeated. There is, however, no reason why, within the single line, there should be any repetition; why there should not be lines (as there are) divisible only into feet of different types. How can the grammatical exercise of scansion make a line of this sort more intelligible? Only by isolating elements which occur in other lines, and the sole purpose of doing this is the production of a similar effect elsewhere. But repetition of effect is a question of pattern.

Scansion tells us very little. It is probable that there is not much to be gained by an elaborate system of prosody, by the erudite complexities of Swinburnian metre. With Swinburne, once the trick is perceived and the scholarship appreciated, the effect is somewhat diminished. When the unex-pectedness, due to the unfamiliarity of the metres to English ears, wears off and is understood, one ceases to look for what one does not find in Swin-burne; the inexplicable line with the music which can never be recaptured in other words. Swinburne mastered his technique, which is a great deal, but he did not master it to the extent of being able to take liberties with it, which is everything. If anything promising for English poetry is hidden in the metres of Swinburne, it probably lies far beyond the point to which Swinburne has developed them. But the most interesting verse which has yet been written in our language has been done either by taking a very simple form, like the iambic pentameter, and constantly withdrawing from it, or taking no form at all, and constantly approximating to a very simple one. It is this contrast between fixity and flux, this unperceived evasion of monotony, which is the very life of verse.

I have in mind two passages of contemporary verse which would be called *vers libre*. Both of them I quote because of their beauty:

> Once, in finesse of fiddles found I ecstasy,
> In the flash of gold heels on the hard pavement.
> Now see I
>
> That warmth's the very stuff of poesy.
> Oh, God, make small
> The old star-eaten blanket of the sky,
> That I may fold it round me and in comfort lie.

This is a complete poem. The other is part of a much longer poem:

> There shut up in his castle, Tairiran's,
> She who had nor ears nor tongue save in her hands,
> Gone—ah, gone—untouched, unreachable!
> She who could never live save through one person,
> She who could never speak save to one person,
> And all the rest of her a shifting change,
> A broken bundle of mirrors . . .!

It is obvious that the charm of these lines could not be, without the constant suggestion and the skilful evasion of iambic pentameter.

At the beginning of the seventeenth century, and especially in the verse of John Webster, who was in some ways a more cunning technician than Shakespeare, one finds the same constant evasion and recognition of regularity. Webster is much freer than Shakespeare, and that his fault is not negligence is evidenced by the fact that his verse acquires this freedom. That there is also carelessness I do not deny, but the irregularity of carelessness can be at once detected from the irregularity of deliberation. (In *The White Devil* Brachiano dying, and Cornelia mad, deliberately rupture the bonds of pentameter.)

> I recover, like a spent taper, for a flash
> and instantly go out.

Cover her face; mine eyes dazzle; she died young.

You have cause to love me, I did enter you in my heart
Before you would vouchsafe to call for the keys.

This is a vain poetry: but I pray you tell me
If there were proposed me, wisdom, riches, and beauty,
In three several young men, which should I choose?

These are not lines of carelessness. The irregularity is further enhanced by the use of short lines and the breaking up of lines in dialogue, which alters the quantities. And there are many lines in the drama of this time which are spoilt by regular accentuation.

> I loved this woman in spite of my heart.
> *The Changeling*
> I would have these herbs grow up in his grave.
> *The White Devil*
> Whether the spirit of greatness or of woman . . .
> *The Duchess of Malfi*

The general charge of decadence cannot be preferred. Tourneur and Shirley, who I think will be conceded to have touched nearly the bottom of the decline of tragedy, are much more regular than Webster or Middleton. Tourneur will polish off a fair line of iambics even at the cost of amputating a preposition from its substantive, and in *The Atheist's Tragedy* he has a final, 'of' in two lines out of five together.

We may therefore formulate as follows: the ghost of some simple metre should lurk behind the arras in even the 'freest' verse; to advance menacingly as we doze, and withdraw as we rouse. Or, freedom is only truly freedom when it appears against the background of an artificial limitation.

Not to have perceived the simple truth that *some* artificial limitation is necessary except in moments of the first intensity is, I believe, a capital error of even so distinguished a talent as that of Mr. E. L. Masters. The *Spoon River Anthology* is not material of the first intensity; it is reflective, not immediate; its author is a moralist, rather than an observer. His material is so near to the material of Crabbe that one wonders why he should have used a different form. Crabbe is, on the whole, the more intense of the two; he is keen, direct, and unsparing. His material is prosaic, not in the sense that it would have been better done in prose, but in the sense of requiring a simple and rather rigid verse-form, and this Crabbe has given it. Mr. Masters requires a more rigid verse-form than either of the two contemporary poets quoted above, and his epitaphs suffer from the lack of it.

So much for metre. There is no escape from metre; there is only mastery. But while there obviously is escape from rhyme, the *vers librists* are by no means the first out of the cave.

> The boughs of the trees
> Are twisted
> By many bafflings;
> Twisted are
> The small-leafed boughs.
> But the shadow of them
> Is not the shadow of the mast head
> Nor of the torn sails.

> When the white dawn first
> Through the rough fir-planks
> Of my hut, by the chestnuts,
> Up at the valley-head,
> Came breaking, Goddess,
> I sprang up, I threw round me
> My dappled fawn-skin. . . .

Except for the more human touch in the second of these extracts a hasty observer would hardly realize that the first is by a contemporary, and the second by Matthew Arnold.

I do not minimize the services of modern poets in exploiting the possibilities of rhymeless verse. They prove the strength of a Movement, the utility of a Theory. What neither Blake nor Arnold could do alone is being done in our time. 'Blank verse' is the only accepted rhymeless verse in English—the inevitable iambic pentameter. The English ear is (or was) more sensitive to the music of the verse and less dependent upon the recurrence of identical sounds in this metre than in any other. There is no campaign against rhyme. But it is possible that excessive devotion to rhyme has thickened the modern ear. The rejection of rhyme is not a leap at facility; on the contrary, it imposes a much severer strain upon the language. When the comforting echo of rhyme is removed, success or failure in the choice of words, in the sentence structure, in the order, is at once more apparent. Rhyme removed, the poet is at once held up to the standards of prose. Rhyme removed, much ethereal music leaps up from the word, music which has hitherto chirped unnoticed in the expanse of prose. Any rhyme forbidden, many Shagpats were unwigged.

And this liberation from rhyme might be as well a liberation *of* rhyme. Freed from its exacting task of supporting lame verse, it could be applied with greater effect where it is most needed. There are often passages in an unrhymed poem where rhyme is wanted for some special effect, for a sudden tightening-up, for a cumulative insistence, or for an abrupt change of mood. But formal rhymed verse will certainly not lose its place. We only need the coming of a Satirist—no man of genius is rarer—to prove that the heroic couplet has lost none of its edge since Dryden and Pope laid it down. As for the sonnet I am not so sure. But the decay of intricate formal patterns has nothing to do with the advent of *vers libre.* It had set in long before. Only in a closely-knit and homogeneous society, where many men are at work on the same problems, such a society as those which produced the Greek chorus, the Elizabethan lyric and the Troubadour canzone, will the development of such forms ever be carried to perfection. And as for *vers libre,* we conclude that it is not defined by absence of pattern or absence of rhyme, for other verse is without these; that it is not defined by non-existence of metre, since even the *worst* verse can be scanned; and we conclude that the division between Conservative Verse and *vers libre* does not exist, for there is only good verse, bad verse, and chaos.

EZRA POUND

Treatise on Metre

The occasion for Pound's "Treatise" is similar to that of Bridges's "Letter": the insensitivity, the legalism, and the deafness evinced by scholars (although I feel that the "professorial pint pots" and the dense "Prof. Wubb" are very insubstantial straw men). Pound's name-calling and tiresome pose of *nil admirari* are in excess of his enterprise, but not uncharacteristic of so much writing on prosody. The polemical vigor carries these aphorisms along, and helps to make Pound's more sensible remarks persuasive and plausible.

Pound's most intriguing and useful insight is his definition of rhythm: "Rhythm is a form cut into time." We have a 'dead' spatial metaphor describing the temporal manifold. Pound's judgment of poetic value rests on the poem's 'music,' and the poet's proper handling of syllabic weights and durations. Behind all Pound's theorizing is the classical dream of a quantitative metric for English verse. Meanwhile, the poet cannot rely on any book of rules for achieving a prosody, a rhythmic style. He must learn, through inspired listening, to manipulate shapes in time.

I

I heard a fair lady sigh: 'I wish someone would write a good treatise on prosody.'

As she had been a famous actress of Ibsen, this was not simple dilettantism, but the sincere wish for something whereof the lack had been inconvenient. Apart from Dante's *De Vulgari Eloquentia* I have encountered only one treatise on metric which has the slightest value. It is Italian and out of print, and has no sort of celebrity.

The confusion in the public mind has a very simple cause: the desire to get something for nothing or to learn an art without labour.

Fortunately or unfortunately, people CAN write stuff that passes for poetry, before they have studied music.

The question is extremely simple. Part of what a musician HAS to know is employed in writing with words; there are no special 'laws' or 'differences' in respect to *that part.* There is a great laxity or vagueness permitted the poet in regard to *pitch.* He may be as great a poet as Mr. Yeats and still think he doesn't know one note from another.

Mr. Yeats probably would distinguish between a *g* and a *b flat,* but he is happy to think that he doesn't, and he would certainly be incapable of whistling a simple melody in tune.

Nevertheless before writing a lyric he is apt to 'get a chune[1] in his head.'
He is very sensitive to a limited gamut of rhythms.

Rhythm is a form cut into TIME, as a design is determined SPACE.

A melody is a rhythm in which the pitch of each element is fixed by the composer.
(Pitch: the number of vibrations per second.)

I said to a brilliant composer[2] and pupil of Kodaly:
These people can't make a melody, they can't make a melody four bars long.
He roared in reply: Four bars, they can't make one TWO bars long!

Music is so badly taught that I don't suggest every intending poet should bury himself in a conservatory. The *Laurencie et Lavignac Encyclopédie de la Musique et Dictionnaire de Conservatoire*[3] has however an excellent section on Greek metric, better than one is likely to find in use in the greek language department of your university.

In making a line of verse (and thence building the lines into passages) you have certain primal elements:

That is to say, you have the various 'articulate sounds' of the language, of its alphabet, that is, and the various groups of letters in syllables.

These syllables have differing weights and durations
    A. original weights and durations
    B. weights and durations that seem naturally imposed on them by the other syllable groups around them.

Those are the medium wherewith the poet cuts his design in TIME.

If he hasn't a sense of time and of the different qualities of sound, this design will be clumsy and uninteresting just as a bad draughtsman's drawing will be without distinction.

The bad draughtsman is bad because he does not perceive space and spatial relations, and cannot therefore deal with them.

The writer of bad verse is a bore because he does not perceive time and time relations, and cannot therefore delimit them in an interesting manner, by means of longer and shorter, heavier and lighter syllables, and the varying qualities of sound inseparable from the words of his speech.

He expects his faculty to descend from heaven? He expects to train and control that faculty without the labour that even a mediocre musician expends on qualifying to play fourth tin horn in an orchestra, and the result is often, and quite justly, disesteemed by serious members of his profession.

Symmetry or strophic forms naturally HAPPENED in lyric poetry when a man was singing a long poem to a short melody which he had to use over and over. There is no particular voodoo or sacrosanctity about symmetry. It is one of many devices, expedient sometimes, advantageous sometimes for certain effects.

It is hard to tell whether music has suffered more by being taught than has verse-writing from having no teachers. Music in the past century of shame and human degradation slumped in large quantities down into a soggy mass of tone.

In general we may say that the deliquescence of instruction in any art proceeds in this manner.

I   A master invents a gadget, or procedure to perform a particular function, or a limited set of functions.

Pupils adopt the gadget. Most of them use it less skilfully than the master. The next genius may improve it, or he may cast it aside for something more suited to his own aims.

II   Then comes the paste-headed pedagogue or theorist and proclaims the gadget a law, or rule.

III   Then a bureaucracy is endowed, and the pin-headed secretariat attacks every new genius and every form of inventiveness for not obeying the law, and for perceiving something the secretariat does not.

The great savants ignore, quite often, the idiocies of the ruck of the teaching profession. Friedrich Richter can proclaim that the rules of counterpoint and harmony have nothing to do with composition, Sauzay can throw up his hands and say that when Bach composed he appears to have done so by a series of 'procedures' whereof the secret escapes us, the hard sense of the one, and not altogether pathetic despair of the other, have no appreciable effect on the ten thousand calves led up for the yearly stuffing.

Most arts attain their effects by using a fixed element and a variable.

From the empiric angle: verse usually has some element roughly fixed and some other that varies, but which element is to be fixed and which vary, and to what degree, is the affair of the author.

Some poets have chosen the bump, as the boundary.

Some have chosen to mark out their course with repetition of consonants; some with similar terminations of words. All this is a matter of detail. You can make a purely empiric list of successful manoeuvres, you can compile a catalogue of your favorite poems. But you cannot hand out a receipt for making a Mozartian melody on the basis of take a crotchet, then a quaver, then a semi-quaver, etc. . . . .

You don't ask an art instructor to give you a recipe for making a Leonardo da Vinci drawing.

Hence the extreme boredom caused by the usual professorial documentation or the aspiring thesis on prosody.

The answer is:

LISTEN to the sound that it makes.

II

The reader who has understood the first part of this chapter has no need of reading the second. Nothing is more boring than an account of errors one has not committed.

Rhythm is a form cut into time.

. . . . .

The perception that the mind, either of an individual or a nation, can decay, and give off all the displeasing vapours of decomposition has unfortunately gone into desuetude. Dante's hell was of those who had lost the increment of intelligence with the capital. Shakespeare, already refining the tough old catholic concept, refers to ignorance merely as darkness.

From the time Thos. Jefferson jotted down an amateur's notes on what seemed to be the current practice of English versification, the general knowledge, especially among hacks, appears to have diminished to zero, and to have passed into infinite negative. I suppose the known maxima occurred in the *North American Review* during Col. Harvey's intumescence. During that era when the directing minds and characters in America had reached a cellarage only to be gazed at across the barriers of libel law, the said editorial bureau rebuked some alliterative verse on the grounds that a consonant had been repeated despite Tennyson's warning.

A parallel occurs in a recent professorial censure of Mr. Binyon's Inferno, the censor being, apparently, in utter ignorance of the nature of Italian syllabic verse, which is composed of various syllabic groups, and not merely strung along with a swat on syllables two, four, six, eight, ten of each line.

You would not expect to create a Mozartian melody or a Bach theme by the process of bumping alternate notes, or by merely alternating quavers and crotchets.

Great obfuscation spread from the failure to dissociate heavy accent and duration.

Other professors failed to comprehend the 'regularity' of classic hexameter.

So-called dactylic hexameter does NOT start from ONE type of verse.

There are, mathematically, sixty-four basic general forms of it; of which twenty or thirty were probably found to be of most general use, and several of which would probably have been stunts or rarities.

But this takes no count either of shifting caesura (pause at some point in the line), nor does it count any of the various shadings

It ought to be clear that the variety starting FROM a colony of sixty-four different general rhythm shapes, or archetypes, will be vastly more compendious, will naturally accommodate a vastly greater amount of real speech, than will a set of variants starting from a single type of line, whether measured by duration or by the alternating heaviness of syllables.

specifically:

ti tum ti tum ti tum ti tum ti tum

from which every departure is treated as an exception.

The legal number of syllables in a classic hexameter varied from twelve to eighteen.

When greek dramatists developed or proceeded from anterior greek prosody, they arrived at chorus forms which are to all extents 'free,' though a superstructure of nomenclature has been gummed on to them by analysers whom neither Aeschylus nor Euripides would ever have bothered to read.

These nomenclatures were probably invented by people who had never LISTENED to verse, and who probably wouldn't have been able to distinguish Dante's movement from Milton's had they heard it read out aloud.

I believe Shakespeare's 'blank verse' runs from ten to seventeen syllables, but have no intention of trying to count it again, or make a census.

None of these professorial pint pots has anything to do with the question.

· Homer did not start by thinking which of the sixty-four permitted formulae was to be used in his next verse.

THE STROPHE

The reason for strophic form has already been stated. The mediaeval tune, obviously, demanded an approximately even number of syllables in each strophe, but as the duration of the notes was not strictly marked, the tune itself was probably subject to variation within limits. These limits were in each case established by the auditive precision of the troubadour himself.

In Flaubert's phrase: 'Pige moi le type!' Find me the guy that will set out with sixty-four general matrices for rhythm and having nothing to say, or more especially nothing germane or kindred to the original urge which created those matrices, and who will therewith utter eternal minstrelsy, or keep the reader awake.

As in the case of Prof. Wubb or whatever his name was, the ignorant of one generation set out to make laws, and gullible children next try to obey them.

III

The populace loved the man who said 'Look into thine owne hearte and write' or approved Uc St Circ, or whoever it was who recorded: 'He made songs because he had a will to make songs and not because love moved him thereto. And nobody paid much attention to either him or his poetry.'

All of which is an infinite remove from the superstition that poetry isn't an art, or that prosody isn't an art WITH LAWS.

But like the laws of any art they are not laws to be learnt by rule of thumb. 'La sculpture n'est pas pour les jeunes hommes,' said Brancusi. Hokusai and Chaucer have borne similar witness.

Pretended treatises giving recipes for metric are as silly as would be a book giving you measurements for producing a masterpiece à la Botticelli.

Proportion, laws of proportion. Pier della Francesca having thought longer, knew more than painters who have not taken the trouble.

'La section d'or'[4] certainly helped master architects. But you learn painting by eye, not by algebra. Prosody and melody are attained by the listening ear, not by an index of nomenclatures, or by learning that such and such a foot is called spondee. Give your draughtsman sixty-four stencils of 'Botticelli's most usual curves'? And he will make you a masterpiece?

Beyond which we will never recover the art of *writing to be sung* until we begin to pay some attention to the sequence, or scale, of vowels in the line, and of the vowels terminating the group of lines in a series.

NOTES

[1] *ch*, Neo-Celtic for t.
[2] Tibor Serly.
[3] Pub. Delagrave, Paris.
[4] Traditions of architectural proportion.

THEODORE ROETHKE

What Do I Like?

Theodore Roethke composes an elegant *jeu d'esprit*. He draws on his own verse for examples of prosodic effect; he also shows how certain rhythms originate in popular verse and early Tudor lyrics. Roethke's immense skill and zest are evidences of a rare spirit. The imagination that shaped his poetry shapes the brilliant analyses here.

Especially valuable are Roethke's observations on what Eliot calls "the contrast between fixity and flux." Indeed, Roethke (doubtless unconsciously) closely approximates a formulation from "Reflections on *Vers Libre*": "the ghost of some simple metre should lurk behind the arras in even the 'freest' verse; to advance menacingly as we doze, and withdraw as we rouse. Or freedom is only truly freedom when it appears against the background of an artificial limitation."

Robert Graves (q.v.) quarrels with (and, in my opinion, misunderstands) this aesthetic principle: that a formal structure exists to be evaded, varied, or departed from. Mere regularity is monotony; unconsidered or unconscious freedom is anarchy. "There is no escape from metre; there is only mastery." And Roethke was one of our modern masters of meter and rhythm.

What do I like? Listen:

> Hinx, minx, the old witch winks,
> The fat begins to fry,

> There's nobody home but Jumping Joan,
> And Father, and Mother, and I.

Now what makes that catchy, to use Mr. Frost's phrase? For one thing, the rhythm. Five stresses out of a possible six in the first line. Though maybe "old" doesn't take quite as strong a stress as the others. And three—keep noticing that magic number—internal rhymes, hinx, minx, winks. And notice too the apparent mysteriousness of the action. Something happens right away—the old witch winks and she sets events into motion. The fat begins to fry, literally and symbolically. She commands—no old fool witch this one. Notice that the second line, "The fat begins to fry," is absolutely regular metrically. It's all iambs, a thing that often occurs when previous lines are sprung or heavily counterpointed. The author doesn't want to get too far from his base, from his ground beat. The third line varies again with an anapest and variations in the "o" and "u" sound: "There's nobody home but Jumping Joan." Then the last line—anapest lengthening the line out to satisfy the ear: "And Father, and Mother, and I."

Sometimes we are inclined to feel that Mother Goose, or the traditional kind of thing, is almost infallible as memorable speech. The phrase is Auden's but this is by no means so. There is another version that goes:

> Hink, mink, the old witch stinks,
> The fat begins to fry
> Nobody's home but Jumping Joan,
> Jumping Joan and I.

Well, the whole situation has obviously altered, for the better perhaps from the standpoint of the speaker at least. But in his excitement he has produced a much inferior poem. First, deleting the "s's" takes some of the force away from the three rhyming words—"Hinx, minx, the old witch winks"—the triad. What's more, he has become tiresomely naturalistic. The old witch stinks—hardly a fresh piece of observation. *Stink*'s a splendid word, but here it is a bore. It is a prerogative of old witches to stink. Part of their stock in trade as it were, and nobody mentions it. Take the change from *minx,* which means of course a pert little vixen of a girl, and carries with it overtones of tenderness or, further back, a wanton, a roaring girl. And the mink, a wonderful little predatory animal with a characteristic odor. But if we keep that in mind the line becomes an olfactory horror. It's some fusty little cave these two have in the absence of father and mother. And their absence takes away the real drama from the situation. It's a roll in the hay, and nothing more.

Allow me another I love:

> I N spells in.
> I was in my kitchin,
> Doin' a bit of stitchin'
> Old Father Nimble,
> Came 'n took ·my thimble.
> I got a great big stone.
> Hit him on the belly bone.
> O U T spells out.

Here we see how light "i" and short "i" and feminine endings can make for speed and rhythmical quickness, velocity and then, with the words following the action, that truly awesome and portentous line with its spondees, "I got a great big stone," and then the sudden speedup in the action, the triumphant release from a frustration, I suppose the Freudians would say, "Hit him on the belly bone. O U T spells out." Take another, a single line, which is always a test. "Great A, little a, bouncing B." There are three shifts of pace—it's a triad again, lovely alliterations, the long full vowels combined. Names themselves can be a love in half the poem:

> Julius Caesar Pompey Green
> Wore a jacket of velveteen.

Here we're cranked up by four trochees in the first line. The second line would be dull by itself, but that first line, the impetus of it, is still bearing us along.

What's my real point by these little examples? It's this. That while our genius in the language may be essentially iambic, particularly in the formal lyric, much of memorable or passionate speech is strongly stressed, irregular, even sprung, if you will. Now we see that the name itself, the direct address, makes for the memorable, for rhythmical interest; often it means an implied dialogue. Take the ridiculous

> Oh Father dear, do ships at sea
> Have legs way down below?
> Of course they do, you goosey you,
> Or how else could they go?

Or, if you can stand my Scots:

> Says Tweed to Till—
> 'What gars ye rin sae still?'
> Says Till to Tweed—'Though ye rin with speed
> And I rin slaw,
> For ae man that ye droon
> I droon twa!'

But, you may protest, these are the rhythms of children, of folk material, strongly stressed—memorable perhaps, but do they appear in poetry today? The answer is yes, certainly in some poets. For instance Auden's

> The silly fool, the silly fool
> Was sillier in school
> But beat the bully as a rule.
>
> The youngest son, the youngest son
> Was certainly no wise one
> Yet could surprise one.
>
> Or rather, or rather
> To be posh, we gather,
> One should have no father.

Then the cryptic and elliptical end:

> Simple to prove
> That deeds indeed
> In life succeed
> But love in love
> And tales in tales
> Where no one fails.

Not all Mother Goosie to be sure. And the 'rather-father' rhyme maybe comes from Sam Johnson's

> If a man who turnips cries,
> Cries not when his father dies,
> It must prove that he would rather
> Have a turnip than a father.

Or take an example from myself, a piece, "I Need, I Need." In the first section the protagonist, a little boy, is very sad. Then there is a jump-rope section in which two children chant in alternate aggressive dialogue. Then their aggression trails off into something else. This goes:

> Even steven all is less:
> I haven't time for sugar,
> Put your finger in your face,
> And there will be a booger.

> A one is a two is
> I know what you is:
> You're not very nice,—
> So touch my toes twice.

> I know you are my nemesis
> So bibble where the pebble is.
> The Trouble is with No and Yes
> As you can see I guess I guess.

> I wish I was a pifflebob
> I wish I was a funny
> I wish I had ten thousand hats,
> And made a lot of money.

> Open a hole and see the sky:
> A duck knows something
> You and I don't
> Tomorrow is Friday.

> Not you I need.
> Go play with your nose.
> Stay in the sun,
> Snake-eyes.

Some of the poems I cherish from the dramatists have heavily pronounced, strongly expressed spot rhythms. They are written to be sung, or maybe danced to. Here from *Ralph Roister Doister:*

> I mun be married a Sunday;
> I mun be married a Sunday;
> Whosoever shall come that way,
> I mun be married a Sunday.

> Roister Doister is my name;
> Roister Doister is my name;

> A lusty brute I am the same;
> I mun be married a Sunday.
>
> Christian Custance have I found;
> Christian Custance have I found;
> A widow worth a thousand pound;
> I mun be married a Sunday.

And so on. Notice that shift in the second stanza, in tone, and feeling—how it goes into another speed rhythmically. George Peele, that wonderful poet, abounds in incantatory effects in the same propulsion. Here is the opening of a dialogue:

> Fair and fair, and twice so fair,
> As fair as any may be,
> The fairest shepherd on our green, A love for any lady.

And later:

> And of my love my roundelay,
> My merry, merry, merry roundelay,
> Concludes with Cupid's curse:
> They that do change old love for new,
> Pray gods they change for worse!

Repetition in word and phrase and in idea is the very essence of poetry and particularly of this kind of poetry. Notice how these poets can and do change the pace, and the change is right psychologically. We say the command, the hortatory, often makes for the memorable. We're caught up, involved. It is implied we do something, at least vicariously. But it can also be very tricky—it can seem to have a factitious strength. The emotion must be strong and legitimate and not fabricated. Thus when Elinor Wylie writes:

> Go study to disdain
> The frail, the overfine

I can't get past the first line. There is no conviction, no natural rhythm of speech. I suppose there must be an element of the startling, or the strange, or the absurd. Yeats is magnificent, often, at getting the right tone, seizing the attention:

> 'Call down the hawk from the air;
> Let him be hooded or caged wild'

or

> Come swish around, my pretty punk,
> And keep me dancing still
> That I may stay a sober man
> Although I drink my fill.

Or Donne's "So, so, breake off this last lamenting kisse, . . ." I think of Bogan's "Come, Break with Time" as a supreme example of this kind of thing.

> Come, break with time,
> You who were lorded
> By a clock's chime
> So ill afforded.
> If time is allayed
> Be not afraid.
>
> *I shall break, if I will.* Break, since you must.
> Time has its fill,
> Sated with dust. Long the clock's hand
> Burned like a brand.
>
> Take the rock's speed
> And the earth's heavy measure.
> Let buried sea
> Drain out time's pleasure,
> Take time's decrees.
> Come, cruel ease.

Here is a strong stress again, and the emotion powerful. We are into the theme immediately, a great theme always but one that few can handle. Say anything new about today. Notice a cunning shift of rhythm in the last stanza, the pick-up in energy. The change reminding me always (and perhaps this is deliberate) of the Wordsworthian

> No motion has she now, no force;
> She neither hears nor sees;
> Rolled round in earth's diurnal course
> With rocks, and stones, and trees.

In some more serious poetry we see again how the direct address can pull us up sharply. We are used to this in spoken language. Maybe we hark back to the condition of the child when we are being told. Almost invariably a dramatic situation, some kind of opposition, is indicated. Thus Charlotte Mew's

> Sweetheart, for such a day
> One mustn't grudge the score;

or Donne's

> When by thy scorne, O murderess, I am dead.

Or the action itself can be dramatic, as in Herbert's "I struck the board, and cry'd 'No more'." Or the situation can be given dramatically, as in Kunitz'

> Within the city of the burning cloud,
> Dragging my life behind me in a sack
> Naked I prowl, . . .

Nor must we forget the rhetorical question, as in W. H. Davies' lovely and little-known poem, "V is for Venus":

> Is that star dumb, or am I deaf?
> Hour after hour I listen here
> To catch the lovely music played
> By Venus down the evening air.
>
> Before the other stars come out,
> Before the Moon is in her place—
> I sit and watch those fingers move,
> And mark the twitching of her face.
>
> Hour after hour I strain my ears
> For the lovely notes that will not come:
> Is it my mortal flesh that's deaf,
> Or that long-fingered star that's dumb?

And he *ends* with a question, you see. To question and to affirm, I suppose, are among the supreme duties of a poet.

But what about the rhythm and the motion of the poem as a whole? Are there any ways of sustaining it, you may ask? We must keep in mind that rhythm is the entire movement, the flow, the recurrence of stress and un-stress that is related to the rhythms of the blood, the rhythms of nature. It involves certainly stress, time, pitch, the texture of the words, the total meaning of the poem. We've been told that a rhythm is invariably produced by playing against an established pattern. Blake does this admirably in "The Poison Tree":

> I was angry with my friend:
> I told my wrath, my wrath did end.
> I was angry with my foe:
> I told it not, my wrath did grow,
>
> And I watered it in fears
> Night and morning with my tears,
> And I sunned it with smiles
> And with soft deceitful wiles.
>
> And it grew both day and night,
> Till it bore an apple bright,
> And my foe beheld it shine,
> And he knew that it was mine,—
>
> And into my garden stole
> When the night had veiled the pole;
> In the morning, glad I see
> My foe outstretched beneath the tree.

The first and third lines in the first stanza have really only two stresses. The lines said in an absolute rush, "I was angry with my friend," "I was angry with my foe." But each is followed by a perfectly regular iambic four-beat line: "I told my wrath, my wrath did end," "I told it not, my wrath did grow." The whole poem is a masterly example of variation in rhythm, of playing against meter. It's what Blake has called "the bounding line," the nervousness, the tension, the energy in the whole poem. And this is a clue to everything. Rhythm gives us the very psychic energy of the speaker, in one emotional situation at least.

But there are slow rhythms too, for we're not always emotionally high. And these, as any practitioner will find, are very difficult to sustain in poetry without boring the reader. Listen to Janet Lewis' "Girl Help":

> Mild and slow and young,
> She moves about the room,
> And stirs the summer dust
> With her wide broom.
>
> In the warm, lofted air,
> Soft lips together pressed,

Soft wispy hair,
She stops to rest,

And stops to breathe,
Amid the summer hum,
The great white lilac bloom
Scented with days to come.

Here we see particularly the effect of texture, especially the vowel sounds as well as the effect of the dentates, the "d's" and "t's." The first line sets the pace. It *can't* be said fast. "Mild and slow and young." It's a little vignette, very feminine, absolutely true emotionally. The drowsy adolescent. But the poem is not static. The girl moves, she stirs, she stops to rest, and stops to breathe. At last, a real pick-up in motion. And the girl, virtually embraced by the season, is part of it herself. It's nonsense, of course, to think that memorableness in poetry comes solely from rhetorical devices, or the following of certain sound patterns, or contrapuntal rhythmical effects. We all know that poetry is shot through with appeals to the unconscious, to the fears and desires that go far back into our childhood, into the imagination of the race. And we know that some words, like *hill, plow, mother, window, bird, fish,* are so drenched with human association, they sometimes can make even bad poems evocative. I remember the first time I heard Robert Frost read, in 1930. Suddenly a line, I think it was from Shakespeare, came into his head. He recited it. "Listen to that," he said. "Just like a *hiss,* just like a *hiss.*" It is what Eliot has called "the auditory imagination." The sinuousness. A rhythm like the tail of a fish, a cadence like the sound of the sea or the arbor bees, a droning, a hissing, a sighing. I find it in early Auden:

Shall memory restore
The steps and the shore,
The face and the meeting place;
Shall the bird live,
Shall the fish dive,
And sheep obey
In a sheep's way;
Can love remember
The question and the answer,
Or love recover
What has been dark and rich and warm all over?

Or to quote from my own "The Lost Son," the protagonist, we are told, is hunting, hunting along the river down among the rubbish, the bug-riddled foliage, by the muddy pond edge, by the bog holes, by the shrunken lake, hunting, in the heat of summer.

> The shape of a rat?
> It's bigger than that
> It's less than a leg
> And more than a nose,
> Just under the water
> It usually goes.
>
> Is it soft like a mouse?
> Can it wrinkle its nose?
> Could it come in the house
> On the tips of its toes?
>
> Take the skin of a cat
> And the back of an eel,
> Then roll them in grease,—
> That's the way it would feel.
>
> It's sleek as an otter
> With wide webby toes
> Just under the water
> It usually goes.

Curiously, we find this primitiveness of the imagination cropping up in the most sophisticated poetry. In Eliot; in Stevens' "She sang beyond the genius of the sea," and he keeps playing with that wavelike repetitive motion until the whole poem reverberates, and resounds to the pitch and swell of the sea itself. Stevens can also intone and doodle platonically. But it's the wildly nutty ones of his that I cherish thus:

> The garden flew round with the angel,
> The angel flew round with the clouds,
> And the clouds flew round and the clouds flew round
> And the clouds flew round with the clouds.
>
> Is there any secret in skulls,
> The cattle skulls in the woods?
> Do the drummers in black hoods
> Rumble anything out of their drums?
>
> Mrs. Anderson's Swedish baby
> Might well have been German or Spanish,

> Yet that things go round and again go round
> Has rather a classical sound.

A real piece of sophisticated looniness. We haven't lost, we have recovered,
in Stevens at least, the secret of being lyrically funny. We are closer, rhythmically I think, to the nursery rhyme, the poem of the common speech. If we
concern ourselves with more primitive effects in poetry, we come inevitably
to consideration, I think, of verse that is closer to prose. And here we jump
rhythmically to a kind of opposite extreme. To many strong stresses, or to a
playing against an iambic pattern, a loosening up, a longer, more irregular
foot. I agree that free verse is a denial in terms. There is, invariably, the
ghost of some other form, often blank verse, behind what is written, or the
more elaborate rise and fall of the rhythmical prose sentence. Let me point
up, to use Mr. Warren's phrase, in a more specific way the difference between the formal poem and the more proselike piece. Mr. Ransom has read
his beautiful elegy, "Bells for John Whiteside's Daughter"; I'd like to read
"Elegy for Jane" on the same theme, a poem, I'm proud to say, Mr. Ransom
first printed.

> I remember the neckcurls, limp and damp as tendrils;
> And her quick look, a sidelong pickerel smile;
> And how, once startled into talk, the light syllables leaped for her,
> And she balanced in the delight of her thought,
> A wren, happy, tail into the wind,
> Her song trembling the twigs and small branches.
> The shade sang with her;
> The leaves, their whispers turned to kissing;
> And the mold sang in the bleached valleys under the rose.
>
> Oh, when she was sad, she cast herself down into such a pure depth,
> Even a father could not find her:
> Scraping her cheek against straw;
> Stirring the clearest water.
>
> My sparrow, you are not here,
> Waiting like a fern, making a spiny shadow.
> The sides of wet stones cannot console me,
> Nor the moss, wound with the last light.
>
> If only I could nudge you from this sleep,
> My maimed darling, my skittery pigeon.
> Over this damp grave I speak the words of my love:

I, with no rights in this matter,
Neither father nor lover.

I think any reader would agree that Mr. Ransom's is a superior piece; the emotion subtler, more complex and kept in control, the psychological distance maintained with great skill. The understatement of "brown study," for instance, and the rhythms, the light "i's," the off-rhymes, the feminine endings—"the body," "study." The whole thing in beautiful balance, a truly classical restraint. Behind this piece, as in a Hardy lyric, lies a whole world. There is an immense tenderness, that rare quality in modern poetry, in Mr. Ransom's elegy. It makes me want to love all of the South, and that's an undertaking! But let me indicate one or two technical effects in my little piece. For one thing, the enumeration, the favorite device of the more irregular poem. We see it again and again in Whitman and Lawrence. "I remember," then the listing, the appositions, and the absolute construction. "Her song trembling," etc. Then the last three lines in the stanza lengthen out:

The shade sang with her;
The leaves, their whispers turned to kissing;
And the mold sang in the bleached valleys under the rose.

A kind of continuing triad. In the last two stanzas exactly the opposite occurs, the final lines being,

Over this damp grave I speak the words of my love:
I, with no rights in this matter,
Neither father nor lover.

There is a successive shortening of the line length, an effect I have become inordinately fond of, I'm afraid. This little piece indicates in a way some of the strategies for the poet writing without the support of a formal pattern—he can vary his line length, modulate, he can stretch out the line, he can shorten. If he is a real master, he can, like Christopher Smart, make virtually every line an entity in itself, a poem, as he does in his magnificent ode to his cat, Jeoffrey. Here are a few excerpts:

For I will consider my Cat Jeoffrey.
For he is the servant of the Living God, duly and daily serving him.
For at the First glance of the glory of God in the East he worships in his way.
For this is done by wreathing his body seven times round with elegant
    quickness.
. . .For he is of the Lord's poor and so indeed is he called by benevolence

perpetually—Poor Jeoffrey! poor Jeoffrey! the rat has bit thy throat.
For I bless the name of the Lord Jesus that Jeoffrey is better.
For the divine spirit comes about his body to sustain it in complete cat.
For he can jump over a stick which is patience upon proof positive . . .
For he can catch the cork and toss it again . . .
For he is good to think on, if a man would express himself neatly . . .
For by stroking of him I have found out electricity . . .
For God has blessed him in the variety of his movements.
For, tho he cannot fly, he is an excellent clamberer.
For his motions on the face of the earth are more than any other quadrupede.
For he can tread to all the measures upon the music.
For he can swim for life.
For he can creep.

It was Lawrence, a master of this sort of poem (I think I quote him more or less exactly), who said, "It all depends on the pause, the natural pause." In other words the breath unit, the language that is natural to the immediate thing, the particular emotion. Think of what we'd have missed in Lawrence, in Whitman, in Charlotte Mew or, more lately, in Robert Lowell, if we denied this kind of poem. There are areas of experience in modern life that simply cannot be rendered by either the formal lyric or straight prose. We need the catalogue in our time. We need the eye close on the object, and the poem about the single incident—the animal, the child. We must permit poetry to extend consciousness as far, as deeply, as particularly as it can, to recapture, in Stanley Kunitz' phrase, "what it has lost to some extent to prose." We must realize, I think, that the writer in freer forms must have an even greater fidelity to his subject matter than the poet who has the support of form. He must keep his eye on the object, and his rhythm must move as a mind moves, must be imaginatively right, or he is lost. On the simplest level, something must happen in this kind of poem. The Smart sort of piece, or the biblical catalogue, is really easier to do than the free poem in the shorter line length. Let me end with a simple and somewhat clumsy example of my own, in which we see a formal device giving energy to the piece, that device being, simply, participial or verbal forms that keep the action going.

BIG WIND

Where were the greenhouses going,
Lunging into the lashing
Wind driving water
So far down the river

All the faucets stopped?—
So we drained the manure-machine
For the steam plant,
Pumping the stale mixture
Into the rusty boilers,
Watching the pressure gauge
Waver over to red,
As the seams hissed
And the live steam
Drove to the far
End of the rose-house,
Where the worst wind was,
Creaking the cypress window-frames,
Cracking so much thin glass
We stayed all night,
Stuffing the holes with burlap;
But she rode it out,
That old rose-house,
She hove into the teeth of it,
The core and pith of that ugly storm,
Ploughing with her stiff prow,
Bucking into the wind-waves
That broke over the whole of her,
Flailing her sides with spray,
Flinging long strings of wet across the roof-top,
Finally veering, wearing themselves out, merely
Whistling thinly under the wind vents;
She sailed until the calm morning,
Carrying her full cargo of roses.

So we'll leave Roethke and his manure machine.

STANLEY KUNITZ

Action and Incantation: A Conversation on Prosody

Stanley Kunitz identifies rhythm as extending "beyond poetry into the arts, into the life itself." In the processes of creation, rhythm can be experienced as pre-verbal activity, as "a complex of thoughts and feelings looking for a language, seeking a language." Such rhythms exist deep in the psyche and have their origins in long forgotten experiences.

Mr. Kunitz speaks as well as writes his poems: the whole making of the poem the cooperating and synthesizing work of voice, ear, and eye. The rhythm of incantation sets the basis of the poem's movement. Earlier in his career Mr. Kunitz composed his verse in formal metrical patterns; more recently he has felt that the constraints of meter set unwanted limitations on the incantatory freedom of the speaking voice. In his recent poems he has both extended and stripped down his prosody; he has allowed himself greater rhythmic flexibility within a short line of three beats. "I am getting down to a functional trimeter line. Three beats seems to be my natural speech pattern." However, this change in prosody, the greater freedom "to write in a middle voice," signals no repudiation of form. Mr. Kunitz takes issue with the concept of "open form": that a poem should have no limits, "no possible closure." There can be no art without the limitations of form, and no form without the "weave and cross-weave" of freedom and constraint.

This conversation was taped on July 2, 1977, in New York City, and published in *Antaeus*. Copyright © 1978 by *Antaeus*. Reprinted by permission.

I am speaking with Stanley Kunitz in the garden of his Greenwich Village house. Our particular subject is prosody; however, I expect that we shall be ranging over a wider area: the whole craft of writing poetry. To begin: a question on the use of the word *prosody*. Among theoreticians especially there is an ongoing dispute about the terminological implications of the word. The linguists seem to feel that the word refers to the vocalic elements in language: matters of voice, intonation, pitch, etc. Poets think of prosody as the science of metrics; the word still carries with it some implications of classical prosody based on quantitative principles. Do you feel that the word is still a viable one?

Stanley Kunitz: I don't know that there is any alternative, any really valid substitute for it. So that even though I think it's true that it means different things to different persons, it still seems to me the only term you can use effectively.

Harvey Gross: Ezra Pound says that prosody concerns itself with "the articulation of the total sound structure of a poem."

Kunitz: I tend to think of it as combining the elements you mention. It has to do with voice and the inflection of voice, the sound of the poem: the way it breathes. But it also has to do with the systematic reduction of it . . .

Gross: . . .the meter itself . . .

Kunitz: . . .the imposition of limits on the voice. I thus use prosody in both senses: as a reconciliation between the constraint of meter and the freedom of the voice.

Gross: Let us move on to another rather troublesome set of terms: rhythm on the one hand, meter on the other. How do you think of these two words: their respective denotations and connotations?

Kunitz: Rhythm to me is the more general term, and extends beyond poetry into the arts, into the life itself. Metrics is a specific application of rhythm; it's a system of measuring rhythm, actually, or defining it. Rhythm is the broad term, metrics is the limiting term.

Gross: Metrics is then the more technical term. Of course, you can say that a non-metrical prosody has rhythm: free verse has rhythm.

Kunitz: Yes, prose has rhythm; it doesn't have meter unless it's highly organized, in which case it's moving toward the condition of the poem.

Gross: Whitehead makes the fascinating distinction that a diamond has too much pattern to have rhythm, a fog has too little pattern to have rhythm. I would like to turn toward the phenomenon of rhythm itself, and then perhaps we can work toward the more specific elements of meter and metrical form. Most of your poetry, as I read it, is metrical . . .

Kunitz: . . .or quasi-metrical . . .

Gross: Certainly your earlier verse is written in the metrical modes.

Kunitz: However, I must say that I don't think of my later poems as metrical at all.

Gross: In *The Testing Tree?*

Kunitz: In *The Testing Tree* and in the poems since *The Testing Tree.*

Gross: I haven't seen those poems: is there a collection available?

Kunitz: No. I am publishing them next spring. ·

Gross: What will the title of your new volume be?

Kunitz: My complete *Collected Poems.*

Gross: In your prose collection, *A Kind of Order, A Kind of Folly,* you come up with this intriguing notion about rhythm: "Even before it is ready to change into language, a poem may begin to assert its buried life in the mind with wordless surges of rhythm and counter-rhythm. Gradually the rhythms attach themselves to objects and feelings ' Would you care to elaborate on this activity of the poetic unconscious?

Kunitz: Because it *is* a pre-verbal activity, it is very hard to describe it in words! But I suspect that when one detects in oneself this surge of rhythm and counter-rhythm, really what you are locating is a complex of feelings.

Gross: Is rhythm, then, as the aestheticians say, "isomorphic" with feeling: a map or symbol of feeling?

Kunitz: It is a complex of thoughts and feelings looking for a language, seeking a language. It is like coming out of that fog you have just mentioned and beginning to shape itself. But the only way it can shape itself, in the beginning, is in wordless rhythms which gradually attach themselves to words. And then that fog becomes palpable. . . .

Gross: Do you ever start out with a rhythm oscillating or vibrating in your unconscious, and then you have an experience and then you see that the rhythm and the experience are related? Or you recall an experience and then the poem becomes, in a sense, the rhythm of that experience?

Kunitz: Usually, what I find is that these rhythms are ancient. They have been buried in me a long time; they have roots in experiences that may be long forgotten . . .

Gross: Childhood experiences, perhaps?

Kunitz: Perhaps. Many times. Certainly, in recent poems that is true. Then something happens today that triggers that old wound, that old joy: whatever it may be. It begins to assert itself, it begins to find its way toward a language. And so you have the combination of something old with something new which then gives you that effect of cross-grain or cross-weave which is to me essential to the making of a poem.

Gross: Do some of these rhythms go back to nursery rhymes or children's poems or memories of particular childhood experiences, like going to the circus?

Kunitz: The events are often the property of childhood; the rhythms are not necessarily out of nursery rhymes. They tend, in my case, to be more complex rhythms because the feelings they are attached to are no longer simply the feelings of the child. They are the feelings of the child combined with the feelings of the man.

Gross: I find in all your poetry, metrical and quasi-metrical, the rhythmic elements richly stylized: heightened to the level of incantation.

Kunitz: Definitely so. This goes back to the way I write my poems: which is by speaking them. My voice, so I've been told by those who have overheard me, is definitely incantatory when I'm making a poem; and even, I think some of that remains after the poem is written and I read the poem aloud to an audience. There is an element of incantation present and this is the rhythm on which the poem rides and builds.

Gross: In your earlier work, when you were writing within the constraints of formal metric and stanza, did you find that these formal elements limited the incantatory freedom of your speaking voice?

Kunitz: That is, of course, the problem of writing in metrical forms. But the meter also offers opportunities: the tension created between the regularity of the ideal pattern and the irregularity of the actual syntax of the poem. Then it is possible to create something that does relate to the natural voice, and yet is a formalized version of it. I think that what happened to me through the years is that eventually I began to feel that the necessity for formalizing the rhythms and the inflections became an impediment; it prevented me from saying certain things that I wanted to say. I wanted, for example, to be able to write in a middle voice, not always in a high style. It was increasingly difficult for me to see how that could be done, so that a good part, I felt, of my experience was cut out of my poems: I couldn't reconcile them with the high style.

Gross: When we move from *The Selected Poems* to *The Testing Tree,* we recognize the dramatic change from formalized meters to freer rhythmic forms. In *The Selected Poems* there seem to be two modes: the flexible iambics of such poems as "The Science of the Night," "Foreign Affairs," and the magnificent *guazzabuglio* of polemic, celebration, and Roman history, "The Thief"; and then there are the other poems composed in stanzas.

Kunitz: The iambic pieces, I feel, anticipate a good deal of later, freer work.

Gross: These poems are always moving against an iambic norm . . .

Kunitz: But not rigidly . . .

Gross: No, hardly, but in the way that much modern blank verse is written . . .

Kunitz: Even Shakespeare!

Gross: Yes, the Shakespeare of the later plays: *The Winter's Tale, The Tempest* . . .

Kunitz: Yes, I think that the late Shakespeare has a very modern sound.

Gross: Although there is a change of prosodic style in *The Testing Tree,* I still hear the same voice. There is one poem, however, "Three Floors," which is written in ballad stanzas.

Kunitz: That is the earliest poem in *The Testing Tree,* and it is closer to my older style.

Gross: I am very much moved by the use of free rhythms in your "Around Pastor Bonhoeffer": certainly one of the most profoundly expressive poems you have written.

Kunitz: That I couldn't possibly have written in a metrical mode.

Gross: You were adapting actual notebook material, records of conversation, and so on.

Kunitz: Yes, and some of it with very little variation from the original entries. But you understand that the voice you still recognize in *The Testing Tree* as being fundamentally the same is, of course, a testimony to the persistence of the psyche—which is, after all, the motor behind the poetry.

Gross: Do you feel that the earlier discipline of the metrical verse gives you an advantage even in your freer verse: namely, that having learned to work in strict forms affords a greater expressive potential? Let me use the analogy of the composer who first learns the rules of harmony, counterpoint, and fugue—then goes on to free composition.

Kunitz: Oh, of course; I think that a poet who doesn't know anything about metrics, who hasn't really practiced the discipline of formal metrics is at a great loss.

Gross: There are many poets who are operating today . . .

Kunitz: . . . who have never learned . . .

Gross: . . . or don't care about it.

Kunitz: But I think that what happens there is that their ear is never finely tuned. The great thing that you learn from the metric discipline is to recognize the beat and the evasion of the beat. That is the great lesson: you train your ear for that.

Gross: You have taught courses in the writing of poetry. Do you ask your students to write exercises in metrical forms, as a matter of ear-training.

Kunitz: In my early years of teaching, when I was teaching under-graduates, yes, I worked very definitely with the metric forms; and found it very helpful to them. Then in the period of the sixties I discovered that the young writers were impatient . . .

Gross: . . . they didn't want to hear about metrics . . .

Kunitz: . . . they didn't want to hear about it. They were rejecting their parents, the social structure, and the metrical tradition. Poetry had to begin anew; it was born that year, that day. And so it was impossible really to do much of anything except surreptitiously about technique, about craft. Recently, a new thing has happened: there is a definite sense of return and an interest in the traditional forms. My students, who are graduate students, are supposed to know about metrical matters; and in the last few years I haven't worked with the metrical disciplines at all: one assumed that the students already had the advantage of that kind of training. But it was a false assumption in many cases. This year, for the first time, my students really asked for instruction in prosody.

Gross: This is fascinating because it brings up the whole question of *Zeitgeist* and prosody in general. When Robert Lowell published *Lord Weary's Castle* in 1946, right after the war, he seemed to have set a prosodic fashion. His book set me to writing rhymed couplets, *terza rima,* sestinas, etc. Very often the impact of a major poet will establish the prosody of a creative age. Similarly, in 1959 when *Life Studies* appeared, we experienced a rerun of freer forms.

Kunitz: I don't think that Lowell, with *Lord Weary's Castle,* really set anything because he derived his style out of the Southern traditionalists: Ransom and Tate in particular. I don't think it was a novelty in that epoch.

Gross: Do you think the main influence during the fifties was Auden—who was a very conscious prosodist?

Kunitz: I think that Auden was the strongest influence through the thirties. Every decade has had a dominant voice which is related to prosody; for example, Eliot certainly was the "voice" of the twenties.

Gross: You can listen to the rhythm of a particular poem and date it.

Kunitz: I tell in my prose book [*A Kind of Order, A Kind of Folly*] the game that Roethke and I used to play. We would dig up the most obscure poem we could find out of the past, and try to date it just by reading it aloud to the other. We got to be so proficient in that game that we rarely missed by more than ten years.

Gross: Do you feel that a revision in our reading of cultural history is going on? We used to divide the nineteenth century into a Romantic, a

Victorian, an Edwardian period; but in the twentieth century we speak of the twenties, thirties, forties, fifties, sixties.

Kunitz: That is the acceleration of the tempo. We experience a faster obsolescence which seems to be built into our society. History itself is turning faster.

Gross: Do you feel that as a threat to the whole enterprise of poetry or to your own practice in particular? Do you believe poets worry about being outmoded?

Kunitz: No, definitely not. The fact remains that if one is honest with self and with work, the fashions, in the end, don't count. One lives through the fashions. And what persists is your own identity. Naturally, there are periods in which the work is admired and periods in which it is unloved. One has to expect that if one lives long enough.

Gross: From about 1660 to the end of the eighteenth century, we had the dominance of a particular prosodic form, the heroic couplet. Then things seem to break up at the time of Wordsworth, and we see the emergence (or re-emergence) of a great variety of metrical modes. We can, I believe, define the prosodic norms of the eighteenth and nineteenth centuries, even recognize the changing period styles. Do you believe we can discern a period style in twentieth-century prosody—more exactly, prosodies? Do you believe that non-metrical verse will emerge as the "period style" for modern prosody, or do you feel that the very concept of "period style" simply does not apply to our age?

Kunitz: Non-metrical verse has swept the field, so that there is no longer any real adversary from the metricians. The defining element of poetry is no longer whether it is metrical or non-metrical: the defining element is something else: it is substantive. Or poetry is defined by a certain inflection of the voice rather than in terms of a particular prosodic practice.

Gross: I think of some of the features of our most recent poetry: the use of surrealist images and radical metaphors; the persistent use of the end-stopped line, ultimately derived from Whitman. . . . Do these usages define our current style?

Kunitz: I don't think that there is a defining element, right now; it seems to me that what we have is an open field. All possibilities are open, even including, I think, metrical verse.

Gross: I noticed in a recent issue of *The New Yorker* two new poems by Donald Justice. They are pointedly metrical, in rhymed quatrains.

Kunitz: I think it is perfectly possible these days to write metrically—if you do it well enough.

Gross: You don't feel that there is any necessity in the experience of the age that requires a particular kind of prosody, namely that we have to be free, therefore we must use non-metrical verse?

Kunitz: I think that's nonsense. You can be free in heroic couplets. In completely unconfined, unrestrained verse, one is a prisoner of infinity; that is the worst kind of bondage because there is no escape from it. In a sense every artist is both a prisoner and a free man: as Goethe said, "Art exists in limits." We cannot deny that. It is better to be a prisoner of a form that you yourself have defined and that you know the limits of.

Gross: I would like to ask about your musical training. In your *A Kind of Order* you tell us: "I was with the Pierian Sodality at Harvard under Walter Piston . . . one day I read John Donne and locked my fiddle-case." You obviously have had considerable musical training.

Kunitz: Yes, many years. Music was my first art, really.

Gross: You don't speak very much about music except in that one passage. I am interested in your giving up one kind of music, the violin, and turning to another, that of John Donne.

Kunitz: I think the reason for my giving up music—which meant performing music—was that I was not satisfied playing somebody else's compositions. That was a sense of limitation that I didn't want; I wanted to write my own music.

Gross: Did you ever do any actual musical composition?

Kunitz: No, I didn't do any composition. I didn't want to play other people's music, that was basically it. In answer, I don't think I would have been a first-rate musician: although I was a good technician.

Gross: To play the violin well, you need a good ear.

Kunitz: My ear was very good, but I never felt that I was really a master of the instrument—even though I did give concerts.

Gross: Do you ever play the violin any more?

Kunitz: No, I haven't played it for years.

Gross: I'd like to explore the matter of John Donne. On the one hand, Donne is often regarded as a very "unmusical" poet: he was sentenced to hanging by Ben Jonson for violating the metrical rules, and so on. On the other hand, some recent critics have heard in Donne's metrical irregularities a highly complex and idiosyncratic "music."

Kunitz: Yes, I think of him as being a musical poet. He is a musician of the passions. That was what I was seeking when I read him and first turned to his art. Those metrical variations, which he should have been hanged for, were really human inflections: exactly the same sort of thing that Hopkins later formalized in his sprung rhythm. Hopkins, by the way, has been a great influence on my prosody, although it isn't obvious.

Gross: It certainly is not obvious. In your earlier poetry, it seems to me, you do work as Donne worked by setting up an initial stanza which then becomes the pattern for the rest of the poem.

Kunitz: Oh yes, and I learned that from Donne. Donne was very much a master for me in that period.

Gross: I don't, however, hear in your poetry that characteristic grating quality that seems so typical of Donne.

Kunitz: Donne did not work with incantation; and I suppose, from the beginning, the incantatory element was for me the other approach to the whole question of prosody, to what I was seeking in poetry.

Gross: There are two poles, then. We have the conversational, the voice, and we have the incantatory.

Kunitz: That's right. And there's a delicate area where the two may meet, but it's a very difficult one to define.

Gross: I'm interested in another thing you say in A Kind of Order: "By and large I prefer the company of painters and sculptors to that of poets." Is that a matter of personalities, or do you feel that the company of painters and sculptors provides a better environment for the practice of your art?

Kunitz: To prove that I prefer the company of painters, I am married to one. I often envy painters and sculptors because there is so much physical release in the plastic arts—an expression, an assertion of the whole body. In the very kinetics, as it were. . . . Poetry is supposedly the sedentary art—that's why I pace, I walk, I talk when I write. I am a physical being.

Gross: Have you ever tried composing into a recording machine?

Kunitz: No, I couldn't think of doing that. I have to see it also. I say it and then I put it down. I write it and then after I write it, after I get a block of it, I type it. I like to see it on the page. And that helps me. The visual element is very important to me, as much as the auditory, but in a different way. The visual element helps me understand the architecture, helps me achieve the architecture. Until I see it on the page, I don't quite know the ultimate shape of the poem. The shaping of the poem, the way it looks on the page, is important, too.

Gross: This seems more evident in The Testing Tree than in the Selected Poems. We find in The Testing Tree very intricately arranged poems like "The Magic Curtain," or "The Testing Tree" itself with its use of triads.

Kunitz: I was just looking at the notebooks and work-sheets for "The Testing Tree" and I see that I started it with flush margins. And then it began sprawling: I didn't know where it was going. It could go on forever.

Gross: Do you use the typewriter when you compose?

Kunitz: I compose first by writing it out on the page. At a certain stage, when I feel I am in control of the rhythms, then I can go to the typewriter and proceed. I go to the typewriter after the poem has really taken charge of me; then I can trust the typewriter, but I have to find the poem on the written page.

Gross: Another matter of craft: did you ever have a teacher who set you exercises in the writing of verse, or did you work it all out for yourself when you were a young man?

Kunitz: I never really had any instruction that I felt benefited me at all. At Harvard I did take a course with Robert Hillyer, who was a very conventional poet. He did assign metrical exercises which I resented and resisted because his ear, I felt, was defective. He wanted absolute regularity. When I wrote a poem with Donneish variations, he would slaughter it!

Gross: Did you study Latin and did you have instruction in classical prosody?

Kunitz: Yes, I studied Latin and the scansion of Latin verse.

Gross: Was this of any use to you?

Kunitz: Let me say that I think it had two influences on me. First, the interest in the roots of language, in the radicals. So that the effort has always been in my poems to use words in terms of their root sense as much as in terms of their current meaning. This is something I learned from Milton: to think of a word as belonging to a secret language, as always containing its root meanings. Second, the interest in quantity, in the lengths of the syllables. Quantity is a factor in my concept of prosody. I am very aware of the time sense: a line to me is very much a time unit. So I am often compensating for a swift passage with a slower passage; I also often work with sounds that are in opposition, for example, short syllables that are formed labially or dentally, and with deep syllables that are formed down in the throat. These are important elements in my concept of prosody: I see them as having to do with time and depth and surface. They are part of the tension of the prosody.

Gross: After you work on a poem, after you establish the lines of verse, do you ever go back and consciously adjust accents, lengths or syllables, metrical ictus?

Kunitz: Yes, revision is often exactly that. I will not be satisfied with the way a line moves. It doesn't interest me; it seems to have just a running sort of movement without enough variation. I want to slow it down, then get it started again; I will change the word with a different vowel sound or consonant until I achieve the right movement.

Gross: Ransom speaks somewhere—and he had a curious theory of meter as "a low grade musical material"—of poets who deliberately roughen up lines of smooth metrical verse for particular effects. Do you think that this was an idiosyncratic notion of Ransom's?

Kunitz: No, I think that it is very true,and I do it myself. I know in conversation with Lowell that he does that too.

Gross: So Lowell follows the tradition of his teacher. In this connection, I think of Ransom's poem "Captain Carpenter." I wonder if the first line originally went

> Captain Decatur rose up in his prime

rather than

> Captain Carpenter rose up in his prime.

Obviously, you can't say "Captain Car-pén-ter . . ."

Kunitz: That reversed second foot . . . Hopkins said that the reversal of the second foot was the most violent of all the reversals.

Gross: In that celebrated and somewhat notorious line from your "Father and Son,"

> The night nailed like an orange to my brow

you reverse that sensitive second foot.

Kunitz: But it is after a caesura. It should be read with a heavy pause after "night,"

> Thĕ níght| | | naíled lĭke | ˘an ór | aňge tó | mȳ brów.

It is easier to reverse the foot after a caesura.

Gross: That deliberate consciousness of metrical matters is, I feel, part of your approach to the writing of poetry.

Kunitz: Yes, and I still work very much in revision in those terms. But to go back to what I was saying about the way the sounds are formed: I don't think there has been an adequate study ever made of the location of the sounds and their relation to prosody. One of the deficiencies in so much of the poetry written by young people nowadays is their lack of awareness of these possibilities: all these influences on the process of the poem. They never think of the element of sound, of the location of sounds. Take a line like

> Full fathom five thy father lies.

The first three words are formed right in the front of the mouth; the next three completely different sounds are formed deep down in the throat. The kinetic force of certain poets is generated by making these jumps from front to back.

Gross: I wonder if any poet has ever achieved the music of the Shakespearean song.

Kunitz: I wish we were closer to song than we are.

Gross: I often feel that poets ought to have musical training, prosodic training, linguistic training . . .

Kunitz: . . . and life training.

Gross: Yes, and life training. As we look back at the prosodies of the various modernist movements, does it make sense to speak of the alternation of freedom and restraint? We have had periods in which the non-metrical or quasi-metrical techniques have dominated followed by periods, notably the thirties and fifties, when we had a return to traditional syllable-stress norms.

Kunitz: Yes, historically that has certainly seemed to be true. We have been, of course, in a long free period. But I do think, as I said earlier, there is now some sense of a return to form. I also think that the whole concept of open form, which was around for a little while, out of Olson largely, the concept that the poem was infinitely open, with no possible closure, was anarchic and a denial of form. The whole concept of form depends on the setting of limits. There has to be a weave and a cross-weave in order to make the cloth. A straight line to infinity is not a poem; there has to be some sense of enclosure in order to complete the poem. There has to be at least an exhaustion of the impulse that began the poem. Aristotle said in his *Poetics* that a painting ten-thousand miles long was an aesthetic impossibility.

Gross: You have published a volume of translations from the great Russian poet Anna Akhmatova. Were you partly attracted to her by her formal qualities? I note that in your translations you use a great many slant rhymes—where in the Russian, I suppose, they are perfect rhymes.

Kunitz: Yes, she is a very formal poet. But that isn't basically why I was attracted to her. I was attracted to her largely by her themes, and by the degree of feeling she managed to assert in her poems without breaking the mold. These poems are full of pain and terrible suffering and yet they retain their validity as poems. They don't crack up.

Gross: What is the metrical form of such a poem as her "Cleopatra"? Is the Russian line analogous to the English iambic?

Kunitz: Yes, the equivalent of an iambic line. But because Russian is such a different language, you cannot really adapt its metrics; it's so free in vowel sounds and rhyming possibilities—because of the inflectional endings there are thousands of rhyming possibilities. And you usually have feminine endings. When Brodsky attacked my translation of Akhmatova, he said that

I had denied her formal virtues. But it isn't true: actually what I am resorting to is what I call functional stressing. The tetrameter lines are still tetrameter in my concept of functional stressing: a four-stressed line with any number of unstressed syllables. But Brodsky didn't hear that.

Gross: I have done some translating from the German, and in dealing with a highly formal poet like Stefan George you often discover yourself "stuffing" the line with polysyllabic adjectives. A German ten-syllable line, with its wealth of inflected forms, breaks down in English to a line of eight or sometimes seven or six syllables.

Kunitz: One of the main differences, I think, between modern poetry and the poetry of another age is in the linear unit. The pentameter line seemed to be natural to the Elizabethan speech pattern—which was highly rhetorical and inflected speech, full of adjectives and adverbs. What has happened is that we are gradually stripping down the language of its ornaments. In our poetry in particular, the movement has been towards a language that relies largely on nouns and verbs without qualifiers. That certainly has been the tendency in my poems: so I am getting down to a functional trimeter line. Three beats seems to be my natural speech pattern. If I were to write in a four-beat or five-beat line, I would have to qualify my nouns in order to fill out the line. But I don't want to do that; I like that stripped quality.

Gross: We have covered a wide sweep of territory in our talk, and I believe you have answered most of the questions I had in mind to ask.

Kunitz: I enjoyed that. This is the first time I have talked about prosody to anybody in a long, long time except to my students.

Gross: You still ask your students to think about prosody?

Kunitz: Even when I wasn't teaching, I was always, in my criticism, talking about what happens to this or that line: why doesn't it sound right, why has the energy leaked out of it? I once made the comment, "I like a poem that rides the beast of an action." That is very important to me, and that has a lot to do with my whole sense of prosody.

DONALD JUSTICE

Meters and Memory

Donald Justice describes himself as "a rationalist defender of the meters."
He is primarily concerned with the traditional metrical ordering of English verse and does not touch upon the larger question of rhythm and its
significances. He is an eloquent spokesman for the mnemonic function of
meter; however, his concept of memory is really a theory of the imagination. Meter serves as stimulus to the processes of creation: the meters "will
have called back the thing itself—the subject—that became the poem."
But the meters do not only stimulate imagination by helping to recollect
the original experience; they also serve to transform and hence fix the
"terror or beauty or plain ordinariness of the original event. . . ." Meters
are artificial in the Renaissance sense; providing aesthetic distance, their
very artifice reminds us "that we are at that remove from life which
traditionally we have called art."

Skeptical of the supposed mimetic function of meter, he points out,
as does Dr. Johnson, that we often "ascribe to the numbers the effects of
the sense." Meters accompany the sense "like a kind of percussion only,
mostly noise." (We are reminded of Ransom's characterization of meter as
a low-grade musical material.) The function of the meters—apart from
their power to set memory and imagination in motion—is architectonic.
Like syntax they serve to articulate the words and the larger elements of
poetic form.

The poet who uses the meters "may feel as deeply as the non-metrical
writer. . . ." A young woman once asked the great pianist and teacher,

Artur Schnabel, whether she should play in time or in accordance with her feelings. Schnabel answered, with his usual wit, "Why not feel in time?" Professor Justice, in rejecting the fallacy of imitative form and its corollary that a disorderly world requires a poetry without meter and syntax, argues that the meters help the poet gain mastery of his subject. And by learning to feel in time, his feelings become both understandable to himself and more truly communicable to his audience.

The mnemonic value of meters seems always to have been recognized. There are, to begin with, the weather saws, counting spells, and the like, which one does more or less get by heart in childhood. But any ornament, however trivial and even meaningless, probably assists the recollection to some degree, if by ornament we mean a device of sound or structure not required by the plain sense of a passage. Repetition obviously functions in this way— anaphora, refrains, even the sort of repetition which involves nothing more than an approximate equivalence of length, as in Pound's Sapphic fragment:

> Spring . . . .
> Too long . . . . .
> Gongula . . . . .

Likewise with such structural features as parallel parts or syllogistic order, whether in verse or prose. For that matter, fine and exact phrasing alone enables the memory to take hold about as well as anything. A friend of mine, at parties, preferred to recite prose rather than verse, usually, as I recall, the opening paragraph of *A Farewell to Arms*.

The purely mnemonic character of a passage, however, contributes very little to its aesthetic power. Often enough rhymes are more effective mnemonically than meters, and occasionally other devices may prove to be. But the meters, where employed at all, are likely to be the groundwork underlying other figurations, hence basic, if not always dominant. Consider a couplet like "Red sky at morning, / Sailor take warning." Here the meters cooperate with the rhymes to fit the lines to one another, not only as lines of verse but as linked parts of a perception. It is no more than a slight exaggeration to claim that the couplet becomes fixed in memory by reason of this sense of fittedness. But few devices of sound are enough in themselves to ensure recall. Should, for example, the sky of the couplet be changed from red to blue, although neither rhyme nor meter would be affected, I cannot believe the couplet would survive. Survival in this case has something to do with aptness of observation, with use, that is, as well as cleverness or beauty.

The kernel of lore provides a reason for keeping the jingle; the jingle preserves the lore in stable form.

Now all this is to consider memory, as is customary, from the viewpoint of an audience, as if a significant purpose of poetry were simply to put itself in the way of being memorized. For my part, when I am at work on a poem, the memory of an audience concerns me less than my own. While the meters and other assorted devices may ultimately make the lines easier for an audience to remember, they are offering meanwhile, like the stone of the sculptor, a certain resistance to the writer's efforts to call up his subject, which seems always to be involved, one way or another, with memory. (Hobbes somewhere calls imagination the same thing as memory.) In any case, memory is going to keep whatever it chooses to keep not just because it has been made easy and agreeable to remember but because it comes to be recognized as worth the trouble of keeping, and first of all by the poet. The audience will find it possible to commit to memory only what the poet first recalls for himself. Anything can be memorized, including numbers, but numbers that refer to something beyond themselves, as to the combination of a safe, are the easier to keep in mind for that reason. Something other than themselves may likewise be hidden in the meters, and an aptness to be committed to memory might almost be taken as a sign of this other presence. Pattern is not enough. The trivial and insignificant pass beyond recall, no matter how patterned, discounting perhaps a double handful of songs and nonsense pieces,[1] where the pattern itself has somehow become a part of what is memorable. But such a result is exceptional. What happens in the more serious and ordinary case is that some recollection of a person, of an incident or a landscape, whatever we are willing to designate as subject, comes to seem worth preserving. The question for the poet is how to preserve it.

One motive for much if not all art (music is probably an exception) is to accomplish this—to keep memorable what deserves to be remembered. So much seems true at least from the perspective of the one who makes it. Nor should any resemblance to the more mechanical functions of camera and tape recorder prove embarrassing; like a literary text in the making, film and tape also permit editing, room enough for the artist. Let emotion be recollected, in tranquillity or turmoil, as luck and temperament would have it. And then what? Art lies still in the future. The emotion needs to be fixed, so that whatever has been temporarily recovered may become as nearly permanent as possible, allowing it to be called back again and again at pleasure. It is at this point that the various aids to memory, and meter most persistently, begin to serve memory beyond mnemonics. Such artifices are, let us say, the fixatives.

Like the chemicals in the darkroom, they are useful in developing the negative. The audience is enabled to call back the poem, or pieces of it, the poet
to call back the thing itself, the subject, all that was to become the poem.

The transcription of experience represented by the meters ought not to
be confused with the experience itself. At best they can perform no more than
a reenactment, as on some stage of the mind. This being so, to object to the
meters as unnatural because unrealistic is to miss the point. Like the odd
mustaches and baggy pants of the old comedians, they put us on notice that
we are at a certain distance from the normal rules and expectations of life.
The effect has been variously called a distancing or a framing. Wordsworth
described it as serving "to divest language, in a certain degree, of its reality,
and thus to throw a sort of half-consciousness of unsubstantial existence over
the whole composition." The meters signify this much at least, that we are at
that remove from life which traditionally we have called art.

Their very presence seems to testify to some degree of plan, purpose,
and meaning. The meters seem always faintly teleological by implication,
even in company with an anti-teleological argument, as the case may be.
They are proof of the hand and ear of a maker (uncapitalized), even in a
poetry which otherwise effaces the self. They seem to propose that an emotion, however uncontrollable it may have appeared originally, was not, in
fact, unmanageable. "I don't know why I am crying" becomes "Tears, idle
tears, I know not what they mean." The difference seems important to me.
The poetic line comes to constitute a sort of paraphrase of the raw feeling,
which will only get broken back down close to its original state in some
future critic's re-paraphrase. The writer in meters, I insist, may feel as deeply
as the non-metrical writer, and the choice whether or not to use meters is as
likely to be dictated by literary fashion as by depth of feeling or sincerity.
Nevertheless, they have become a conventional sign for at least the desire for
some outward control; though their use cannot be interpreted as any guaran-
tee of inner control, the very act of writing at all does usually imply an
attempt to master the subject well enough to understand it, and the meters
reinforce the impression that such an attempt is being made and perhaps
succeeding. Even so, the technology of verse does not of itself affirm a
philosophy, despite arguments to the contrary. Certain recent critics have
argued that even syntax is now "bogus," since the modern world contains no
such order as that implied in an ordinary sentence, much less a metrical one.
But the imitation theory underlying this argument seems naive and unhis-
torical, for it was never the obligation of words or of word-order to imitate
conditions so reflexively. Syntax deals, after all, primarily with word-order,

not world-order, and even the meters, or so it seems to me, can imitate only by convention.

Let me take a simple case. Yvor Winters once offered his line "The slow cry of a bird" as an example of metrical imitation, not strictly of a birdcall itself but of "the slowness of the cry." The convention would seem to be that two or more strong syllables in succession carry associations of slowness and heaviness, while two or more weak syllables in succession carry contrary associations of rapidity and lightness: melancholy on the one hand, playfulness on the other. But the displacement of a stress from *of* to *cry* in the Winters line, bringing two stresses together, fails to slow the line down, as I hear it. Substitute for this "The *quick* cry of a bird," and the two weak syllables following *cry* can be said to do as much to speed the line up, or as little. But whether the cry is to sound quick or slow, the metrical situation itself remains, practically speaking, identical. If any question of interpretation arises from the reversed foot, the meaning of the reversal must depend on the denotation of the adjective rather than on the particular arrangement of syllables and stresses, for denotation overrides any implication of the meters apart from it. Though apparently agreed on by generations of poets, the minor convention on which Winters was depending is hardly observed any longer except in criticism or occasionally the classroom. Nor was it, for that matter, observed by Milton in his great melancholy-playful pair, "Il Penseroso" and "L'Allegro," or if observed, then only to be consciously played against. Composers of music for the movies learned early that direct imitation of a visual image through sound was best restricted to comic effects (pizzicati, trombone glissandi, staccato bassoons). Pushed far enough, and that is not very far at all, the results of metrical imitations can seem similarly cartoonlike:

> I sank to the pillow, and Joris, and he;
> I slumbered, Dirck slumbered, we slumbered all three.

In any case, simple imitation by means of rhythm would seem to be more plausible in free verse, with its greater flexibility, and most workable in prose, which is allowed any and every arrangement of syllables. Wordsworth ascribes to the meters a different power, finding in them a "great efficacy in tempering and restraining the passion by an intertexture of ordinary feeling," and, he goes on to add, "of feeling not strictly and necessarily connected with the passion." The meters move along in their own domain, scarcely intersecting the domain of meaning, except in some illusory fashion or by virtue of conventions nearly private. The responsibility they bear to the sense, comic writing aside, is mostly not to interfere. But so effacing themselves they will have accomplished all that they must accomplish in relation to the sense. Speech they can and do imitate, from a little distance, but rarely by quoting, that is to say, by attempting to become speech. Song they perhaps are or can become, their natural inclination; no question in that of imitating anything outside their own nature.

Whether their nature really embodies an imitation of natural processes may be arguable. But I do not think the meters can be, in any such sense, organic. A recognition of this, conscious or not, has been reason enough for their rejection by contemporary organicists, poets and critics both. The meters seem more to resemble the hammer-work of carpenters putting together a building, say, than waves coming in to shore or the parade of seasons. We do inhale and exhale more or less rhythmically, as long as we stay healthy; our hearts do beat without much skipping, for years on end. Breath and heart are the least remote of these similitudes, but any connection between them and the more or less regular alternation of weak and strong syllables in verse seems doubtful to me and, valid or not, need carry no particular prestige. In urban life, far from the Lake Country of 1800, are to be found analogies as appropriate as any from nature, if no more convincing. Signals timed to regulate the flow of traffic not only seem analogous but at times remarkably beautiful, as on a nearly deserted stretch of Ninth Avenue in New York City at three a.m., especially in a mild drizzle. If the meters do represent or imitate anything in general, it may be nothing more (or less) than some psychological compulsion, a sort of counting on the fingers or stepping on cracks, magic to keep an unpredictable world under control.

Where the meters are supposed to possess anything of an imitative character, the implicit purpose must be to bring the poetic text closer to its source in reality or nature by making it more "like" the thing it imitates. Such an illusion may be enhanced if the poet's conviction is strong enough to persuade an audience to share his faith, but such conversions are more likely to be accomplished through criticism than through poetry alone. The twin illusions of control and understanding seem more valuable to me than this illusion of the real or the natural, since it is through these, I suspect, that the meters are more firmly connected to memory. To remember an event is almost to begin to control it, as well as to approach an understanding of it; incapable of recurring now, it is only to be contemplated rather than acted on or reacted to. Any sacrifice of immediate reality is compensated for by these new perspectives. The terror or beauty or, for that matter, the plain ordinariness of the original event, being transformed, is fixed and thereby made more tolerable. That the event can recur only in its new context, the context of art, shears it of some risks, the chief of which may anyhow have been its transitory character.

If for an audience the meters function in part to call back the words of the poem, so for the poet they may help to call the words forth, at the same time casting over them the illusion of a necessary or at least not inappropriate fitness and order. There is a kind of accrediting in the process, a warrant that things are being remembered right and set down right, so long as the meters go on working. In this way the meters serve as a neutral and impersonal check on self-indulgence and whimsy; a subjective event gets made over into something more like an object. It becomes accessible to memory, repeatedly accessible, because it exists finally in a form that can be perused at leisure, like a snapshot in an album. Memory itself tends to act not without craft, but selectively, adding here to restore a gap, omitting the incongruous there, rearranging and shifting the emphasis, striving, consciously or not, to make some sense and point out of what in experience may have seemed to lack either. That other presence of which I spoke earlier—the charge of feeling, let us say, which attaches perhaps inexplicably to the subject, what the psychologist might call its *affect*—is not much subject to vicissitudes and manipulations of this sort, except for a natural enough diminution. It remains, but more than likely beneath the surface.

The meters are worth speculating about because they are so specific to the medium, if not altogether essential. Without them nothing may, on occasion, be lost; with them, on occasion, something may be gained, though whatever that is probably has little or nothing to do with sense or ostensible subject. This, in fact, appears to be the sticking point, that in themselves the meters signify so little. It seems a mistake for a rationalist defender of the meters to insist on too much meaningfulness. Let us concede that the effects of the meters are mysterious, from moment to moment imprecise, often enough uncertain or ambiguous. Like Coleridge's incense or wine, however, their presence may "act powerfully, though themselves unnoticed." To which he adds an interesting comparison to yeast—"worthless," as he says, "or disagreeable by itself, but giving vivacity and spirit to the liquor" in right combination. Meters do accompany the sense, like a kind of percussion only, mostly noise. Over and above syntax, they bind the individual words together, and the larger structural parts as well, over and above whatever appearance of logic survives in the argument; as a result, the words and parts seem to cohere, more perhaps than in plain fact may be the case. How they assist the recollection is by fixing it in permanent, or would-be permanent, form. This, for the poet, may be the large and rather sentimental purpose which gives force to all their various combining and intersecting functions.

NOTE

[1]Nonsense may be the condition, in any case, to which devices of sound in themselves aspire.

Appendixes

Glossary of Terms

This is not a complete glossary of prosodical terminology but rather a list of hard words that have turned up in the previous essays. The student interested in more complete glossing should consult Karl Shapiro and Robert Beum's excellent *A Prosody Handbook* (New York: Harper & Row, 1965). For much useful information, especially on Greek and Latin metrics, the student will also want to look at the *Encyclopedia of Poetry and Poetics*, edited by Alex Preminger *et al.* (Princeton, 1974).

ACCENTUAL VERSE. Verse measured by count of stresses alone. In accentual verse the number of stressed syllables is usually constant; the number of unstressed syllables can vary considerably. A favorite nursery rhyme, "Oranges and Lemons," is a fine example of accentual verse, four stresses to the line:

Bull's eyes and targets || say the bells of St. Marg'ret's.
Brickbats and tiles || say the bells of St. Giles'.
Oranges and lemons || say the bells of St. Clement's.

See remarks under *Strong-stress verse.*

ACCIDENCE. Grammatical inflection as it occurs in gender, number, case, person, voice, etc.

ADONIC. A metrical scheme in Latin and Greek poetry. It consisted of a dactyl and a spondee: $- \cup \cup \mid - -$
The adonic forms the last line in the Sapphic (q.v.) stanza.

ALEXANDRINE. Originally the French verse line of twelve syllables. As the carry-all metric of French poetry, it stands analogous to the iambic pentameter in English. Its appearance in English verse has been contemptuously remarked by Pope; the second line below is meant as a horrible example:
A needless Alexandrine ends the song,

That, like | a wound | ed snake | drags its | slow length | a long.

The English Alexandrine contains six feet and six metrical stresses.

ANACRUSIS. An extra syllable, or syllables, occuring in a metrical pattern. It is like the up-beat preceding the main accent in a musical bar. The last line of the stanza below is preceded by an extra unstressed syllable: an anapest for the expected iamb:

O what can ail thee, knight-at-arms,
So haggard, and so woe-begone?

The squirrel's granary is full,
Ănd thĕ hár | vĕst's dóne.
>
> Keats, *La Belle Dame Sans Merci*

ANAPHORA. Strictly speaking, a rhetorical rather than a prosodical device. However, anaphora, the repetition of a syntactical figure at the head of a line, can have rhythmical significance. Whitman uses anaphora with great freedom and effect:

Passing the visions, passing the night,
Passing, unloosing the hold of my comrades' hands,
Passing the song of the hermit bird and the tallying song of my soul. . . .
>
> *When Lilacs Last in the Door-Yard Bloom'd*

ARSIS. A much confused term. Greek prosodists regarded the thesis as the long syllable of the foot, the arsis the remaining short syllables. However, the Latin theorists reversed the meaning of the two terms; arsis became the long syllable, and thesis the short syllables of a foot.

BRACHYCATALECTIC. A line lacking two syllables of its normal metrical scheme is called brachycatalectic. In the stanza below, the indented lines lack the two unstressed syllables of the normal dactylic foot; the omitted syllables are marked by a caret (∧):

Pále beĕch ănd | píne sŏ blŭe
Sét iñ oñe | cláy, ∧ ∧
Bóugh tŏ boŭgh | cán nŏt yŏu
Líve oŭt yŏur | dáy? ∧ ∧
>
> Thomas Hardy

CAESURA (CESURA). A pause in the line of verse occasioned by normal syntactical phrasing or grammatical sense. Though of great prosodical importance, the caesura does not form part of the regular metrical scheme. Shakespeare often splits the metrical foot with a pronounced caesura (marked here with the double bar):

Whŏse ác | tiŏn ís | nŏ strónger | ĕr || thán | ă flówer. . . .
>
> *Sonnet 65*

CATALEXIS, CATALECTIC. Literally truncation. The omission of an expected final syllable in a line of verse. Trochaic lines are frequently catalectic, lacking the final unstressed syllable:

Pí piñg | dówn thĕ | vál leўs | wíld, ∧
Pí piñg | sóngs ŏf | pléas ant | glée, ∧
Oń ă | clóud Ĭ | sáw ă | chíld, ∧
Ańd hĕ | láugh iñg | sáid tŏ | mé. . . ∧
>
> William Blake

Lines lacking two omitted syllables are brachycatalectic (q.v.).

COUNTERPOINT, COUNTERPOINT RHYTHM. Gerard Manley Hopkins coined this term to designate the simultaneous appearance of two rhythms in a line of verse: "... two rhythms ... in some manner running at once and we have something answerable to counterpoint in music. ...." A line of iambic pentameter verse may be counterpointed by the reversal of certain sensitive feet, usually the second and the fourth:

$$\text{Cáp taĭn} \mid \text{Cár pĕn} \mid \text{tĕr róse} \mid \text{úp iň} \mid \text{hǐs príme.} \dots$$

John Crowe Ransom

Successive spondees will also counterpoint a line of iambic verse:

$$\text{Góod stróng} \mid \text{thíck stú} \mid \text{pĕ fý} \mid \text{iňg ín} \mid \text{cĕnse smóke.} \dots$$

Browning

DECASYLLABIC. Containing ten syllables. A 'regular' line of English iambic pentameter is normally decasyllabic: however, dramatic blank verse may show great irregularity in syllable count:

> Do anything but this thou doest. Empty
> Old receptacles, or common shores, of filth;
> Serve by indenture to the common hangman.
> Any of these ways are yet better than this.
> For what thou professest, a baboon, could he speak,
> Would own a name too dear. Oh, that the gods
> Would safely deliver me from this place!
> Here, here's gold for thee.

Shakespeare, *Pericles,* IV, vi

DIPODIC VERSE. Verse structured so that the metrical unit encompasses two feet. Good examples of dipodic verse may be found in the patter songs from the Gilbert and Sullivan operettas:

$$\text{Ăs sóme} \mid \text{dăy ít} \mid \text{măy háp} \mid \text{pĕn that} \mid \text{ă víc} \mid \text{tǐm múst} \mid \text{bĕ fóund,}$$
$$\text{Ŏf sŏ cí e tý's ŏf fend ĕrs} \mid\mid \text{who míght wéll bĕ ŭn dĕr gróund} \dots$$

The Mikado

The first line is scanned as conventional iambic heptameter; however, it is clear that the syllables marked with the double accent (//) receive the stronger stress. The scansion in the second line recognizes the double foot or dipody of two strong stresses separated by the strong medial pause or caesura. Such verse is sometimes termed double-iambic. Its descent from Old English strong-stress meter (q.v.) should be noted.

ELISION. The practice of running together a final unstressed, or short, vowel with the initial vowel or mute consonant of the following syllable. Elision allows greater freedom in building the line in conformity with the metrical scheme. Elision is a regular feature of Latin versification:

Pŏl lĭ ŏ̯ĕt | īn cĭ pĭ | ēnt māg | nī prō | cē dĕ rĕ | mēn sēs ...

Virgil, Ecloga IV

The final 'o' of Pollio and the initial 'e' of et count, in the metrical scheme, as one syllable. Milton introduced elision in the blank verse of Paradise Lost, adapting the rules of quantitative verse for English syllable stress verse:

Hurl'd head | long flam | ing from | the E the | real Sky. ...

I, 45

END STOPPING. The practice of adjusting the syntax of the verse-line to the length of the line itself, as in these lines from James Thomson's The Seasons:

> See, Winter comes, to rule the vary'd Year,
> Sullen, and sad with all his rising Train;
> Vapours, and Clouds, and Storms. Be these my Theme,
> These, that exalt the Soul to solemn Thought,
> And heavenly Musing. Welcome, kindred Glooms!

Winter, 1–5

See Enjambment.

ENDECASILLABO. See Hendecasyllabic.

ENJAMBMENT. The practice of "running a line over" so that "the sense be variously drawn out from one Verse into another," as in these lines from Keats:

> A thing of beauty is a joy forever:
> Its loveliness increases; it will never
> Pass into nothingness; but still will keep
> A bower quiet for us, and a sleep
> Full of sweet dreams, and health, and quiet breathing.

Endymion, I, 1–5

FEMININE ENDING. A hypermetrical (q.v.) line with a final unstressed syllable. The first four lines of Hamlet's famous soliloquy have feminine endings:

> To be, or not to be: that is the question:
> Whether 'tis nobler in the mind to suffer
> The slings and arrows of outrageous fortune,
> Or to take arms against a sea of troubles. ...

Shakespeare, Hamlet, III, i, 56–59

HENDECASYLLABIC. A line of eleven syllables. Chaucer's lines may be thought of as hendecasyllabic if we pronounce the final 'e.' The first two lines of The Canterbury Tales may be hendecasyllabic; the second two are decasyllabic:

> Whan that Aprille with his shoures soote
> And droghte of March hath perced to the roote

> And bathed every veyne in swich licour
> Of which vertu engendred is the flour.

See *Decasyllabic*.

HEXAMETER. In classical prosody the meter of both Homer's *Iliad* and Virgil's *Aeneid*. It was originally a quantitative line of six feet, conforming to this paradigm:

$$— \cup \cup \quad — \cup \cup \quad — \cup \cup \quad — \cup \cup \quad — \cup \cup \quad — —$$
$$1 \qquad 2 \qquad 3 \qquad 4 \qquad 5 \qquad 6$$

The pattern, as may be seen, was five dactyls with a spondee in the sixth position. However, a spondee may substitute for a dactyl in any position except the last; a spondee rarely occurs in the fifth position: when it does, the entire line is named 'spondaic.' The opening line of the *Aeneid* scans:

$$\overline{\text{Ar}} \text{ ma } \breve{\text{vir}} \mid \overline{\text{um}} \text{ qu}\breve{\text{e}} \text{ c}\breve{\text{a}} \mid \overline{\text{no}} \overline{\text{Troi}} \mid \overline{\text{ae}} \overline{\text{qui}} \mid \overline{\text{pri}} \text{ m}\breve{\text{is}} \text{ a}\breve{\text{b}} \mid \overline{\text{or}} \overline{\text{is}} \dots$$

Longfellow adapted the quantitative hexameter to syllable-stress meter for his *Evangeline*.

HYPERMETRICAL. A line of verse containing more syllables than the paradigm allows. The loose blank verse of the Jacobean dramatists is characteristically hypermetrical; the lines often run to eleven, twelve, or more syllables:

> Why, no 'tis most apparent: this precise fellow
> Is the duchess' bawd:—I have it to my wish!
> This is a parcel of intelligency
> Our courtiers were cased up for: it needs must follow
> That I must be committed on pretence
> Of poisoning her; which I'll endure and laugh at.
>
> Webster, *The Duchess of Malfi*, II, iii

IAMBIC TRIMETER. In classical verse a line of three iambic dipodies (double feet):

$$\overline{\text{ad}} \overline{\text{sum}} \mid \text{pro } \breve{} \overline{\text{fun}} \| \overline{\text{do}} \overline{\text{Tar}} \mid \text{ta } \breve{} \text{rie} \cdot \| \overline{\text{miss}} \overline{\text{us}} \mid \text{spe } \breve{} \overline{\text{cu}}$$
$$\wedge$$
$$\text{Seneca}$$

This line was used with great freedom in dramatic dialogue, especially in later Roman comedy.

ICTUS. The heavy stress in classical verse, usually falling on the long syllable of the foot. However, metrical ictus and normal word accent do not necessarily coincide; Robert Bridges quotes this line from Virgil where normal word accent contradicts (or 'combats') the metrical expectation:

$$\overline{\text{Flu}} \text{ mi } \breve{} \text{ na } \breve{} \mid \text{qu}\overline{\text{e}} \text{ an ti} \mid \overline{\text{quos}} \overline{\text{sub}} \mid \overline{\text{ter}} \overline{\text{la}} \mid \overline{\text{ben}} \text{ ti } \breve{} \text{a } \breve{} \mid \overline{\text{mu}} \overline{\text{ros}} \dots$$

INTERNAL RHYME.   Rhyme occurring within the line of verse, as

> The fair breeze *blew,* the white foam *flew,*
> The furrow followed free;
> We were the *first* that ever *burst*
> Into that silent sea.
> Coleridge, *The Rime of the Ancient Mariner,* 103–106

ISOCHRONIC, ISOCHRONISM.   Some prosodists ('timers' and musical scanners) maintain that English meter is composed of units of equal time. Musical scanners believe that the foot is equivalent to the musical bar and that each foot occupies the same time interval. Others feel that isochronism is illusory, created by "the total effect of metrical organization which seemingly eliminates temporal discrepancies."

PARADIGM.   In grammar all the inflected forms of a part of speech, arranged in systematic order. A *metrical paradigm* abstracts the ideal form of a particular metrical arrangement; thus the paradigm of the iambic pentameter line consists of five iambic feet in consecutive arrangement:

$$\breve{\text{The}}\ \acute{\text{pro}} \mid \breve{\text{per}}\ \acute{\text{stu}} \mid \breve{\text{dy}}\ \acute{\text{of}} \mid \breve{\text{man}}\ \acute{\text{kind}} \mid \breve{\text{is}}\ \acute{\text{man}}. \ldots$$

The paradigm is often departed from; in the following line a trochee substitutes (q.v.) for an iamb in the first foot:

$$\acute{\text{Cha}}\ \breve{\text{os}} \mid \breve{\text{of}}\ \acute{\text{Thought}} \mid \breve{\text{and}}\ \acute{\text{Pas}} \mid \breve{\text{sion}},\ \acute{\text{all}} \mid \breve{\text{con}}\ \acute{\text{fus}}'\text{d}. \ldots$$

SAPPHIC, SAPPHICS.   A Greek stanzaic form named after the poetess Sappho— who may or may not have invented it. Its paradigm consists of three lines of Lesser Sapphics

$$-\ \cup \mid -\ \text{--} \mid -\ \cup\ \cup \mid -\ \cup \mid -\ -$$

Followed by a fourth line, an Adonic (q.v.):

$$-\ \cup\ \cup \mid -\ -$$

Swinburne, among others, has adapted the Sapphic stanza to English:

> All the night sleep came not upon my eyelids,
> Shed not dew, nor shook nor unclosed a feather,
> Yet with lips shut close and with eyes of iron
> Stood and beheld me.
> *Sapphics*

SEPTENARY.   A line consisting of seven metrical feet, as in T. S. Eliot's

> The yellow fog that rubs its back upon the window-panes . . .

SESTINA. A complicated Provençal verse form, invented, supposedly, by Arnaut Daniel. A sestina is a poem of thirty-nine lines divided into six stanzas of six lines each, and an envoy of three lines. Each stanza repeats the end-words of the first stanza in a new arrangement; the envoy repeats all six words in a set pattern. Because of the insistent repetitions of the end-words, the sestina adapts itself to both incantation and polemic. A good example of the incantatory sestina is Auden's "Hearing of harvests rotting in the valley"; of the polemical sestina, Pound's "Sestina: Altaforte."

SPRINGING. A strong rhythmic disturbance in the metrical line. 'Springing' is only possible in syllable-stress meter; it is a basic conflict between the paradigmatic meter and the disturbing element. It is similar to counterpointing (q.v.); however, in counterpointing the basic metrical structure is still felt. A 'sprung' line loses its sense of firm metrical organization and moves toward greater freedoms. A line may be sprung by an intrusive monosyllabic foot:

Thrŏugh shárp | séas | ĭn wín | tĕr níghts | dŏth páss. . . .

Wyatt

Ĭ nŏ lóng | ĕr stríve | tŏ stríve | towárds | sŭch thíngs. . . .

T. S. Eliot

Nŏ stréngth | ŏf mán, | ŏr fíer | cĕst wíld | béast | cŏuld wĭth stánd. . . .

Milton, *Samson Agonistes*

A line also may be sprung by the wholesale use of substitution; the spondee in the third position and trochees in the first, and in the very sensitive fourth position effectively spring this line:

Lóok ăt | thĕ stárs! | lóok, lóok | úp ăt | thĕ skíes!

Hopkins, *The Starlight Night*

SPRUNG RHYTHM. A verse form invented and described by Gerard Manley Hopkins. In sprung rhythm the lines move out of recognizable syllable-stress metric and cannot be scanned by syllable, stress, and foot. Some poems in sprung rhythm are actually written in strong-stress meter; other poems are in what amounts to free verse. Hopkins' *The Wreck of the Deutschland* shows a complex stress metric; *The Leaden Echo and the Golden Echo* is a free-verse rhapsody.

STRONG-STRESS VERSE. Accentual verse as it appears in the basic Old English pattern of the four-stress line. A medial caesura divides the line into two parts:

Across the cloud	pointed with light
Darts the tongue	of the roaring plane
Earth explodes	under its fire
Searing the stone	consuming the air
No hawk, no Harpy	disputes its place
Poised at the sun	death is less sure.

SUBSTITUTION.   In syllable-stress verse the practice of replacing the expected foot with one of a different character. The line below substitutes a trochee for an iamb at the third position:

$$\text{His sil} \mid \text{ver skin} \mid \text{laced with} \mid \text{his gol} \mid \text{den blood.} \ldots$$

Shakespeare, Macbeth, II, iii, 118

Here is a good example of 'counterpoint' rhythm releasing great emotional power.

SYLLABIC VERSE.   Strictly speaking, verse measured by count of syllables alone. French prosody is syllable counting; in this stanza by Gautier, we find eight syllables in the line:

> Une femme mystérieuse,
> Dont la beauté trouble mes sens,
> Se tient debout, silencieuse,
> Au bord des flots retentissants.

Coerulei Oculi

Many attempts have been made, especially by contemporary poets, to adapt syllabic metric to English. Marianne Moore, W. H. Auden, and Thom Gunn have devised syllabic forms for their poetic contents.

SYLLABLE-STRESS VERSE.   The traditional syllable, stress, and foot prosody of English poetry.

THESIS.   See ARSIS.

Selected Bibliography

Part One lists older studies, mostly published before 1930. Part Two lists items through the late sixties and early seventies: a period of great activity, especially for linguistic studies of 'metricality.' The student will also wish to consult Karl Shapiro's *A Bibliography of Modern Prosody* (Baltimore, 1948), and Karl Shapiro's and Robert Beum's *A Prosody Handbook* (New York, 1965) whose "A Selected Bibliography" lists items through 1963. Rae Ann Nager's bibliographical study, included in W. K. Wimsatt's *Versification* (pp. 204–16), is useful if somewhat idiosyncratic. This bibliography does not repeat the information provided for the essays in this collection.

PART ONE

1. ABERCROMBIE, LASCELLES. *Principles of English Prosody.* London, 1929.
2. ALDEN, RAYMOND MACDONALD. *English Verse: Specimens Illustrating Its Principles and History.* New York, 1902 (republished 1929).
3. ALLEN, GAY WILSON. *American Prosody.* New York, 1934.
4. BARKAS, PALLISTER. *A Critique of Modern English Prosody, 1880–1930.* Halle, 1934.
5. BAUM, PAULL F. *The Principles of English Versification.* Cambridge, Mass., 1922.
6. BRIDGES, ROBERT. *Milton's Prosody.* Oxford, 1921.
7. CROLL, MORRIS W. *Style, Rhetoric, and Rhythm.* Edited by J. Max Patrick *et al.* Princeton, N.J., 1966. Contains the essay "The Rhythm of English Verse," published in 1929. Croll is a ·'musical scanner' in the tradition of William Thomson and Sidney Lanier.
8. GUEST, EDWIN. *A History of English Rhythms.* 2 vols. London, 1838. New edition, edited by Walter W. Skeat, 1882. Reprinted by Haskell House Publishers, New York, 1968.
9. HAMID, ENID. *The Metres of English Poetry.* London, 1930.
10. JACOB, CARY T. *The Foundation and Nature of Verse.* New York, 1918.
11. LANIER, SIDNEY. *The Science of English Verse.* New York, 1880. Reprinted with introduction by P. F. Baum, Baltimore, 1945.
12. LANZ, HENRY. *The Physical Basis of Rime.* Palo Alto, 1931.
13. MAYOR, JOSEPH B. *A Handbook of Modern English Metre.* London, 1903.
14. OMOND, T. S. *A Study of Metre.* London, 1903.
15. OMOND, T. S. *English Metrists / Being a sketch of English prosodical / criticism from Elizabethan times / to the present day.* Oxford, 1921. Clouded-crystal-ball depart-

ment: speaking of Gerard Manley Hopkins, Omond tells us, "I cannot believe that [his] poems deserve or will receive attention from even the most determined seeker after novelties (p. 263).

16. PATMORE, COVENTRY. "Essay on English Metrical Law." In *Amelia*, London 1878.

17. SAINTSBURY, GEORGE. *A History of English Prosody*. 3 vols. London, 1906–1910. The classic historical study.

18. SAINTSBURY, GEORGE. *Historical Manual of English Prosody*. First published in 1910. Reprinted with introduction by Harvey Gross, New York: Schocken Books, 1966.

19. SAINTSBURY, GEORGE. "Some Recent Studies in English Prosody." *Proceedings of the British Academy*, vol. IX. London: Oxford University Press, 1919.

20. SCHIPPER, JAKOB. *Englische Metrik / In historischer und systematischer / Entwicklung dargestellt. Erster Theil: Altenglische Metrik* [from Old English to the Scottish Chaucerians]. Bonn, 1881. *Zweiter Theil: Neuenglische Metrik* [from the early Tudor poets to the later nineteenth century]. Bonn, 1888.

21. SCHIPPER, JAKOB. *A History of English Versification*. Oxford, 1910. [translation of *Grundriss der englischen Metrik*, Wien 1895].

22. SCHRAMM, WILBUR L. *Approaches to a Science of English Verse*. Iowa City, 1935.

23. SMITH, EGERTON. *The Principles of English Metre*. London, 1923.

24. STEELE, JOSHUA. *An Essay Towards Establishing the Melody and Measure of Speech*. London, 1775. The *Essay* appeared again in 1779 (with additions), under the title *Prosodia Rationalis*. Reprinted in facsimile by The Scolar Press Limited, Menston, England, 1969. Steele is the first English theorist who uses an elaborate system of musical symbols to notate not only meter but also the other prosodic features of language: pitch, duration, intensity, etc.

25. STEWART, GEORGE. *The Technique of English Verse*. New York, 1930. Reissued by Kennikat Press, Port Washington, New York, 1966.

26. SYMONDS, JOHN ADDINGTON. *Blank Verse*. London, 1895. A book that Eliot seems to have known. Like Eliot Symonds acknowledges the great virtuosity and freedom of 'Websterian blank verse.'

27. THOMSON, WILLIAM. *The Rhythm of Speech*. Glasgow, 1923.

PART TWO

28. ATTRIDGE, DEREK. *Well-weighed Syllables*. London: Cambridge University Press, 1974. A full and sympathetic treatment of the Elizabethan experiments in classical meters.

29. BEAVER, JOSEPH C. "Current Metrical Issues," *College English* 33, 2 (November 1971), 177–97. Offers refinements on Halle-Keyser.

30. BLACKMUR, R. P. "Lord Tennyson's Scissors." In *Form and Value in Modern Poetry*, pp. 369–88. Garden City, New York, 1957.

31. CHATMAN, SEYMOUR. *A Theory of Meter*. The Hague, 1965. A linguist's account of metrical phenomena.

32. CHATMAN, SEYMOUR, ed. *Literary Style: A Symposium.* London and New York, 1971. Contains W. K. Wimsatt's "The Rule and the Norm: Halle and Keyser on Chaucer's Meter."

33. CHATMAN, SEYMOUR, ed. *Approaches to Poetics: Selected Papers from the English Institute* [1972]. New York and London, 1973.

34. COOPER, GROSVENOR, and LEONARD B. MEYER. *The Rhythmic Structure of Music.* Chicago, 1960.

35. DAVIE, DONALD. *Articulate Energy: An Enquiry into the Syntax of English Poetry.* New York, 1958.

36. "English Verse and What It Sounds Like." [A symposium] *Kenyon Review,* XVIII, 3 (Summer 1956), 411–77. Contains the following articles: Harold Whitehall, "From Linguistics to Criticism"; Seymour Chatman, "Robert Frost's 'Mowing': an Inquiry into Prosodic Structure"; Arnold Stein, "Donne's Prosody"; Seymour Chatman, "Mr. Stein on Donne"; Arnold Stein, "A Note on Meter"; John Crowe Ransom, "The Strange Music of English Verse."

37. FRASER, G. S. *Metre, Rhyme, and Free Verse.* London, 1970. An excellent short introduction to the subject.

38. FREEMAN, DONALD C. *Linguistics and Literary Style.* New York, 1970. Contains a valuable section on "Approaches to Metrics": articles by Seymour Chatman, John Thompson, Halle and Keyser, *et al.*

39. FRYE, NORTHROP. *Anatomy of Criticism.* Princeton, N.J., 1957. See "The Rhythm of Recurrence: Epos," pp. 251–62; "The Rhythm of Association: Lyric," pp. 270–81.

40. FRYE, NORTHROP. ed. *Sound and Poetry: English Institute Essays, 1956.* New York and London, 1957.

41. FRYE, NORTHROP. *The Well-Tempered Critic.* Bloomington, Ind., 1963.

42. FUSSELL, PAUL. *Theory of Prosody in Eighteenth Century England.* New London, Conn., 1954. Reprinted by Archon Books, 1966.

43. "Generative Metrics." *Poetics* 12 (April 1974). Articles by Joseph C. Beaver, Wolfgang Klein, Dudley L. Hascall, Jacqueline Guéron, A. Walter Bernhart, and Karl Magnuson.

44. GROSS, HARVEY. *Sound and Form in Modern Poetry.* Ann Arbor, Mich., 1964. Reprinted by Ann Arbor Paperbacks AA 141, 1968. A study of prosody from Thomas Hardy to Robert Lowell.

45. HALLE, MORRIS, and SAMUEL J. KEYSER. "Chaucer and the Study of Prosody," *College English,* 28 (December 1966), 187–219. Pioneering essay in generative metrics; first proposes the theory of the stress maximum.

46. HALLE, MORRIS, and SAMUEL J. KEYSER. "Illustration and Defense of a Theory of the Iambic Pentameter," *College English,* 33 (November 1971), 154–76.

47. HALLE, MORRIS, and SAMUEL J. KEYSER. *English Stress: Its Form, Its Growth, and Its Role in Verse.* New York, 1971.

48. HALPERN, MARTIN. "On the Two Chief Metrical Modes in English." *PMLA* 77 (1962), 177–86.

49. HAMM, VICTOR M. "Meter and Meaning." *PMLA* 69 (1954), 695–710.
50. HEMPHILL, GEORGE, ed. *Discussions of Poetry: Rhythm and Sound.* Boston, 1961.
51. LOTZ, JOHN. "Notes on Structural Analysis in Metrics," *Helicon* 4 (1942), 119–46. Budapest and Leipzig.
52. MALOF, JOSEPH. *A Manual of English Meters.* Bloomington, Ind., 1970.
53. MCCAULEY, JAMES. *Versification: A Short Introduction.* East Lansing, Mich., 1966.
54. NABOKOV, VLADIMIR. *Notes on Prosody.* New York, 1968.
55. PERLOFF, MARJORIE. *Rhyme and Meaning in the Poetry of Yeats.* The Hague, Paris, 1970.
56. PREMINGER, ALEX, *et al.*, eds. *Princeton Encyclopedia of Poetry and Poetics. Enlarged Edition.* Princeton, N.J., 1974.
57. RIFFATERRE, MICHAEL. "Describing Poetic Structures: Two Approaches to Baudelaire's 'les Chats'." In *Structuralism,* edited by Jacques Ehrmann. Garden City, N.Y., 1970. A structuralist reading which takes into account the poem's prosodic features.
58. SEBEOK, THOMAS A., ed. *Style in Language.* Cambridge, Mass., and New York, 1960. An important collection. Includes a section on metrics with contributions by John Lotz, Seymour Chatman, Benjamin Hrushovski, John Hollander, W. K. Wimsatt, and Monroe C. Beardsley. Also includes Roman Jakobson's important "Linguistics and Poetics."
59. SHAPIRO, KARL. *A Bibliography of Modern Prosody.* Baltimore, 1948.
60. SHAPIRO, KARL, and ROBERT BEUM. *A Prosody Handbook.* New York, Evanston, and London, 1965. Includes a glossary of prosodic terms and a selected bibliography which lists items to 1963.
61. THOMPSON, JOHN. *The Founding of English Metre.* New York and London, 1961.
62. TRAGER, G. L., and H. L. SMITH, JR. *An Outline of English Structure.* Norman, Okla., 1951.
63. TURCO, LEWIS. *The Book of Forms: A Handbook of Poetics.* New York, 1968.
64. WELLEK, RENÉ, and AUSTIN WARREN. *Theory of Literature.* 3rd ed. New York, 1962. See Chapter 13, "Euphony, Rhythm, and Metre." The authors make the crucial distinction "between performance and pattern of sound." Metrics is the study of patterns of sound, and "cannot be based only on the study of individual recitals."
65. WIMSATT, W. K. "One Relation of Rhyme to Reason," in *The Verbal Icon.* Lexington, Ky., 1954. An important study of the semantic resonances of rhyming words.
66. WIMSATT, W. K. "The Rule and the Norm: Halle and Keyser on Chaucer's Meter." *College English,* 31 (May 1970), 774–88.

Contributors

ROBERT GRAVES (1895 —)

Despite his manifold activities as historical novelist, anthropologist, translator, classicist, and communicant of The Church of The White Goddess, Graves regards himself as primarily a poet. He has published more than a hundred books and is the father of eight children. He was Professor of Poetry at Oxford University in 1961.

PAUL FUSSELL (1924 —)

Professor Fussell holds degrees from Pomona College and Harvard University. His earlier book on prosody was *Theory of Prosody in Eighteenth Century England* (1954); his recent book, *The Great War and Modern Memory,* received a National Book Award (1975). Professor Fussell teaches at Rutgers University.

ROBERT BRIDGES (1844–1930)

In his long life Bridges was physician, poet, prosodist, and Poet Laureate (1913–1930). He was friend to and literary executor for Gerard Manley Hopkins. He published Hopkins' poems in 1918, twenty-nine years after the death of the poet.

I. A. RICHARDS (1893 —)

I. A. Richards is one of our century's most influential literary and educational theorists. He is the intellectual father of the New Criticism, and with C. K. Ogden the inventor of Basic English. The earlier part of his career was spent at Cambridge University; from 1944 until his retirement in 1963, he was Professor of English at Harvard University. His many books include *Principles of Literary Criticism* (1924), *Practical Criticism* (1929), and *Coleridge on Imagination* (1934).

JOHN HOLLANDER (1929 —)

Professor Hollander holds degrees from Columbia University and Indiana University; he also held a three-year appointment as Junior Fellow in the Society of Fellows at Harvard. His first book of poems was *A Crackling of Thorns* (1958). Subsequent books of poems include *Types of Shape,* (1969), *The Night Mirror* (1971), and *The Head of the Bed* (1974). He has also published *The Untuning of the Sky: Ideas of Music in English Poetry,* 1500–1700. Professor Hollander teaches at Yale University.

OTTO JESPERSEN (1860–1943)

Jespersen's masterwork is the seven-volume *A Modern English Grammar,* published during the years 1909–1931. His other writings include *The Philosophy of*

Grammar (1924) and *Growth and Structure of the English Language* (nine editions, first published in 1905).

YVOR WINTERS (1900–1968)

Poet, critic, and influential teacher, Yvor Winters taught at Stanford University until his death in 1968. Alan Swallow published his *Collected Poems* in 1960. Winters is also the author of *Primitivism and Decadence* (1937), a study of Edward Arlington Robinson (1946), and *In Defense of Reason* (1947).

WILLIAM K. WIMSATT (1907–1975)

William K. Wimsatt held degrees from Georgetown and Yale Universities. From 1939 he taught at Yale, and from 1965 until his death he was Frederick Clifford Ford Professor of Literature. His publications include three collections of critical essays, *The Verbal Icon* (1954), *Hateful Contraries* (1965), and *Day of the Leopards* (1976); and (with Cleanth Brooks) *Literary Criticism: A Short History* (1957).

MONROE C. BEARDSLEY (1915 —)

Professor Beardsley holds undergraduate and graduate degrees from Yale University. His books include *Aesthetics: Problems in the Philosophy of Criticism* (1958), and *The Possibility of Criticism* (1970). Since 1969 he has been Professor of Philosophy at Temple University.

MORRIS HALLE (1923 —)

Professor Halle studied at the City College of New York, at the University of Chicago, and at Columbia University. He holds a Ph.D. from Harvard University. He has taught at the Massachusetts Institute of Technology since 1951. His books include *Fundamentals of Language* (with Roman Jakobson), 1956; *The Sound Patterns of English* (with Noam Chomsky), 1968; *English Stress: Its Form, Its Growth, and Its Role in Verse* (with Samuel J. Keyser), 1971. A *Festschrift for Morris Halle* was published in 1973.

SAMUEL J. KEYSER (1935 —)

Professor Keyser studied at George Washington University and at Merton College, Oxford. He holds a Ph.D. in Linguistics from Yale University. Since 1965 he has taught at Brandeis University. He has collaborated with Morris Halle on *English Stress: Its Form, Its Growth, and Its Role in Verse*. He is also the co-author (with Paul M. Postal) of *Beginning English Grammar* (1976).

CHARLES L. STEVENSON (1908—)

Professor Stevenson holds undergraduate degrees from Yale University and Cambridge University; his Ph.D. is from Harvard University. He taught philosophy at the University of Michigan from 1946 until his retirement in 1977. He is the author of *Ethics and Language* (1944, 1960), and *Facts and Values* (1963).

T. S. ELIOT (1888–1965)

T. S. Eliot held the position in English tradition previously occupied by Ben Jonson, Dryden, and Samuel Johnson—that of a literary dictator. Consequently he was extravagantly admired, and, in recent years, resented. Nevertheless he was for my generation the "strong poet" whose influence had to be assimilated and resisted.

EZRA POUND (1885–1972)

Pound's personality made a permanent impression on modern letters. That he is our Dante and the *Cantos* our *Divina Commedia* remain open questions. My preference is for his early work: *Cathay, Mauberley,* and the magnificent *Homage to Sextus Propertius*—perhaps his best executed poem.

THEODORE ROETHKE (1907–1963)

Theodore Roethke was born in Saginaw, Michigan. He attended the University of Michigan and Harvard University. In the years before his death he taught at the University of Washington. His was a Dionysian spirit, tormented by his despairs and ecstasies. In his poems he was an exquisite craftsman, a master of traditional metric as well as of the freer measures. His *Collected Poems* was published in 1966.

STANLEY KUNITZ (1905 —)

Mr. Kunitz holds degrees from Harvard University. He published his first book of poems, *Intellectual Things,* in 1930. His *Selected Poems* (1958) was awarded the Pulitzer Prize: *The Testing Tree* appeared in 1970. Mr. Kunitz has taught at Columbia University since 1963. His *Collected Poems* is scheduled for publication in 1979. His other books include *A Kind of Order, A Kind of Folly* (1975), and (with Max Hayward) *Poems of Akhmatova (1973).*

DONALD JUSTICE (1925 —)

Professor Justice holds degrees from the University of Miami and the University of Iowa. His books of poems include *The Summer Anniversaries* (1960), *Night Light* (1967), and *Departures* (1973). He teaches in the Program in Creative Writing at the University of Iowa.